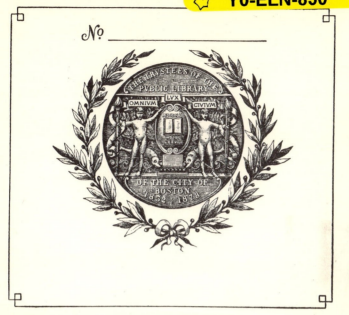

# SOCIAL THOUGHT

## AMONG THE

# EARLY GREEKS

# SOCIAL THOUGHT
## AMONG THE
# EARLY GREEKS

JOSEPH B. GITTLER

*Department of Sociology*
*The University of Georgia*

PREFACE BY

WILLIAM F. OGBURN

ATHENS

THE UNIVERSITY OF GEORGIA PRESS

1941

In Memory of

HAROLD HIRSCH

# PREFACE

FEW there are who realize how indebted we are to the Greeks for our civilization. Yet we have probably contributed to our cultural possessions less ourselves than we received from the Greeks. To know something of these fundamental contributions from around the Aegean, which saw the dawn of civilization, to the origin of our own culture is the mark of an educated person. The author has made the acquisition of this knowledge most attractive; for out of the treasure house of all that made the glory that was Greece, he has picked gems. They are brilliant in the setting that he has given them, a setting of interpretation and history, made with sympathetic understanding.

That the author is a sociologist as well as a student of Greek thought is not an accident, for thought and culture are social in origin. It was once thought that our ideas derived solely from our biological brain, and that the Greeks were a people with more than their quota of inherited genius. But whatever were the racial gifts of the Greeks, it is now recognized that any such expression of inherited abilities must be through the social milieu, which means long cultivation in the mores of the people. Science, literature and philosophy, anywhere, are the outgrowth of the social life of the time. Hence the aptness of the title, "Social Thought Among the Early Greeks," and the appropriateness of a sociologist's making the correlations between social conditions and ideologies.

It is also interesting to observe that this contribution to the understanding of Greek culture comes from a professor in a Southern university, and that it is published by the University of Georgia Press, for it is my impression that the South and the

Southern universities show relatively more evidence of appreciation and influence of classic antiquity than is found in any other section of the United States.  They resemble England and the English universities in this respect.  We may hope that young men and young women in other parts of the United States, as well as in the South, will gain much from this book.

WILLIAM FIELDING OGBURN

# ACKNOWLEDGEMENTS

The preparation of such a work as this has called for help and guidance from numerous sources. It is, therefore, with deep appreciation that I wish to acknowledge the assistance given to me by the following persons: To Dr. William F. Ogburn, my teacher, for his encouragement, advice, and patience in reading the original manuscript; to Edward M. Shils of the University of Chicago for his reading and constructive criticism of the manuscript; to Calvin S. Brown for his corrections of the manuscript; to H. Frazier Moore and Ralph Stephens of the University of Georgia Press for their unfailing attention to the multitudinous details that constantly arose in connection with the release of the volume; to Sol I. Golden, to whom I am deeply grateful for his unfailing friendship and encouragement; to B. O. Williams for his reading of the page-proofs; to my students, Elizabeth Pierce, who worked devotedly at many tasks in connection with the volume, and Max Cooper, Morris Brody, Bernice Shanker, Sarah Bolgla, Adel Weiss for their clerical help; to Elizabeth Creighton for typing part of the manuscript; to Louise Hollingsworth and Louise Fant of the University of Georgia Library; and to my wife, whose name rightfully belongs alongside that of the author.

For permission to quote copyrighted material I should like to make grateful acknowledgement to the following publishers: A. & C. Black, Ltd., for quotations from *The Early Greek Philosophy* by John Burnet; Charles Scribner's Sons for quotations from *Source Book in Ancient Philosophy* by C. M. Bakewell; The Clarendon Press for quotations from *The Public Orations of Demosthenes,* and from Jowett's translation of

*Thucydides* and Plato's *Dialogues* and *Republic;* E. P. Dutton and Company for quotations from *Greek Economics* translated by M. L. W. Laistner, and *Greek Historical Thought* translated by Arnold J. Toynbee; Harvard University Press for quotations from volumes in The Loeb Classical Library; Kegan Paul, Trench, Trubner & Company, Ltd., for a quotation from *First Philosophers of Greece* by Arthur Fairbanks; and The Macmillan Company for quotations from *The Odyssey,* translated by Butcher and Lang; *The Iliad,* translated by Lang, Leaf, and Myers; *The History of Herodotus,* translated by G. C. Macaulay; *The Works of Xenophon,* translated by H. G. Dakyns; and *Sophocles,* translated by Arthur S. Way.

J. B. G.

# CONTENTS

xi

# CHAPTER I

## INTRODUCTION

Among the nations which stand out in the course of history as having done most to promote human knowledge, human art, and human culture, the Greeks are first in the judgment of all competent observers.—J. P. MAHAFFY [1]

The gain to sociology would be great if the workers on the grand scale could have at their service separate monographs which would undertake impartially to gather and systematize the sociological material in such documents as the Vedas, the Zend-Avesta, the Eddas, the Hebrew Scriptures, the Kalevala, the Nibelungen Lied, the Homeric poems, and the like.—A. G. KELLER [2]

IT SHOULD be stated at the outset that the author agrees with those who differentiate social thought from sociology. There is a distinction between the two, just as there is a distinction between social philosophy and sociology. Social thought consists of reflections on one's fellow-men—their institutions, customs, human problems, and human relations. It has its roots in a sensitivity to and an awareness of the all-pervading social atmosphere. Social thought is merely the expression of this awareness.

Social thought, *per se*, does not discriminate between the political, the economic, and the ethical. All thoughts that are related to the associated life of man can be considered as social thinking. The field consists of a body of beliefs, ethical ideas, and dogmas of behavior and practices, as well as a body of knowledge and theory. A statement as to what should prevail among men is as much a part of social thought as the finding of what does exist among men. It may accept and condone; it may attack and criticize; or it may hope and plan for the new.

Social thought can hardly be considered a science or a discipline. A science must possess a body of knowledge, theories, and generalizations. Ethical pronunciations remove any field from the realm of the scientific. Thus it might be said that social thought is the reflections about man by men at a given time and place.

## 1. DIFFERENCE BETWEEN SOCIAL THOUGHT AND SOCIOLOGICAL THOUGHT

The social thoughts of a person consist of his ideas about social phenomena. In order to think about social phenomena it is not necessary to be conscious of any fundamental axis of inquiry, any methods, any concepts, or any frame of reference —these are what distinguish a science and a discipline from random thought. Hence, before we can speak of sociological thought we must know what concepts and methods of sociology are present in a social thinking. Sociology, to distinguish it from social thought, consists of a body of knowledge, employing various methods and concepts, which seeks to determine the facts of human behavior by virtue of the fact that man lives in groups. It studies human relations in so far as they can be interpreted on the premise of group life. Thus, while sociological thought (as well as political thought, economic thought, and so on) is part of social thought, social thought is not necessarily sociological thought.

Not all sociologists accept this difference. Some identify sociology with social thought; others do not. This moot question has caused differences of opinion as to the origins of sociology. On that account, numerous sociologists hold a variety of diverse views in regard to the beginnings of sociology as an intellectual discipline. We might classify these conceptions of the origins of sociology into the following groups: (1) the theory that sociology dates back to ancient times and to the Greeks in particular (this view is upheld by Spann, Bogardus,

Lichtenberger, Menzel, Ellwood, and Hankins); (2) the conception of the origin of sociology in the seventeenth and eighteenth centuries (this is supported by such men as Sombart, Brinkmann, and Tonnies); (3) the view that it begins in the romantic period of about 1800 (Small, von Below, and Baxa believed in this conception); (4) the idea that the nineteenth century is the period which gave rise to sociology (this theory has such adherents as Barth, Oppenheimer, H. Weber, Gothein, Freyer, Squillace, von Stein, and von Mohl); (5) and the theory which places the origins of sociology in the twentieth century (von Wiese strongly supports this theory).

For our purposes it will not be necessary to treat the arguments for and against each of the classifications that these sociologists give, but we will limit ourselves to a short consideration of the first group—those that consider sociology as having begun in ancient and classical times.

The members of this group consider sociological thought to be synonymous with social thought. Hence they place the beginnings of sociology with the beginnings of civilization itself. They argue that the underlying purpose of sociology is the study of human behavior. Any conception of man, society, state, or human values finds a rightful place in the sociological realm. And since such conceptions have existed since earliest times, sociological beginnings must be placed there.[3]

If there is a justification for believing that any of the ancient civilizations produced *sociological* thought, Adolf Menzel [4] appears to present the most legitimate arguments. He points out that it is a mistaken notion that the Greeks possessed social philosophies only, in contra-distinction to a value-free sociology, or that they failed to distinguish between state and society.[5] It is interesting to note that in his analysis Menzel discovers that the problems and fields of present-day sociology were known to the Greeks. He states that the sociological schools of thought handled by Pitirim Sorokin in his *Contemporary Sociological Theories* were included in various

Greek writings.  As he says, "Wenn man das inhaltsreiche Werk von P. Sorokin über die soziologischen Theorien der Gegenwart zu Hand nimmt und die Kapitelüberschriften findet: die mechanistische, die biologische, die psychologische, die ökonomische, die formale Soziologie usw., so muss man feststellen, dass die Ansätze zu allen diesen methodischen Richtungen bereits in der griechischen Wissenschaft gegeben sind." [6]

The present writer lays no claim to an extensive discovery of sociological thought among the early Greeks.  He does contend, however, that there are indisputable traces of undifferentiated sociological, political, anthropological, and economic ideas in early Greek literature.[7]

To the extent that one may discern the sociological (also the anthropological, the economic, and the political) sources in the social thought of the early Greeks, we have pushed back the historical frontiers of our science.  The concepts, methods, and problems of this discipline may not always be explicitly stated.  But in so far as a statement tends to discover or explain, without preestablished biases and dogmas, a phase of the associated life of man and that which affects this association, there is implicit an historical source of sociology.

Since the writer is a sociologist by profession, it is evident that his interest is focussed on the sociological.  But what has been said about the sources of historical sociology can be said for the other social sciences as well.  Where dogmas and maxims of behavior instead of analyses and statements of social facts among the early Greeks appear, we can relegate them only to the "discipline" of social thought.  Nevertheless, they remain valuable historically.  For undifferentiated social thought is the forerunner of scientific social thought (differentiated social thought).  Both of these, then, help toward a better understanding of a field of social knowledge.  Accepting the difference between sociology and social thought does not obviate the importance of the study of social thought and social thinking as precursory to sociology.

## 2. IMPORTANCE OF GREEK SOCIAL THOUGHT

As a field develops there is a felt need for a knowledge and understanding of the origin of its concepts and its objectives. Many scholars have recognized the essential need for histories of their particular fields. Although the emphasis in this volume has been on a background for the sociologist, the book should prove valuable to students working in all the allied fields.

A knowledge of the social thought of the past leads to a keener understanding of contemporary social thinking as well as to a clearer perception of contemporary society as a whole. For it is these ideas of the past that mold present-day attitudes, institutions, customs, social groups, and social forms. Then, too, a familiarity with the character and the fate of past social thought may guard us from the danger of making the same errors. No student of early Greek thought can fail to see a parallel between events and ideas of that period and of our own.

A perusal of Greek social thought will undoubtedly make for humility in contemporary students. It has been said that "The ancients have stolen all of our good ideas." Similarly an old adage illustrates the same point: "The Greeks had a word for it." Although it cannot be stated that all our contemporary ideas are to be found in Greek literature, many present-day thinkers, unfamiliar with the material, will be astounded to learn how many of them are to be found there. Thus it is hoped that the material here presented will serve as a ballast to the eager student prone to be carried away by every sharp gust of controversial thinking. A sound foundation in what has gone before may make for a keener perception and a more profound sense of values in the analyses of the present.

Greek writings have had an astonishingly wide influence on all western civilizations. If we were to examine closely modern religion, morality, science, politics, and literature, we should find the deep imprint of the Greek mind. Since the time they were first composed, Greek writings have been bearing fruit.

Many of our modern problems, such as the freedom of women, propaganda, dictatorship, corrupt politics, the class struggle, democracy, totalitarianism, reforestation, and soil erosion, are discussed and analyzed in the living pages of Greek literature.

The Greek contribution to civilization was not a material one. Indeed, the technological and economic life of Greece was more backward than that of many of her contemporaries, but her intellectual attainments have scarcely been surpassed. The post-Socratic Greeks, especially, succeeded in liberating men's minds from the superstition, fear, and intolerance which were characteristic of earlier civilizations. Rationalism was upheld as the highest good, and all thought was subjected to merciless scrutiny in the light of the material world. Free inquiry and scientific questioning were fostered to a greater degree than in any preceding time, or for a countless number of years after the decline of the Greek world. It was this spirit of free inquiry which might be thought of as the forerunner of modern science. The Greeks were the first people to establish education as a social institution. Prior to this time education was largely the function of the family or tribe, and was devoted, for the most part, to the imparting of group tradition and custom. The Greeks, however, widened the scope of education to include philosophy and the acquisition of new knowledge. In political thought and political institutions the Greeks advanced far. They surpassed all previous ages in both sculpture and architecture. Greek literature, both prose and poetry, reached heights that have seldom been equaled. The major contribution of the Greeks lay in their philosophy of life—in their emphasis not only on pleasing the Gods, but on the necessity for human happiness. As their culture developed there was a marked emphasis upon the secular and a trend away from the sacred. Greek civilization was backward in its technological and economic development as well as in its ability to cope with the problems of war, peace, and national unity, but its achievements in other fields stand as a monument to its people.

The preceding statement must not be taken to include the

entire course of Greek civilization from its advent to its close. Nor could it apply at any one time to all the Greeks. Many of the Greek city-states made very little contribution to this achievement. Nor were the earlier Greeks—the Homeric Greeks, and the Greeks of the ninth, eighth, and seventh centuries—as "secular" as the foregoing paragraphs would indicate. The statement clearly covers the period shortly before, during, and after the Attic age and is applicable only to a portion of the Greek people.[8] The earlier Greeks still formed a "sacred" civilization.[9] At the point at which we first catch a glimpse of the social thought of the Greeks they are still in the mythological age, as is seen in the poems of Homer and Hesiod.

There are various classifications of the cultural periods of Greek history from the archaeological remains (indicating a Neolithic period) down to the Hellenistic age (after Alexander the Great). For our purposes it was found convenient and expedient to arrange the Greek periods of social thought in accordance with the forms of literature dominant in various periods. In making this classification, it was not necessary to distort the social thought in order to fit it into the established categories. There is a significant connection between the "type" of social thought and the forms of literary expression. It might be stated here that since the culture periods of Greek (as well as any other) civilization are reflected in the forms of literary expression, the literary periods correspond quite appropriately to the Greeks' periods of social thought and culture. This is especially true of the early periods of Greek culture.

### 3. Periods of Early Greek Social Thought

It has been the general practice in the treatment of the history of social thought to begin with Plato, gliding over pre-Platonic Greek thought almost entirely. Several volumes have appeared dealing with pre-Greek social thought, including Egyptian, Hindu, Chinese, and Hebrew social thinking. In these works, there is a woeful neglect of the early Greek (pre-

Platonic) thought on the one hand, and of the social thought to be found in the writings and documents of other thinkers during Plato's and Aristotle's time—in Greek drama, oratory, historical writings, and so on.   It is these two gaps that *Social Thought Among the Early Greeks* endeavors to fill.

It will be demonstrated that although the pre-Socratic Greeks did not systematically discuss social phenomena, they made a meaningful contribution to the history of social thought. In fact, it is important to understand the connection between the Orient, Africa, and Asia Minor, and the later Platonic Greek social thought.   It was found that early Greek social thought falls into the following literary periods: (1) the Age of Homer and Hesiod (1250–700 B.C.); (2) the Lyric Age (700–500 B.C.); (3) the Attic Age (500–300 B.C.).   A description of each of these periods is to be found at the beginning of its chapter.   The last period (500–300 B.C.) covers and includes Plato and Aristotle.   This book, however, does not include the ideas of these two men, since Plato and Aristotle have been handled by a countless number of scholars and their writings have been interpreted in many fashions.   The author did not feel that an inclusion of them was essential, since they are so readily accessible in other treatments.   For those who are interested in the social writings of these men source references have been provided in the appendices.

A complete survey of Greek social thought would also have to include a treatment of the post-Attic period, or the Hellenistic age, as it is usually called.   The social writings of this age have also received multifold treatments, and a separate appendix indicating the sources of the social ideas of this period is also included.

### 4. THE GENERAL NATURE AND THE COMMON ASPECTS OF EARLY GREEK SOCIAL THOUGHT

The social thought peculiar to each period and to each writer can be ascertained in the succeeding chapters.   It is, however, important to discover the common aspects of the social thinking in all of the three periods dealt with in this book. It is certainly obvious that no single idea can survive in identical form or content, or remain unchanged over a period of nine hundred years. Nevertheless, several propositions as to the general nature of social thought among the early Greeks suggest themselves.

First, by the close of the Attic period, Greek social thought had touched upon every conceivable phase of social life. Since the Greek mode of life led to social experiences as multifold and as varied as those of contemporary life, it can be said that the Greeks reflected on, and spoke about every phase of present-day social problems. The difference lies in the emphasis rather than in the actual content. They concentrated on those problems which were most consistently pressing in their life. They discussed industry, but—it is to be expected—few references are found regarding the effects of technology, because, although tools existed then, they played a minor part in shaping social events as compared with the technology of contemporary life (note the development of technocracy). Slavery was an important aspect of their way of life, but slavery in the modern world has virtually disappeared. We, therefore, have ceased to think of slavery; they thought about it a great deal.

Second, reason played a major role in Greek civilization. It was reason that always seemed to determine Greek action, whether it led to success or not. Throughout Greek literature the characters are seemingly motivated by reason, and less by emotion. In fact, appeals to beware of oratorical subterfuges which might cause emotional unbalance are made time and time again in Aristophanes' dramas. What Pericles says of the Athenians applies only in a lesser degree to all Greeks: "We have a peculiar power, of thinking before we act, and of acting too, whereas other men are courageous from ignorance, but hesitate upon reflection." [10]

Third, to say that the Greeks were motivated by reason is to distinguish reason as a type of reflection as distinguished from emotion.  But this does not mean that the Greeks were exempt from a life of emotion or from emotional attachments to a pre-existing way of life.  The truth of the matter is that the age of Homer and Hesiod, and a portion of the Lyric age, might be "ideally typed" as sacred societies—that is, "Communities in which a sort of emotional halo encircles the ways of the fathers and thereby prevents their profanation by change." [11] But this "sacred" way of life gradually wanes as we approach the Attic period, which very definitely exemplifies a 'secular' way of life.  That is, mental mobility, habitual abstraction (the product of the comparison of peoples), rationalism, and individuation become the *modus vivendi*.[12]  Thus reflections on justice and the nature of the state, comparative estimates of different types of governments, an analysis of the problem of what is wealth, a critical evaluation of the theory of communism by Aristophanes, an exposition on the first principles of economics by Socrates in Xenophon's *Oeconomicus*—all these become possible with the development of abstraction. For "weaknesses of democracy" [13] can be pointed out only when a mode of life may be abstracted and typified as democracy.

Fourth, early Greek social thought is unscientific.  It is unscientific in the sense that no attempts at empirical investigation of impressions and ideas are in evidence.  This does not mean that Greek social thought does not embody the authors' experiences.  On the contrary, these men display an acute and sensitive recording of their submergence in the ocean of social experience.  But this experience is casual.  Their assertions are not arrived at in any systematic way.  Little attempt is made to verify concepts.  Greek social thought, therefore, must be studied as a spontaneous rather than an intentional, methodical body of knowledge.

However, in so far as we today have come to recognize various methods of social investigation as necessary, and inasmuch as insight is one of these methods, we must respect the validity of these writers' observations.  For there is little doubt that Greek literature displays a wide and penetrating insight into the problems of the social world.

Fifth, the Greeks, especially those of the Lyric and Attic ages, present a modern version of the nature of human nature. Many of them recognized, in general, the acquired and developmental aspects of human nature. Some considered man's nature inborn and innate, but a goodly number stated the opposite point of view—that culture and human associations shape and account for man's human nature. As Theognis says, "The bad are not all bad from the womb, but have learnt base works and wanton outrage from friendship with the bad because they thought all they said was true." [14]

Communication, including discourse and language, is recognized as the fundamental means for the individual's development as a human and cultural self. As Isocrates puts it, "because there has been implanted in us the power to persuade each other and to make clear to each other whatever we desire, not only have we escaped the life of wild beasts, but we have come together and founded cities and made laws and invented arts; and, generally speaking, there is no institution devised by men which the power of speech has not helped us to establish." [15]

Aristophanes recognizes imitation as a factor operating in social life. Alcman suggests that human motives are not externally observable, but are often concealed, and therefore difficult to ascertain. This fact suggests the subjectivity of social phenomena. There is present in Greek writings the idea, then, that human nature is a non-inherited, becoming nature.

Sixth, it has been often pointed out that among the pre-Greek thinkers there existed no conception of the group as a unit in the social structure. [16] The same can be said about the Greeks. A social situation was noted in its relation to the individual, rarely in its relation to the group. The concept of the group in its various aspects was almost completely neglected. However, there are some outstanding exceptions to this statement. Although there did not exist a conception of the group *per se,* there did exist a conception of the "greater" group, the mass of humanity, the Great Society. There are constant references to humanity and the masses.

The state also is a strong concept in the Attic age. This is conceived of as a unit and a social plurel over and above the sum of the individuals that go to make up the state. However, no distinction is made between state and society. This lack of differentiation between these concepts does not eliminate the fact that the Greeks possessed and dealt with a concept of the human plurel.

The concept of the human plurel takes even more concrete form when the Greeks repeatedly recognize and refer to the existence of social classes and to a division of labor in society. More, Isocrates states the existence of ethnocentric tendencies for some groups.[17] This implicitly takes cognizance of the existence of differential structural units as component parts of society.

Seventh, in modern sociological literature the concept of social forces plays an important role. By social forces is meant those factors which motivate human behavior. They are considered to be the dynamic, impelling activations operating in human behavior, including such concepts as interests, desires, wishes, and attitudes. It is indeed interesting to note that some awareness of these social forces is to be found in Greek literature. Xenophon distinctly noted in society the forces analogous to W. I. Thomas' wish for recognition. As he says, "ambitious, emulous natures feel the spur of praise, since some natures hunger after praise no less than others crave for meat and drink." [18] Many writers seem to have been impressed by the driving, determinant force exerted by wealth and poverty on society. The importance attached to these economic factors operating in society can legitimately be construed as a recognition of the existence of the wish for security as a social force.

Eighth, there is among the Greeks in all three periods a rather interesting knowledge of distinct and specific social processes—the type of actions *per se,* involved in human association. Hesiod, for example, believes in and depicts the strife inherent in society.[19] Heraclitus considers opposition the cause for human association.[20] Euripides wrote that "our life is conflict all." [21]

Ninth, social control—its nature and its operation—comes in for an extensive treatment in all the literature. The most prominent form of control was thought to be the gods' control of human activity. Man's activity is dependent on the will of the gods. Offended gods punish man for his oversight in the religious observances and sacrifices.

A second source of social control is found in the concept of Fate. This idea is similar to the notion that human events are pre-determined and inevitable. Fate controls human events. Sophocles writes these words for the chorus in one of his plays:

> "Full many a thing do men by seeing learn;
> But ere he see, no prophet may discern
> What lot for him shall leap from fates' dark urn." [22]

But fate and the gods are not the only sources of social control. Tradition, leadership, oratory, public opinion, propaganda, law, wealth, old age, and the effect of physical environment on human life are all treated as forms of social control. References to these in the text are too numerous to mention and will be readily discovered by the reader in the subsequent chapters.

Tenth, probably the most important characteristic of Greek social thought in all of the three periods is that it is ethical in nature. How a state should be constructed, how the state should control, how the individual should conduct himself, how he should act toward others—are problems that appear again and again. War is sometimes upheld, sometimes condemned. No profound attempts are made to discover the causes of war. At one time hedonism is upheld as a criterion of behavior; later the moderate life is praised. In short, the ethical strongly permeates all the Greek writings.

## 5. Method of Presenting Early Greek Social Thought

Frequently, writers of histories of thought formulate arbitrary theories and then proceed to establish these preconceived ideas by forcibly fitting in various "quotations" and eliminating those which tend to disprove their theories. Then, too, many have, on the basis of a few obscure lines, written much interpretive matter out of all proportion to the text. This study has attempted to avoid these pitfalls by presenting, in their own words, the ideas expressed by the various writers. The writer has conceived his role to be one of discovering, selecting, and arranging in as unbiased manner as possible the material of the early Greek authors which will be significant for the student of the social sciences.

In choosing excerpts characteristic of the concepts of the Greek writers, I have been guided by the literature itself. For it is evident that in many works dealing with the Greeks their literature has been treated in the light of present-day events, and much that has been attributed to them becomes problematical in consequence. The following study, therefore, proceeded at the outset to select all the excerpts from virtually all the Greek writings which had a social content. Then the excerpts were classified into various categories of social thought. These constitute the sections under each chapter and historical period of early Greek social thought. The categories were selected inductively. No *à priori* classification of Greek social thought was kept in mind before the selection of the excerpts. Rather, the inherent connection of the excerpts suggested the classifications. That which seemed obscure or necessitated a great deal of far-fetched interpretation has been excluded.

Another approach to our presentation of the social ideas of the early Greeks is through the sociology-of-knowledge method. Much is being written and said at present about the sociology-of-knowledge method or "Wissensoziologie." Its application to the history of ideas and social thought is highly appropriate.

The principal thesis of the sociology of knowledge is that "there are modes of thought that cannot be adequately understood as long as their social origins are obscured." [23] "Intellectual life and thought are conceived as operating within a social milieu, which pervades the thought so as to influence its mode and form. It attempts to understand thought in relation to its place in the historical-social scene. Ideas, thought patterns, and the preconceived standards of the cognitive process have their roots in the situational, existential framework." [24]

The author has kept the sociology-of-knowledge method in mind in presenting this study. It is important to understand and know not only what the Greeks had to say about various social questions and problems, but also why and how they came to say what they did. What were the social conditions which impelled or conditioned their views regarding various questions? What were the social forces which were conducive to the seeking of answers to problematical situations? In short, attempts are made to account for the social basis of social thought.

How is this done? At the beginning of each chapter, and before the presentation of the excerpts, a historical setting of the period dealt with is included. The historical settings include descriptions of the political events of the period, the form of government, the economic system, the daily life, the familial groups and their social relations, the religious practices and beliefs, and the painting, architecture, and other artistic achievements—anything which might be responsible for the bringing about of certain social thoughts and reflections. The lives of the writers are appended in the notes to each chapter. These too can often account for certain beliefs, propensities, and interests.

However, no attempt was made to go all the way with the sociology-of-knowledge method. For that would mean accounting for the literature itself—its style, its motifs—and its authors' characters. We are concerned, for the most part, with accounting for the social themes considered and pointing out, as far as possible, what these themes were in the social thought of the time.

It must also be understood that a straight-line determinism between social forces and social thought is an impossibility. The sociology-of-knowledge method does not purport to posit any theory of social determination. It merely seeks to establish the facts of social conditioning of social thought. It would be difficult to prove that any group of ideas is solely socially determined—if it could be proved at all. While social thought may be accounted for as springing from the milieu in which the "thinking" person may be found, the ideas and thoughts may be due to personal and individualistic factors. That is, one's intellectual capacities, his logical precision, may often be responsible for the creation of a particular idea or solution while the general field of thought in which the idea floats may be socially determined. The social milieu sets the limits in which one's ideas can operate. Furthermore, forceful arguments to show that social ideas are the result of immanent development can be garnered, for, what one thinks about his surroundings may depend on what was thought. While this fact tends to make the social (in this case the social can be thought of as the cultural base as propaedeutic to a special social thinking) responsible for social thought, it is one of inherent and immanent influence rather than external, existential influence. The facts of the social surroundings are given; the thoughts are excerpted; the reader will draw his own conclusions.

It might also be pointed out that this book was not written for Greek scholars. Nor was any attempt made to resolve the problems of interpretation of source material, etymology, and authorship. I accepted what is extant and what the commonly accepted authorships are. No attempt is made to quibble about meanings or translations of words and phrases. These matters have but a slight bearing on the approach in this study; they are left for the students of philology. I have selected commonly recognized authoritative translations, which have altered little in the last century. For our purposes, the nuances in the meanings brought out by various translators make little difference. For present day students, especially those of the social sciences, who are no longer receiving classical training, this book is written, with the hope of bridging a gap in their knowledge, and then giving them a better foundation for their own social thinking.

# CHAPTER II

## THE AGE OF HOMER AND HESIOD

AT THE end of the sixteenth century and the beginning of the fifteenth century B.C., there were three great powers dominating the east and the eastern coast of the Mediterranean. These were the powerful Egyptian Empire, the Hittite Kingdom in Asia Minor, and the alliance of the Aegean kingdom led by Crete.

The Cretan era (1550–1100 B.C.), often referred to as the Late Minoan or Mycenaean age, found civilization centered about the King at the palace of Cnossus. Shortly before, and during this period, continuous waves of migration of Indo-European peoples coming from the west side of the Black Sea pushed forward into the Greek peninsula. They did not stop there, for in the course of time they succeeded in taking over the entire Aegean world as well as Cretan civilization. These migrations not only covered the Greek mainland, but drove south, pressing the inhabitants out of their homes. About 1400 B.C., a branch of this group called the Dorians moved into Crete, successfully destroyed Cnossus, and dealt the final blow to Cretan leadership. From 1300 to 1000 B.C., the Greeks took possession of the remaining islands, along with the coast of Asia Minor. In the twelfth century B.C. (1192–1183), a Greek expedition captured the city of Troy at the end of a long siege. This is the war celebrated by Homer in the *Iliad*. Thus, in less than a millennium the Greeks took possession of the entire Greek peninsula as well as all the Aegean world. Consequently, the three thriving centers of civilization of the fifteenth century—Egypt, the Hittite Empire in Asia Minor, and Crete—are succeeded by a new civilization, the Greek.

These migrations extended over a vast period of years. The exact number of migrations is not known, but there were surely several. The factor of geography, combined with economic conditions, kept migrating stocks and portions of stocks welded together. It kept them divided into small economic and political units. Greece was never able to create a large and centralized political system. Among these units, which had within them the seed of the city-state, the tie of a common language was ever present. It might be more accurately stated that there was a tie of a common dialect of the one Greek language. The various dialects throw much light on the process of settlement of the Greek stocks in Greece. There is a sharp distinction between three of these dialects and they, in all probability, indicate three successive waves of migration. They are called the Arcadian or Aeolian-Achaian (which is said to be the oldest of the three), followed by the Ionian, and lastly, the Dorian.

The Greek world was divided by them. In northern Greece, which included Thessaly, central Greece with the exception of Attica, and all the north-west of Peloponnese, the Achaian-Aeolian dialect was spoken. The central Peloponnese and the island of Cyprus used the Arcadian dialect. Attica, Euboea, and almost all the Aegean islands (particularly the large ones, such as Imbros, Chios, Samos, Lemnos and Naxos) used the Ionian dialect. The Dorian dialect was found in Aetolia, in the south and east of Peloponnese, and in the southern islands of the Aegeans, including Crete and Rhodes. It also influenced the language of Boeotia and Thessaly. Similarly, Asia Minor was divided by these three groups. On the northern coast of the Aegean and that of the Black Sea, which includes Cyme, Smyrna, and Lesbos, we find the Aeolic dialect. The central coast was Ionian, and a small portion to the south near Rhodes and Crete was Dorian.

The organization of the early Greek settlements is described by Homer in the *Iliad* and *Odyssey*. In them he depicts the political, social, and economic organization of these communities. The epics are enacted during the period of the redistribution of Greek peoples. Homer called this Indo-European group which was coming into Greece, the "Achaeans." Through his eyes, the essential characteristics of the life of these people are revealed to us. Almost all the communities seem to have had similar economic, social and political institutions, intangibly connected with the Aegean phase, through which they had all passed.

The aristocracy, consisting of a few families who led the clan, comprised the ruling class in this Homeric Age. All the members of this group traced their descent to a god or hero. One of their number was the king, who directed the activities of the clan at all times. The clan was divided into sub-groups called *phratries* or brotherhoods, whose main functions were of a religious and military nature. Below the ruling families, we find the rest of the population also divided into various groups. Their status depended upon their social and economic position. Some members of this plebian mass owned land, while others were in the position of serfs. Some were laborers; others were artisans.

The land was divided in the following manner. Wood and pasture lands were reserved for the use of all. Special land was kept for the king. The king's councillors and the leaders of troops in wartime were allotted large estates. These were cultivated by their slaves and tenants. The freeman was allowed a piece of land for his house in the city and a field for cultivation in the country. There was no outright ownership of land by an individual. Ownership rights were vested in the family. Toutain points out, however, that joint ownership by an entire family existed side by side with individual ownership. Since war was ever present in this society, there was always an abundance of slaves.

Farming practices among the Greeks at this period consisted of simple cultivation of the soil, along with stock raising. The cultivation of olive trees and vines developed slowly. The common farm animals were cattle, swine, goats, and sheep.

Horses were owned only by the wealthy aristocratic families. A man's wealth was frequently measured by the size of his herd. As in all simple agricultural societies, little was bought and all necessities were produced in the home. Every member of the family had specific chores. The men plowed, sowed, reaped, herded cattle, milked, and hunted. The women spun, wove, washed, and cooked. Work was considered a good, no humiliation being attached to any sort of labor. In *The Odyssey*, Odysseus boasts of his ability in farming and carpentry. Penelope, his queen, is described as weaving daily with her maidens. The slaves usually were assigned the most menial tasks. Custom and religion, however, assured them humane treatment in the household.

The artisan, too, had his place in this society. He was called upon to perform all the difficult tasks which required craftsmanship. Ship building, house building, and similar work was done by the artisan, who received payment for his work. The merchants were also important components of this society. Priests and physicians were respected, as were the skilled singer and musician.

Commerce was regarded as an essential part of life during the Aegean age. The Greeks themselves had no metals and were at a loss without them. From the Aegeans, they learnt the art of navigation, and there was great desire to obtain the fine metal objects produced by the Egyptians. However, these early Greeks had little with which to trade, since most of their wealth lay in slaves and cattle. Consequently, their trading expeditions were in reality a form of piratical enterprise. These ventures were dangerous and not always successful. What objects they brought into the country, whether bought or stolen, were coveted by all. Local men often imitated these Eastern products, thus improving the local products.

The political system of Greece was, in all probability, much the same as that of the Aegean age. Each kingdom had its own king, supported by the clan and his companions-at-arms. The king inherited both his wealth and the right to rule from the gods.  Absolute power was his only upon the battlefield. There was no constitution to check his powers, but he was called to account by the council of elders and the popular assembly.  The council members had the same titles and the same honors as the king.  Homer speaks of them as "sceptre-bearing kings" and "fosterlings of Zeus."  The members of the council were on equal footing with the king at all times. They reprimanded him, disobeyed him, and gave him advice freely.

The council of elders consisted of about twelve men who were chosen either because of their descent or because of their success in battle.  The king always made a place on the council for the man of exceptional military ability.  Once a seat was established it became hereditary.  Voting was not used to decide issues; a discussion lasted until there was unanimous agreement.  The duties of the king as well as the councillors were never defined.  All worked together as equals, directing the affairs of the community in war and peace.

Although the king held the members of the plebian class in contempt, he dared not disregard their will.  Both in peace and war all men were called to the Assembly.  Usually the issues presented to the Assembly had been previously discussed by the elders.  They were always questions which vitally affected the people.  The king or his councillors would present his views to the commons.  They, in turn, would shout if they agreed to the proposal, or remain silent if they disapproved.  In general, their opinions were regarded as final.  It can easily be discerned that in these meetings lay the seeds of the democracy which was to flower in such Greek city-states as Athens.  At this period, however, the leaders allowed only as much democracy as was necessary.  The spirit of the ruling group was the powerful determinant in all decisions.

The city itself was small.  The king, his nobles, and his slaves lived within it, as did the agricultural class.  This latter group had their fields close by the city so that they were readily accessible. The artisans and merchants dwelt there as well. The fortification of the city was quite poor.

The gods had human form in Homeric religion. All were beautiful with the exception of Hephaestus, the lame smith. They differed from man in that they led a life of ease, feasted on nectar and ambrosia, and never died. Superior strength, beauty, and wisdom were also theirs. But they also had human failings. Pain and suffering, defeat and disappointment, were part of their lives. Even their knowledge and power were limited, although Zeus possessed the greatest wisdom and cunning. Dwelling together atop Olympus as a large family, they spent much time in feasting. Quarreling among them was frequent, just as it was among mortal families. Often they sat together in council with Zeus as presiding officer. Moral restraint was not an attribute of the gods, for sinning was as frequent among them as it was among mortals. Thus they possessed the qualities of man, both good and evil. Zeus was regarded with awe because of his great strength and wisdom. Man was close to the gods, and each man performed the religious rites for his family. Here and there were small temples tended by priests, but their influence was not very great.

The burial system of the Homeric Greeks was cremation. The corpse was burned, the ashes placed in an urn, and the urn buried. A pillar was usually placed at the site of the burial. After death, all souls passed on to Hades, beneath the earth. There they lived as shades, pale and unhappy. The shade of Achilles says to Odysseus, "Speak not comfortably to me of death, glorious Odysseus. I should rather be upon the field as the servant of another, of one who had no land and little property, than a king of all the dead." [1]

One must not infer that Homer lived during this period. Homer and the "Homeric Age" do not belong to the same epoch. The man Homer lived at some time during the ninth or eighth century. Thus the *Iliad* and the *Odyssey* were composed then. Whether such a person as Homer existed, and whether he was the original or sole author of these two epics, is a question to be left to those more steeped in classical philological discoveries. To the student of social thought, authorship is comparatively unimportant. The chief interest lies in the social thought that is to be found in these writings. Who wrote what and when it was written are of vital importance for accuracy in the history of Greek literature *per se*. We, however, are concerned with an approximation of time, place and authorship in order to evaluate the social thinking of the period.

Certain facts or truths, however, have been generally accepted about Homer. The first of these facts is that he lived in an era later than the one which he describes. Second, the *Iliad* and the *Odyssey* constitute the earliest specimens of Greek literature and hence Greek thought. Indeed, Xenophanes, the first writer in whose works we find mention of Homer's name, says, "From the beginning, for all have learned from him." [2] Third, the age he depicted existed in actuality. He was able to point out its main features with considerable accuracy, although dates cannot be assigned with exactness to the Homeric Age in human history. Fourth, the subsequent influence of Homer's writings was very great. Plato called him, "The poet wise in all things."

The circumstances of his life are not known with any degree of certainty. The date of his birth has been placed variously between 1050 and 850 B.C. Herodotus, the first man to attempt to fix the date of Homer's birth, argued that Homer had lived about four hundred years before. That is, he assigned Homer to the year 850 B.C. In regard to his place of birth, there is also great question. Many cities laid claim to him because of his fame. Smyrna has been most widely accepted as the place because much of his writing seemed to have its center there. The island of Chios may also have had the distinction, for it is said that he did much of his work there. Homer's dialect was a mixed one. It was substantially Ionic with wide use of Aeolic forms and words. Legend tells of a blind bard, who wandered from place to place earning his living by minstrelsy. [3]

Homer's two great epics were the *Iliad* and the *Odyssey*. The *Iliad* tells the story of the siege of Troy. The action takes place in the last year of the Trojan War, with most of the scenes laid either in camp or on the battlefield, and has soldiers as its chief characters. A great deal of space is given over to vivid descriptions of battles. The hero of the epic is Achilles, who has almost god-like characteristics. He quarrels with Agamemnon over a captive girl and in anger refuses to do battle even to help his friends. Patroclus, his dearest companion, goes into battle wearing armour borrowed from Achilles. In this encounter Hector, leader of the Trojans, succeeds in killing Patroclus. In grief and anger Achilles vows to avenge his comrade's death. He pursues Hector, kills him and mutilates his body in defiance of all codes of honor, but is finally stayed by Priam, Hector's father, who comes to ransom his dead son's body. Stirred by pity, Achilles gives the old man Hector's corpse. There is another tale unfolded in the *Iliad* as well—that of the fall of Troy. Troy has been besieged for ten long years because Paris, a Trojan, has stolen Helen, the wife of Menelaus. The Trojans stand by Paris and in consequence suffer disaster. Hector is the Trojan hero, and we are shown the cost of this war to him, his wife, and his family. In the end he is slain by Achilles, and the fall of Troy is finally accomplished.

The *Odyssey* is in the fullest measure a tale of adventure. Briefly, it deals with the wanderings of Odysseus on his way home from Troy. In the first section, we catch a glimpse of his home ten years after the Trojan War. Penelope, his wife, is beset by vulgar suitors who constantly annoy her, beseeching that she choose one of their number as a husband. She is unwilling to do so, since she has no knowledge as to her husband's whereabouts. It is not even known whether Odysseus is alive or dead. Her young son, Telemachus, sets out to discover news of his father. The second section deals with Odysseus' adventures since he has departed from Troy. These occurrences are in reality a loosely-bound group of old folk-tales about

monsters and unknown seas.   In them we meet the one-eyed
Polyphemus, the sorceress Circe, Calypso, Nausicaa, and many
others.   After many of these strangely exciting adventures,
Odysseus returns to his own fireside.   The remainder of the
story deals with his activities at home.   He ultimately kills all
his wife's suitors.   In the final scenes a conversation between
the shades of the dead suitors and the shades of the dead heroes
of the *Iliad* takes place.   This is the connecting link between
the two epics.

These stories told by Homer reveal a segment of an age
variously referred to as the Age of Homer and Hesiod, the Epic
Age, the Dark Age and the Middle Age.   This period, as generally accepted, extended from about 1250 to 700 B.C.   These
epics give us the first Greek poetry as well as the first glimmer-
ing of Greek history.   Life in Greece before the time of these
poems is known only through archaeological remains.   The
*Iliad* and the *Odyssey* are heroic epics, and although the events
they describe may be imaginary, it is difficult to believe that we
are not seeing an accurate picture of a way of life.

Homer's great effects are of "emotion expressed in action." [4]
It is perhaps true, as many have declared, that Homer does
not reveal explicitly his own judgments on life and society.   It
is nevertheless true that he reveals clearly the type of man he
admired.   It is also true that he observed the life about him
keenly.   Although there is little subjective bias in these works,
his ideas can be surmised by the deeds of his characters.   It
does not greatly matter who says a particular phrase if we can
gather from the whole that there is general agreement and
acceptance of particular views.   These views cannot, perhaps,
be attributed to Homer, but it may certainly be said that they
are views characteristic of Homeric writings.   These views are
also indicative of Homer's identification with the aristocratic
class and their ideals.   C. M. Bowra has pointed out that
Homer, "sang for princes and was concerned almost entirely
with them.   The bards whom he depicts in the *Odyssey* are
servants of kings, at whose court they live and for whose

pleasure they sing.   His own condition must have been like theirs, for his portrayal of them is too detailed and too sympathetic to be anything but a transcript from life.   Moreover his whole story is of kings, whom he calls 'Zeus-born.'   Their only critic, Thersites, is presented in an unfavorable, even hostile light, and the harsh punishment meted out to him by Odysseus is regarded as perfectly justified.   Being of humble position as the servant of princes, Homer says nothing about himself and passes no moral judgments.   He is not the social equal of his patrons and he attributes all that he says to the divine spirit of the Muse.   Moreover, the conception of manhood which he accepts is that of an age when the only men who mattered were kings who had power enough to fight successful battles and to be leaders of armies.   Such men need more than physical prowess; they must be wise in counsel and eloquent of tongue.   The basis of their ethics is highly individualistic." [5] The picture Homer presented was full of the life of kings.   But everywhere he injects into the scene the poor and humble, making no comment about their plight, but obviously feeling great sympathy for them.   It is not unlikely that he himself lived a life similar to theirs.   His works indicate clearly the sharp separation of classes in this society.   Homer was never able to speak of it, probably because of his own position, which must have been precarious.

What Homer found impossible to say, what he found impossible to describe—that is, the plight of the peasant in all his misery—came from the pen of another, Hesiod.   Toward the close of the eighth century B.C., the heroic, adventurous world of which the bards loved to sing faded, and with it went their art.   In its place came the pressing problems of the times.   The poor peasant farmer struggling for the bare necessities of life intruded on the thoughts of men.   The theme of the new literature was the peasant's life.

The farmers (members of the *demos*) were in a desperate situation.   The man who could support himself and his family with products from his scanty fields was fortunate.   Work on the farm was unceasing, clothes consisted of goat skins, and all sorts of privations were suffered. Debt was an ever-present misery. When it became too pressing, the farmers had to forfeit their farms. Many became day laborers and, what was far worse, slaves.

Thus it came about that the bards who had sung the songs of the heroes disappeared. Men heard a new song on behalf of the needy and humble. Hesiod, an unknown farmer, spoke of the drudgery and despair of the farmer's lot. In this, there was a complete reversal of Homer's theme. To Hesiod, the petty kings were not heroes, but bitter enemies of his class. He hated them because he saw in them a degenerate people, ruling without justice. In his *Works and Days,* he warns that Zeus could and would be invoked to halt their cruelty. Hesiod's works are pessimistic in the extreme, for he saw a life that was difficult and lacking in justice. The contrast between Homer and Hesiod was nowhere greater. Homer sang of an idealized picture of the past, while Hesiod saw only the hardship and toil of the life he and his neighbors led. His writing pointed out that the glories of which Homer spoke belonged only to the privileged few.

The facts of Hesiod's life have been obscured by the years. From his own *Works and Days,* we learn that his father became a trader because of his poverty in Cyme, and after sailing the seas for a time settled at Ascra in Boeotia. Here, presumably, the poet was born, although the point has been raised that he might have been born in Cyme and migrated to Ascra with his father. The father apparently became a fairly prosperous farmer, and upon his death left his land to his two sons, Hesiod and Perses. A disagreement over the division of the property arose and the quarrel was taken to court. In *Works and Days,* Hesiod maintains that the unjust decision was due to bribery on his brother's part. He sets out therefore in this work to admonish Perses, to give him advice about farming, general ideas about morality, and some information about navigation.

The dates of Hesiod's life are debatable. General opinion

holds that he lived in the first half of the eighth century, some-
what later than Homer.  Unquestionably he was a farmer, for
his work is saturated with agricultural knowledge.  That his
life must have been difficult can be readily seen in his writings.
His writings inspired a large number of imitators long after
his death.

Two works are attributed to Hesiod, *Works and Days* and
the *Theogony*.  Of the two, *Works and Days* is the more important.  The title is apt, since it dealt with the work of the
farmer and the days on which this work was to be done.  In
the first part of the poem Hesiod addresses his brother Perses,
with whom he has quarreled over the settlement of his father's
property.  He reprimands Perses for bribing the judges in
order that they might give him the larger share of the estate.
He then goes on to relate the necessary tasks on a farm, and in
the last section of the poem, he gives the propitious days for
carrying on this work.  The poem draws a complete picture of
the daily struggle for existence experienced by the Boeotian
farmer.  It is peppered with prudent everyday knowledge, and
shadowed by overtones of bitter despair and hopelessness.

The authorship of the *Theogony* has been questioned from
time to time.  General opinion, however, imputes the work to
Hesiod.  The poem is divided into two parts—the first describes the creation of Nature; the second deals with the birth
of the Gods.  It presents an extraordinarily interesting study
of early Greek religion.  The material for this work was undoubtedly gathered from old hymns, myths, and folk tales.

Quotations are given in the text from various extant writings referred to as the *Homeric Hymns,* the *Epigrams of
Homer,* and the *Contest of Homer and Hesiod.*  Homeric
Hymns containing about thirty-four poems stylistically classed
with Homer and Hesiod, have come down to us anonymously.
Each narrates some legend in connection with a particular
god.  In the *Hymn to Ares,* the poet lauds the god Ares and all
his virtues, praying that he may be saved from weakness of
soul and from feebleness.

The *Contest of Homer and Hesiod* in its present form dates back to the death of Hadrian. However, there is some evidence pointing to an earlier version written by Alcibiades about 400 B.C. The work as we know it today seems to be an amalgamation of two versions, much of it unclear in regard to the life of Homer. The poem may be divided into four sections. The first part relates the descent of Homer and the relative dates of Homer and Hesiod. The second part describes their contest at Chalcis. The third gives us a version of Hesiod's death. The final division deals with Homer's wanderings, as well as the circumstance of the creation of his epics.

*The Homeric Epigrams* are derived from various sources. Most of them occur in the pseudo-Herodotean *Life of Homer*. Some of the material in this work is drawn from the *Contest of Homer and Hesiod* as well as numerous other ancient works. Whether any of them actually go back to Homer's time is an unanswered problem.

In the social thought of the age of Homer and Hesiod, several concepts stand out prominently. These ideas were grouped and classified into seven categories: (1) *The Gods and Their Relation to Man;* (2) *Homeric Idea of Fate;* (3) *Ideas on Society;* (4) *Ideas on the Family;* (5) *Social Ethics of Homer and Hesiod;* (6) *The Decline of Man;* (7) *Principles of Economy and Rural Economy*. Many of these categories are self-explanatory. A brief description of them follows.

*The Gods and Their Relation to Man:* Homer conceived of the gods as superior men, with distinct personalities and functions, having all man's characteristics, both good and bad. They are men without the burdens of mankind—old age, weakness, responsibility. Often Homer points to their weaknesses with obvious delight. Their relation to man was a thing of caprice, for they aided those whom they loved and brought trouble to those whom they disliked.[6] Men who failed to offer sacrifices or who neglected to fulfill a vow were punished.[7] To

THE AGE OF HOMER AND HESIOD

some extent the gods were the guardians of right and the avengers of wrong.[8]

*Homeric Idea of Fate:* Homer believed, too, in the inevitability of events. Though he provided all things in nature with a guiding spirit, the actions of men followed a given course. Affairs went on in accordance with antecedent possibilities. These elements of the inevitable and probable constitute the fundamentals of the Homeric conception of fate as an all-pervading, resistless power inherent in circumstances and in the nature of men, events, and gods—a power essentially blind and implacable, utterly helpless to be or act in any other way than it does, a necessity for all, a necessity unto itself.[9]

*Ideas on Society:* It has been previously shown that Homer sang the song of the privileged class in society. It is to be expected, therefore, that he recognized the existence of social classes. And indeed he did, for we find many examples in his epics. Odysseus, in chiding the common soldier, cries, "sit still and hearken to the words of others who are thy betters." [10] While Homer constantly endorses the rule of the 'upper class,' Hesiod cries out on behalf of the Greek masses. Society, as he saw it, was filled with social abuses, distress, strife, and competition.[11] Also included in this section are passages which indicate that the writers of this period recognized the concept of division of labor in society. There is also an excerpt which might be considered a forerunner of the Malthusian doctrine.

*Ideas on the Family:* Both in Homer's and Hesiod's writings, there is much praise of the family and family life. Homer conceived the family as the foundation of social well-being and happiness. For Hesiod, the family was an economic blessing. Much love and tenderness is expressed for children. The family, of necessity, was a self-contained unit, protecting the lives and property of its members, and avenging its wrongs both individually and collectively. The mother held a position of honor in Homeric society, being regarded as a noble creature because she produced illustrious sons. Her name was often lauded even upon the battlefields. It must be remembered in this regard that for a family line to become extinct at that time was considered the greatest misfortune that could befall human beings. Hence the glorification of the mother who produced sons may be readily understood.[12]

*Social Ethics of Homer and Hesiod:* Homer looked backward in history to find the qualities of men that he most admired. Since the age of which he wrote was an era of constant warfare and personal heroism, he extolled the merits of the warrior as the highest good. Loyalty, courage, bravery, and clever war strategy were the greatest virtues of man. Hesiod, on the other hand, possessed a completely different set of values. He spoke little of the heroic virtues and lauded hard work. He seemed to feel that only through the sweat of ones brow could great things be achieved. His judgments were not based on life as it should have been, but on life as it was for him and his neighbors. He scorned those who would not recognize the struggle necessary to existence. In this exposition of the fight to live he always upheld the golden mean. There is an interesting contrast of ideas here; in some measure we find the same contrasting ethical values in the modern world.[13]

*The Decline of Man:* Hesiod, in his *Works and Days,* seeks to impress his brother Perses with the concept that it is the law of God for man to work hard. From this point, he goes on to elucidate the reasons for life's hardship. He seemed to believe in the law of deterioration as firmly and dogmatically as the past century believed in the law of progress. He conceived mankind as having passed through various ages —those of gold, silver, bronze, and, in his own time, iron. In the wonderful golden age, "men lived like gods, without sorrow . . . and dwelt in ease and peace upon their lands with many good things rich in flocks; and when they died it was as though they were overcome with sleep." The silver age was "less noble by far." These men grew up in one hundred years and were then killed by Zeus, "because they could not keep from wronging one another, nor would they sacrifice on the holy altars of the blessed ones as it is right for men to do wherever they dwell." Then came the age of bronze. The men of this age were, "terrible and strong: they loved the woeful works of the war god . . . these were destroyed by their own hands." Between this age and the iron age the poet inserts the age of heroes, "the race before our own. Grim war and dread battle destroyed a part of these, some at seven-gated Thebes and some at Troy." Finally we are at Hesiod's own age. Of this age he says, "men never rest from labor and sorrow by day and from perishing by night." "Would," says the poet, "that I were not among this generation, but had either died before or been born afterwards." [14]

*Economy and Rural Economy:* The excerpt under this classification comes from Hesiod's *Works and Days*. The passage is readily understandable and of keen interest. Hesiod exhorts his brother Perses to accept his lot in society, that of hard work, rather than depend on the work of others. Hesiod outlines a plan of work best suited for his brother. This can be construed as a plan suitable for anyone depending on the working of land for his livelihood. [15]

## 1. THE GODS AND THEIR RELATION TO MAN

### (Homer, *Odyssey*, I, 46–62) [16]

In the following selection, Pallas Athene prays to Zeus to have Odysseus, who is returning to Ithaca after his successful participation in the Trojan War, delivered to his kingdom. It depicts the dependence of man's activity on the good will of the gods.

"O father, our father Cronides, throned in the highest; that man assuredly lies in a death that is his due; so perish likewise all who work such deeds! But my heart is rent for wise Odysseus, the hapless one, who far from his friends this long while suffereth affliction in a seagirt isle, where is the navel of the sea, a woodland isle, and therein a goddess hath her habitation, the daughter of the wizard Atlas, who knows the depths of every sea, and himself upholds the tall pillars which keep earth and sky asunder.  His daughter it is that holds the hapless man in sorrow: and ever with soft and guileful tales she is wooing him to forgetfulness of Ithaca.  But Odysseus yearning to see if it were but the smoke leap upwards from his own land, hath a desire to die.  As for thee, thine heart regardeth it not at all, Olympian! What! did not Odysseus by the ships of the Argives make thee free offering of sacrifice in the wide Trojan land?  Wherefore wast thou so wroth with him, O Zeus?"

(Homer, *Odyssey*, I, 230–244)

In this excerpt and in the ones that follow, Homer observes ill-luck and evil resulting from the neglect of the gods.  Below, Telemachus, the son of Odysseus, is answering Pallas Athene, who is visiting Telemachus in Ithaca, bidding him call an assembly of the people, and go in search of his father.

"Sir, forasmuch as thou questionest me of these things, and inquirest thereof, our house was once like to have been rich and honourable, while yet that man was among his people. But now the gods willed it otherwise, in evil purpose, who have made him pass utterly out of sight as no man ever before. Truly I would not even for his death make so great sorrow, had he fallen among his fellows in the land of the Trojans, or in the arms of his friends when he had wound up the clew of war. Then would the whole Achaean host have builded him a barrow, and even for his son would he have won great glory in the after days.  But now the spirits of the storm have swept him away inglorious.  He is gone, lost to sight and hearsay, but for me hath he left anguish and lamentation; nor henceforth is it for him alone that I mourn and weep, since the gods have wrought for me other sore distress."

(Homer, *Iliad*, XXIII, 862–871) [17]

Teukros, the great archer, forgetful of Apollo, fails to win the prize.

. . . then arose the strength of the chief Teukros, and
Meriones arose, Idomeneus' brave brother in arms.  And they
took lots and shook them in a brazen helm, and Teukros drew
the first place by lot.  Forthwith he shot an arrow with power,
but made no vow to offer a famous hecatomb of firstling lambs
to the Lord of archery.  The bird he missed—Apollo grudged
him that—but struck the cord beside its foot, where the bird
was tied, and the keen dart cut the cord clean away.  Then the
bird shot up toward heaven, and the cord hung loose toward
earth; and the Archaians shouted.  Then Meriones made
haste, and took from Teukros' hand the bow;—an arrow he
had ready, while the other aimed—and vowed withal to far-
dating Apollo a famous hecatomb of firstling lambs.  High up
under the clouds he saw the pigeon; there, as she circled round,
he struck her in the midst beneath her wing, and right through
went the dart, and fell back and fixed itself in the ground
before Meriones' foot; . . .

(Homer, *Odyssey,* XIV, 83–84)

Homeric ethics were closely tied with the Greeks' conception of the
gods.

"Verily the blessed gods love not froward deeds, but they
reverence justice and the righteous acts of men."

(Homer, *Odyssey,* XVIII, 130–142)

"Nought feebler doth the earth nurture than man, of all the
creatures that breathe and move upon the face of the earth.
Lo, he thinks that he shall never suffer evil in time to come,
while the gods give him happiness, and his limbs move lightly.
But when again the blessed gods have wrought for him sorrow,
even so he bears it, as he must, with a steadfast heart.  For the
spirit of men upon the earth is even as their day, that comes
upon them from the father of gods and men.  Yea, and I too
once was like to have been prosperous among men, but many
an infatuate deed I did, giving place to mine own hardihood
and strength, and trusting to my father and my brethren.

Wherefore let no man forever be lawless any more; but keep quietly the gifts of the gods, whatsoever they may give."

(Homer, *Iliad*, II, 591–600)

Homer is here recounting all the hosts of the Achaians and Trojans. We have an indication here how highly regarded the gods were and how quickly offenses against the gods were punished.

And of them that dwelt in Pylos and lovely Arene and Thryon the fording-place of Alpheios, and in stablished Aipy, and were inhabitants of Kyparisseis and Amphigeneia and Pteleos and Helos and Dorion—when the muses met Thamyris, the Thracian, and made an end of his singing, as he was faring from Oichalia, from Eurytos the Oichalian; for he averred with boasting that he would conquer, even did the Muses themselves sing against him, the daughters of aegis-bearing Zeus; but they in their anger maimed him, moreover they took from him the high gift of song and made him to forget his harping. . . .

(Homer, *Iliad*, IX, 533–539)

Below we find how quickly the offended gods punish man for any oversight in his religious observances. Artemis, who is forgotten in sacrifice, sends a plague to the neglectful.

For Artemis of the golden throne had brought a plague upon them, in wrath that Oineus offered her not the harvest first-fruits on the fat of his garden land; for all the other gods had their feast of hecatombs, and only to the daughter of great Zeus offered he not, whether he forgat or marked it not; and therein sinned he sore in his heart. So the Archer-goddess was wroth and sent against him a creature of heaven, a fierce wild boar, white-tusked, that wrought sore ill continually on Oineus' garden land; many a tall tree laid he low utterly, even root and apple blossom therewith. But him slew Meleagros the son of Oineus, having gathered together from many cities huntsmen and hounds; for not of few men could the boar be slain, so mighty was he; and many an one brought he to the grievous pyre.  But the goddess made much turmoil over him and tumult concerning the boar's head and shaggy hide, between the Kuretes and great-hearted Aitolians.

(Homer, Odyssey, I, 32–43)

Zeus speaks out in a council of the gods.

"Lo you now, how vainly mortal men do blame the gods! For of us they say comes evil, whereas they even of themselves, through the blindness of their own hearts, have sorrows beyond that which is ordained.  Even as of late Aegisthus, beyond that which was ordained, took to him the wedded wife of the son of Atreus and killed her lord on his return, and that with sheer doom before his eyes, since we had warned him by the embassy of Hermes the keen-sighted, the slayer of Argos, that he should neither kill the man, nor woo his wife.  For the son of Artreus shall be avenged at the hand of Orestes, so soon as he shall come to man's estate and long for his own country.  So spake Hermes, yet he prevailed not on the heart of Aegisthus, for all his good will; but now hath he paid for all."

(Hymn to Ares, The Homeric Hymns, VIII, l. 1–18) [18]

In the Hymn to Ares after praising the God by enumerating his attributes, the author prays to be delivered from feebleness and weakness of soul, and also from impulses to wanton and brutal violence.

Ares, exceeding in strength, chariot-rider, golden-helmed, doughty in heart, shield-bearer, Saviour of cities, harnessed in bronze, strong of arm, unwearying, mighty with the spear, O defence of Olympus, father of warlike Victory, ally of Themis, stern governor of the rebellious, leader of righteous men, sceptred King of manliness, who whirl your fiery sphere among the planets in their sevenfold courses through the aether wherein your blazing steeds ever bear you above the third firmament of heaven; hear me, helper of men, giver of dauntless youth!  Shed down a kindly ray from above upon my life, and strength of war, that I may be able to drive away bitter cowardice from my head and crush down the deceitful impulses of my soul.  Restrain also the keen fury of my heart which provokes me to tread the ways of blood-curdling strife. Rather, O blessed one, give you me boldness to abide within the harmless laws of peace, avoiding strife and hatred and the violent fiends of death.

## 2. Homeric Idea of Fate

The first group of excerpts below tends to show fate as an inevitable and all-prevailing force inherent in all natures, including man, things, and gods.

### (Homer, *Odyssey*, VII, 188–200)

"Now that the feast is over, go ye home and lie down to rest; and in the morning we will call yet more elders together, and entertain the stranger in the halls and do fair sacrifice to the gods, and thereafter we will likewise bethink us of the convoy, that so without pain or grief yonder stranger may by our convoy reach his own country speedily and with joy, even though he be from very far away.  So shall he suffer no hurt or harm in mid passage, ere he set foot on his own land; but thereafter he shall endure such things as Fate and the stern spinning women drew off the spindles for him at his birth when his mother bare him."

### (Homer, *Iliad*, XVII, 441–447)

The horses and men grieved over Patroclus' death.  His own horses wept.

And when the son of Kronos beheld them mourning he had compassion on them, and shook his head and spake to his own heart: "Ah, hapless pair, why gave we you to king Peleus, a mortal man, while ye are deathless and ever young?  Was it that ye should suffer sorrows among ill-fated men?  For methinketh there is nothing more piteous than a man among all things that breathe and creep upon the earth."

### (Homer, *Iliad*, VI, 144–149)

Diomedes and Glaukos met in battle.  Diomedes inquired of Glaukos who he was.

Then Hippolochus' glorious son made answer to him: "Great-hearted Tydeides, why enquirest thou of my generation? Even as are the generations of leaves such are those likewise of men; the leaves that be the wind scattereth on the earth, and the forest buddeth and putteth forth more again, when the season of spring is at hand; so of the generations of men one putteth forth and another ceaseth."

(Homer, *Iliad*, XX, 119–131)

Hera is speaking about Aineias, who is going to meet the son of Peleus in battle.

"Come then, be it ours to turn him back straightway; or else let some one of us stand likewise beside Achilles and give him mighty power, so that he fail not in his spirit, but know that they who love him are the best of the Immortals, and that they who from of old ward war and fighting from the Trojans are vain as wind. All we from Olympus are come down to mingle in this fight that he take no hurt among the Trojans on this day—afterward he shall suffer whatsoever things Fate span for him with her thread, at his beginning, when his mother bore him. If Achilles learn not this from voice divine, then shall he be afraid when some god shall come against him in the battle; for gods revealed are hard to look upon."

(Homer, *Iliad*, VI, 482–493)

Hector is bidding farewell to his wife Andromache.

So spake he and laid his son in his dear wife's arms; and she took him to her fragrant bosom, smiling tearfully. And her husband had pity to see her, and caressed her with his hand, and spake and called upon her name: "Dear one, I pray thee be not of oversorrowful heart; no man against my fate shall hurl me to Hades; only destiny, I ween, no man hath escaped, be he coward or be he valiant, when once he hath been born. But go thou to thine house and see to thine own tasks, the loom and distaff, and bid thine handmaidens ply

their works; but for war shall men provide and I in chief of
all men that dwell in Ilios."

(Homer, Iliad, XVIII, 112-121)

Achilles is grieved for Patroclus' death and is determined to avenge it.

"But bygones will we let be, for all our pain, curbing the
heart in our breasts under necessity.  Now go I forth that I may
light on the destroyer of him I loved, on Hector: then will
I accept death whensoever Zeus willeth to accomplish it and
the other immortal gods.  For not even the mighty Herakles
escaped death, albeit most dear to Kronian Zeus the king, but
Fate overcame him and Hera's cruel wrath.  So also shall I, if
my fate hath been fashioned likewise, lie low when I am dead."

(Homer, Odyssey, XX, 73-78)

"Now while fair Aphrodite was wending to high Olympus,
to pray that a glad marriage might be accomplished for the
maidens, and to Zeus she went whose joy is in the thunder,
for he knows all things well, what the fates give and deny to
mortal men. . . ."

### 3. IDEAS ON SOCIETY

(Hesiod, Works and Days, l. 11-41) [18]

Hesiod depicts the strife inherent in society.

So after all, there was not one kind of Strife alone, but all
over the earth there are two.  As for the one, a man would
praise her when he came to understand her; but the other is
blameworthy: and they are wholly different in nature.  For one
fosters evil war and battle, being cruel: her no man loves; but
perforce, through the will of the deathless gods, men pay
harsh Strife her honour due.  But the other is the elder daughter
of dark Night, and the son of Cronos who sits above and dwells
in the aether, set her in roots of the earth: and she is far kinder
to men.  She stirs up even the shiftless to toil; for a man grows
eager to work when he considers his neighbor, a rich man who

hastens to plough and plant and put his house in good order; and neighbor vies with his neighbor as he hurries after wealth. This Strife is wholesome for men. And potter is angry with potter, and craftsman with craftsman, and beggar is jealous of beggar, and minstrel of minstrel.

Perses, lay up these things in your heart, and do not let the Strife who delights in mischief hold your heart back from work, while you peep and peer and listen to the wrangles of the courthouse. Little concern has he with quarrels and courts who has not a year's victuals laid up betimes, even that which the earth bears, Demeter's grain. When you have got plenty of that, you can raise disputes and strive to get another's goods. But you shall have no second chance to deal so again: nay, let us settle our dispute here with true judgment which is of Zeus and is perfect. For we had already divided our inheritance, but you seized the greater share and carried it off, greatly swelling the glory of our bribe-swallowing lords who love to judge such a cause as this. Fools! They know not how much more the half is than the whole, nor what great advantage there is in mallow and asphodel.[19]

(Homer, *Iliad*, II, 1–206)

The following selection presents an interesting view of public life. At the same time it affords information on social classes and social feelings as Homer conceived them. It is worth noting the vast pretensions of the king and his councilors, and their decisive hatred for the common people. It will at the same time give us an insight into the social implications of Homeric religion.

Now all other gods and chariot driving men slept all night long, only Zeus was not holden of sweet sleep; rather was he pondering in his heart how he should do honour to Achilles and destroy many beside the Achaians' ships. And this design seemed to his mind the best, to wit, to send a baneful dream upon Agamemnon, son of Atreus. So he spake and uttered to him winged words: "Come now, thou baneful Dream, go to the Achaian's fleet ships, enter into the hut of Agamemnon son of Atreus, and tell him every word plainly as I charge thee. Bid him call to arms the flowing haired Achaians with all speed, for that now he may take the wide-wayed city of the Trojans. For the immortals that dwell in the halls of Olympus are no longer divided in counsel, since Hera hath turned the minds of all by her beseeching, and over the Trojans sorrows hang."

So spake he, and the Dream went his way when he had heard the charge. With speed he came to the Achaians' fleet ships, and went to Agamemnon son of Atreus, and found him sleeping in his hut, and ambrosial slumber poured over him. So he stood over his head in seeming like unto the son of Neleus, even Nestor, whom most of all the elders Agamemnon honoured; in his likeness spake to him the heavenly Dream:

"Sleepest thou, son of wise Atreus tamer of horses! To sleep all night through, beseemeth not one that is a counsellor, to whom peoples are entrusted and so many cares belong. But now hearken straightway to me, for I am a messenger to thee from Zeus, who though he be afar yet hath great care for thee and pity. He biddeth thee call to arms the flowing-haired Achaians with all speed, for that now thou mayest take the wide-wayed city of the Trojans. For the immortals that dwell in the halls of Olympus are no longer divided in counsel, since Hera hath turned the minds of all by her beseeching, and over the Trojans sorrows hang by the will of Zeus. But do thou keep this in thy heart, nor let forgetfulness come upon thee when honeyed sleep shall leave thee."

So spake the Dream, and departed and left him there, deeming in his mind things that were not to be fulfilled. For indeed he thought to take Priam's city that very day; fond man in that he knew not the plans that Zeus had in mind, who was willed to bring yet more grief and wailing on Trojans alike and Danaans throughout the course of stubborn fights. Then woke he from sleep, and the heavenly voice was in his ears. So he rose up sitting and donned his soft tunic, fair and bright, and cast around him his great cloak, and beneath his glistering feet he bound his fair sandals and over his shoulder cast his silver studded sword, and grasped his sires' sceptre, imperishable forever, wherewith he took his way amid the mail-clad Achaians' ships.

Now went the goddess Dawn to high Olympus, foretelling daylight to Zeus and all the immortals; and the king bade the clear-voiced heralds summon to the assembly the flowing haired Achaians. So did those summon, and these gathered with speed.

But first the council of the great hearted elders met beside the ship of King Nestor the Pylos-born, and he that had assembled them framed his cunning counsel: "Hearken my friends. A dream from heaven came to me in my sleep through the ambrosial night, and chiefly to goodly Nestor was very like in shape and bulk and stature. And it stood over my head and charged me saying: 'Sleepest thou, son of wise Atreus tamer of horses? To sleep all night through beseemeth not one that is a counsellor to whom peoples are entrusted and so many cares belong. But now hearken straightway to me, for I am a messenger to thee from Zeus, who though he be afar yet hath great care for thee and pity. He biddeth thee call to arms the flowing haired Achaians with all speed, for that now thou mayest take the wide-wayed city of the Trojans. For the Immortals that dwell in the palaces of Olympus are no longer divided in counsel, since Hera hath turned the minds of all by her beseeching, and over the Trojans' sorrows hang by the will of Zeus. But keep thou this in thy heart.' So spake the dream and was flown away, and sweet sleep left me. So come, let us now call to arms as we may the sons of the Achaians. But first I will speak to make trial of them as is fitting, and will bid them flee with their benched ships; only do ye from this side and from that speak to hold them back."

So spake he and sate him down; and there stood up among them Nestor, who was King of sandy Pylos. He of good intent made harangue to them and said: "My friends, captains and rulers of the Argives, had any other of the Achaians told us this dream we might deem it a false thing, and rather turn away therefrom; but now he hath seen it who of all the Achaians avoweth himself far greatest. So come, let us call to arms as we may the sons of Achaians."

So spake he, and led the way forth from the council, and all the other sceptred chiefs rose with him and obeyed the shepherd of the host; and the people hastened to them. Even as when the tribes of thronging bees issue from some hollow rock, ever in fresh procession, and fly clustering among the flowers of spring, and some on this hand and some on that fly thick; even so from ships and huts before the low beach marched forth their many tribes by companies to the place of assembly. And in their midst blazed forth Rumour, messenger of Zeus, urging them to go; and so they gathered. And the place of assemblage was in an uproar, and the earth echoed again as the hosts sate them down, and there was turmoil. Nine heralds restrained them with shouting, if perchance they might refrain from clamour, and hearken to their kings, the fosterlings of Zeus. And hardly at the last would the people sit, and keep them to their benches and cease from noise. Then stood up lord Agamemnon bearing his sceptre, that Hephaistos had wrought curiously. Hephaistos gave it to king Zeus son of Kronos, and then Zeus gave it to the messenger-god, the slayer of Argus; and king Hermes gave it to Pelops, the charioteer, and Pelops again gave it to Atreus, shepherd of the host. And Atreus dying left it to Thyestes rich in flocks, and Thyestes in his turn left it to Agamemnon to bear, that over many islands and all Argos he should be lord. Thereon he leaned and spake his saying to the Argives:

"My friends, Danaan warriors, men of Ares' company, Zeus Kronos' son hath bound me with might in grievous blindness of soul; hard of heart is he, for that erewhile he promised me and pledged his nod that not till I had wasted well-walled Ilios should I return; but now see I that he planned a cruel wile and biddeth me return to Argos dishonoured, with the loss of many of my folk. So meseems it pleaseth most mighty Zeus, who hath laid low the head of many a city, yea, and shall lay low;

for his is highest power. Shame is this even for them that come after to hear; how so goodly and great a folk of the Achaians thus vainly warred a bootless war; and fought scantier enemies, and no end thereof is yet seen. For if perchance we were minded, both Achaians and Trojans, to swear a solemn truce, and to number ourselves, and if the Trojans should gather together all that have their dwellings in the city, and we Achaians should marshall ourselves by tens and every company chose a Trojan to pour their wine, then would many tens lack a cupbearer: so much, I say do the sons of the Achaians outnumber the Trojans that dwell in the city. But allies from many cities, even warriors that wield the spear, are therein, and they hinder me perforce, and for all my will suffer me not to waste the populous citadel of Ilios. Already have nine years of great Zeus passed away, and our ships' timbers have rotted and the tackling is loosed; while our wives and little children sit in our halls awaiting us; yet is our task utterly unaccomplished wherefor we came hither. So come, even as I shall bid let us all obey. Let us flee with our ships to our dear native land, for now shall we never take wide-wayed Troy."

So spake he, and stirred the spirit in the breasts of all throughout the multitude, as many as had not heard the council. And the assembly swayed like high sea waves of the Icarian Main, that east wind and south wind raise, rushing upon them from the clouds of father Zeus; and even as when the west wind cometh to stir a deep cornfield with violent blast, and the ears bow down, so was all the assembly stirred, and they with shouting hasted toward the ships; and the dust from beneath their feet rose and stood on high. And they bade each man his neighbour to seize the ships and drag them into the bright salt sea, and cleared out the launching-ways, and the noise went up to heaven of their hurrying homewards; and they began to take the props from beneath the ships.

Then would the Argives have accomplished their return against the will of fate, but that Hera spake a word to Athene: "Out on it, daughter of aegis-bearing Zeus, unwearied maiden!

Shall the Argives indeed flee home-ward to their dear native land over the sea's broad back?  But they would leave to Priam and the Trojans their boast, even Helen of Argos, for whose sake many an Achaian hath perished in Troy, far away from his dear native land.  But go now amid the host of the mail-clad Achaians; with thy gentle words refrain thou every man, neither suffer them to draw their curved ships down to the salt sea."

So spake she, and the bright-eyed goddess Athene disregarded not, but went darting from the peaks of Olympus, and came with speed to the fleet ships of the Achaians.  There found she Odysseus standing, peer of Zeus in counsel, neither laid he any hand upon his decked black ship, because grief had entered into his heart and soul.  And bright-eyed Athene stood by him and said: "Heaven-sprung son of Laertes, Odysseus of many devices, will ye indeed fling yourselves upon your benched ships to flee homeward to your dear native land?  But ye would leave to Priam and the Trojans their boast, even Helen of Argos, for whose sake many an Achaian hath perished in Troy, far from his dear native land.  But go thou now amid the host of the Achaians, and tarry not; and with thy gentle words refrain every man, neither suffer them to draw their curved ships down to the salt sea."

So said she, and he knew the voice of the goddess speaking to him, and set him to run, and cast away his mantle, the which his herald gathered up, even Eurybates of Ithaca, that waited on him.  And himself he went to meet Agamemnon, son of Atreus, and at his hand received the sceptre of his sires, imperishable for ever, wherewith he took his way amid the ships of the mail-clad Achaians.

Whenever he found one that was a captain and a man of mark, he stood by his side, and refrained him with gentle words: "Good sir, it is not seemly to affright thee like a coward, but do thou sit thyself and make all thy folk sit down. For thou knowest not yet clearly what is the purpose of Atreus' son; now is he but making trial, and soon he will afflict the sons of the Achaians. And heard we not all of us what he spake in the council? Beware lest in his anger he evilly entreat the sons of the Achaians. For proud is the soul of heaven-fostered kings; because their honour is of Zeus, and the god of counsel loveth them."

But whatever man of the people he saw and found him shouting, him he drave with his sceptre and chode him with loud words: "Good sir, sit still and hearken to the words of others that are thy betters; but thou art no warrior, and a weakling, never reckoned whether in battle or in council. In no wise can we Achaians all be kings here. A multitude of masters is no good thing; let there be one master, one king, to whom the son of crooked-counselling Kronos hath granted it, [even the sceptre and judgments, that he may rule among you]."

(Homer, Iliad, XIII, 725–734)

Polydamas here counsels Hector to withdraw from the battle and plan a better strategy. In the following passage, Homer gives evidence of recognizing a division of labor and specialized aptitudes existing in society.

Polydamas came near valiant Hector and said: "Hector, thou art hard to be persuaded by them that would counsel thee; for that god has given thee excellence in the works of war, therefore in council also thou art fair to excel other men in knowledge. But in nowise wilt thou be able to take everything on thyself. For to one man has god given for his portion the works of war, [to another the dance, to another the lute and song,] but in the heart of yet another hath far-seeing Zeus placed an excellent understanding, whereof many men get gain, yea he saveth many an one, and himself best knoweth it."

(Homer, Odyssey, VIII, 165–177)

The men of the court of King Alcinous are conducting sports and one of them challenges Odysseus to show his prowess. Odysseus becomes angered and answers him in the following fashion. Once again we notice Homer's realization of a division of labor in society based on differential innate capacities among men.

Then Odysseus of many counsels looked fiercely on him and said: "Stranger, thou hast not spoken well; thou art like a man presumptuous. So true it is that the gods do not give every gracious gift to all, neither shapeliness, nor wisdom, nor skilled speech. For one man is feebler than another in presence, yet the god crowns his words with beauty, and men behold him and rejoice, and his speech runs surely on his way with a sweet modesty, and he shines forth among the gathering of his people, and as he passes through the town men gaze on him as a god. Another again is like the deathless gods for beauty, but his words have no crown of grace about them; even as thou art in comeliness pre-eminent, nor could a god himself fashion thee for the better, but in wit thou art a weakling."

(Homer, *Odyssey*, XV, 390–401)

Homer pictures the joy and satisfaction of human intercourse between understanding men. Odysseus and Eumaeus are supping in Eumaeus' hut, Odysseus asks Eumaeus' story—how he came to wander from his country. Eumaeus answers:

"Stranger, since thou askest and questionest me thereof give heed now in silence and make merry, and abide here drinking wine. Lo, the nights now are of length untold. Time is there to sleep, and time to listen and be glad; thou needest not turn to bed before the hour; even too much sleep is vexation of spirit. But for the rest, let him whose heart and mind bid him, go forth and slumber, and at the dawning of the day let him break his fast, and follow our master's swine. But let us twain drink and feast within the steading, and each in his neighbours' sorrows take delight, recalling them, for even the memory of griefs is a joy to a man who hath been sore tried and wandered far."

(Cyclic Epics, *Cypria*, l. 16–23) [20]

In the following excerpt it is interesting to note a prototype of the theory of Malthus.

Once on a time was Earth by the races of men made weary,
Who were wandering numberless over the breadth of her
 bosom.
Zeus with pity beheld it, and took in his wise heart counsel
How to relieve of her burden the Earth, life-giver to all
 things,
Fanning to flame that terrible struggle, the war upon Troia.
So should the burden by death be removed; and they in the
 Trood
Perished the heroes; the counsel of Zeus was brought to
 fulfillment.

### 4. IDEAS ON THE FAMILY

#### (Homer, *Odyssey*, VI, 179–185)

Homer, through Odysseus, extols and praises the institution of the family. In the following quotation Odysseus is addressing Nausicaa, who welcomes and feeds Odysseus when he meets her during his wanderings.

"And may the gods grant thee all thy heart's desire: a husband and a home, and a mind at one with his may they give —a good gift, for there is nothing mightier and nobler than when man and wife are of one heart and mind in a house, a grief to their foes, and to their friends a great joy, but their own hearts know it best."

#### (Hesiod, *Works and Days*, 695–721)

Bring home a wife to your house when you are of the right age, while you are not far short of thirty years nor much above; this is the right age for marriage. Let your wife have been grown up four years, and marry her in the fifth. Marry a maiden, so that you can teach her careful ways, and especially marry one who lives near you, but look well about you and see that your marriage will not be a joke to your neighbors. For a man wins nothing better than a good wife, and, again nothing worse than a bad one, a greedy soul who roasts her man without fire, strong though he may be, and brings him to a raw old age.

Be careful to avoid the anger of the deathless gods.  Do not make a friend equal to a brother; but if you do, do not wrong him first, and do not lie to please the tongue.  But if he wrong you first, offending either in word or in deed, remember to repay him double; but if he ask you to be his friend again and be ready to give you satisfaction, welcome him.  He is a worthless man who makes now one and now another friend; but as for you, do not let your face put your heart to shame.

Do not get a name either as lavish or as churlish; as a friend of rogues or as a slanderer of good men.

Never dare to taunt a man with deadly poverty which eats out the heart; it is sent by the deathless gods.  The best treasure a man can have is a sparing tongue, and the greatest pleasure, one that moves orderly; for if you speak evil, you yourself will soon be worse spoken of.

(Homer, Iliad, VI, 476–481)

Great sympathy for children is pictured.  Men and women love their children.  Hector, below, prays that his son's fame may surpass his own.

"O, Zeus and all ye gods, vouchsafe ye that this my son may likewise prove even as I, pre-eminent amid the Trojans, and as valiant in might, and be a great king of Ilios.  Then may men say of him, 'Far greater is he than his father' as he returneth home from battle; and may he bring with him blood-stained spoils from the foeman he hath slain, and may his mother's heart be glad."

(Homer, Iliad, XXIV, 503–521)

Priam comes to fetch his son Hector's body from Achilles and moves Achilles to great pity for him.  Homer once again depicts the importance and the love of children in Homeric society.

"Yea, fear thou the gods, Achilles, and have compassion on me, even me, bethinking thee of thy father.  Lo, I am yet more piteous than he, and have braved what none other man on earth hath braved before, to stretch forth my hand toward the face of the slayer of my sons."

Thus spake he, and stirred within Achilles desire to mal lament for his father. And he touched the old man's hand and gently moved him back. And as they both bethought them of their dead, so Priam for man-slaying Hector wept sore as he was fallen before Achilles' feet, and Achilles wept for his own father, and now again for Patroklos, and their moan went up throughout the house. But when noble Achilles had satisfied him with lament, and the desire thereof departed from his heart and limbs, straightway he sprang from his seat and raised the old man by his hand, pitying his hoary head and hoary beard, and spake unto him winged words and said: "Ah hapless! many ill things verily thou hast endured in thy heart. How durst thou come alone to the ships of the Achaians and to meet the eyes of the man who hath slain full many of thy brave sons—of iron verily is thy heart."

(Homer, *Odyssey*, XI, 487–493)

The following passage is cited to illustrate again the close ties between parent and child. Homer makes the absent hero inquire tenderly about his son.

"Even so I spake, and he straightway answered me and said: 'Nay, speak not comfortably to me of death, oh great Odysseus. Rather, would I live on ground as the hireling of another, with a landless man who had no great livelihood, than bear sway among all the dead that be departed. But come, tell me tidings of that lordly son of mine—did he follow to the war to be a leader or not?' "

(Homer's *Epigrams*, XIII) [18]

Children are a man's crown, towers of a city; horses are the glory of a plain, and so are ships of the sea; wealth will make a house great, and reverend princes seated in assembly are a goodly sight for folks to see. But a blazing fire makes a house look more comely on a winter's day, when the son of Cronos sends down snow.

(Homer, *Iliad*, XXII, 477–514)

Homer pities the orphan child made orphan by the death of his father in war.  Andromache is lamenting the death of Hector, killed in battle.

"O Hector, woe is me! to one fate then were we both born, thou in Troy in the house of Priam, and I in Thebe under woody Plakos, in the house of Eëtion, who reared me from a little one—ill-fated sire of cruel-fated child.  Ah, would he had begotten me not.  Now thou to the house of Hades beneath the secret places of the earth departest, and me in bitter mourning thou leavest a widow in thy halls: and thy son is but an infant child—son of unhappy parents, thee and me—nor shalt thou profit him, Hector, since thou art dead, neither he thee.  For even if he escape the Archaians' woeful war, yet shall labour and sorrow cleave unto him hereafter, for other men shall seize his lands.  The day of orphanage sundereth a child from his fellows, and his head is bowed down ever, and his cheeks are wet with tears.  And in his need the child seeketh his father's friends, plucking this one by cloak and that by coat, and one of them that pity him holdeth his cup a little to his mouth, and moisteneth his lips, but his palate he moisteneth not.  And some child unorphaned thrusteth him from the feast with blows and taunting words, 'Out with thee, no father of thine is at our board.'  Then weeping to his widowed mother shall he return, even Astyanax, who erst upon his father's knee ate only marrow and fat flesh of sheep; and when sleep fell on him and he ceased from childish play, then in bed in his nurse's arms he would slumber softly nested, having satisfied his heart with good things; but now that he hath lost his father he will suffer many ills, Astyanax—that name the Trojans gave him, because thou only wert the defence of their gates and their long walls.  But now by the beaked ships, far from thy parents, shall coiling worms devour thee when the dogs have had their fill, as thou liest naked; yet in these halls lieth raiment of thine, delicate and fair, wrought by the hands of women.  But verily all these will I consume with burning fire—to thee no profit, since thou wilt

never lie therein, yet that this be honour to thee from the men
and the women of Troy."

(Hesiod, *Theogony*, l. 591–612)

For from her is the race of women and female kind; of her
is the deadly race and tribe of women who live amongst mortal
men to their great trouble, no helpmeets in hateful poverty, but
only in wealth.   And as in thatched hives bees feed the drones
whose nature is to do mischief—by day and throughout the
day until the sun goes down the bees are busy and lay the white
combs, while the drones stay at home in the covered skepo and
reap the toil of others into their own bellies—even so Zeus who
thunders on high made women to be an evil to mortal men, with
a nature to do evil.   And he gave them a second evil to be the
price for the good they had:  whoever avoids marriage and the
sorrows that women cause and will not wed, reaches deadly old
age without anyone to tend his years, and though he at least has
no lack of livelihood while he lives, yet, when he is dead, his
kinsfolk divide his possessions amongst them.   And as for the
man who chooses the lot of marriage and takes a good wife
suited to his mind, evil continually contends with good:  for
whoever happens to have mischievous children, lives always
with unceasing grief in his spirit and heart within him; and this
evil cannot be healed.

(Homer, *Odyssey*, XI, 271–280)

In Homer's works incest is objected to in so far as it unites mother
and son.   No objection is raised to cases of marriage between brother and
sister, nephew and aunt, uncle and niece.   In the following passage
Oedipus is pursued by the avenging deity (Erinyes) of his mother after
she commits suicide by hanging.   Incest between son and mother was considered a mortal crime.

"And I saw the mother of Oedipus, fair Epicaste, who
wrought a dread deed unwittingly, being wedded to her own
son, and he that had slain his own father wedded her, and
straightway the gods made these things known to men.   Yet he

abode in pain in pleasant Thebes, ruling the Cadmaeans, by reason of the deadly counsels of the gods. But she went down to the house of Hades, the mighty warder; yea, she tied a noose from the high beam aloft, being fast holden in sorrow; while for him she left pains behind full many, even all that the Avengers of a mother bring to pass.

(Homer, Odyssey, X, 1–12)

Odysseus comes to the island of Aeolian where he is entertained by King Aeolus. In the following excerpt, Odysseus describes the practice of incest among the inhabitants of the island. The passage is illustrative of the tolerance of fraternal incest.

"Then we came to the isle Aeolia, where dwelt Aeolus, son of Hippotas, dear to the deathless gods, in a floating island, and all about it is a wall of bronze unbroken, and the cliff runs up sheer from the sea. His twelve daughters too abide there in his halls, six daughters and six lusty sons: and, behold, he gave his daughters to his sons to wife. And they feast evermore by their dear father and their kind mother, and dainties innumerable lie ready to their hands. And the house is full of the savour of feasting, and the noise thereof rings round, yea in the courtyard, by day, and in the night they sleep each one by his chaste wife in coverlets and on jointed bedsteads."

### 5. Social Ethics of Homer and Hesiod

(*Of the Origin of Homer and Hesiod, and of Their Contest,* Sect. 315) [18]

The author of this work is unknown. It dates back to the time of Hadrian, and describes a poetical contest between Homer and Hesiod at Chalcis.

And so, as the story goes, the two went to Chalcis and met by chance. The leading Chalcidians were judges together with Paneides, the brother of the dead king; and it is said that after a wonderful contest between the two poets, Hesiod won in the following manner: he came forward into the midst and put Homer one question after another, which Homer answered. Hesiod then began: "Homer, son of Meles, inspired with wisdom from heaven, come, tell me first what is best for mortal man?"

Homer: "For men on earth 'tis best never to be born at all; or being born, to pass through the gates of Hades with all speed."

Hesiod then asked again: "Come, tell me now this also, god-like Homer: what think you in your heart is most delightsome to men?"

Homer answered: "When mirth reigns throughout the town, and feasters about the house, sitting in order, listen to a minstrel; when the tables beside them are laden with bread and meat, and a wine-bearer draws sweet drink from the mixing-bowl and fills the cups: this I think in my heart to be most delightsome."

(Homer, *Odyssey*, XVIII, 215–232)

Penelope speaks to her son Telemachus and expresses her fear as to the consequence of his living in the evil atmosphere of her home, which is beset by wooers seeking to win her in Odysseus' absence. Homer points out that right conduct is the result of wisdom.

But she spake to Telemachus, her dear son:

"Telemachus, thy mind and thy thoughts are no longer stable as they were. While thou wast still a child, thou hadst a yet quicker and more crafty wit, but now that thou art great of growth, and art come to the measure of manhood, and a stranger looking to thy stature and thy beauty might say that thou must be some rich man's son, thy mind and thy thoughts are no longer right as of old. For lo, what manner of deed has been done in these halls, in that thou hast suffered thy guest to be thus shamefully dealt with! How would it be now, if the stranger sitting thus in our house, were to come to some harm all through this evil handling? Shame and disgrace would be thine henceforth among men."

Then wise Telemachus answered her: "Mother mine, as to this matter I count it no blame that thou art angered. Yet have I knowledge and understanding of each thing, of the good and of the evil; but heretofore I was a child.  Howbeit I cannot devise all things according to wisdom, for these men in their evil counsel drive me from my wits, on this side and on that, and there is none to aid me."

(Hesiod, *Works and Days*, l. 248–265)

Hesiod rebukes the philosophy held by the kings of his day that it is better to be wicked than just.  Injustices practiced by the 'princes' shall be duly punished by the gods.  The following passage illustrates also the relation of the gods to man.

You princes, mark well this punishment you also; for the deathless gods are near among men and mark all those who oppress their fellows with crooked judgements, and reck not the anger of the gods.  For upon the bounteous earth Zeus has thrice ten thousand spirits, watchers of mortal men, and these keep watch on judgements and deeds of wrong as they roam, clothed in mist, all over the earth.  And there is virgin Justice, the daughter of Zeus, who is honoured and reverenced among the gods who dwell on Olympus, and whenever anyone burts her with lying slander, she sits beside her father, Zeus, the son of Cronos, and tells him of men's wicked heart, until the people pay for the mad folly of their princes who, evilly minded, pervert judgement and give sentence crookedly.  Keep watch against this, you princes, and make straight your judgements, you who devour bribes; put crooked judgements altogether from your thoughts.

(Hesiod, *Works and Days*, l. 39–47)

Hesiod praises the life of moderation.

Fools!  They know not how much more the half is than the whole nor what great advantage there is in mallow and asphodel.

For the gods keep hidden from men the means of life.  Else you would easily do work enough in a day to supply you for a full year even without working; soon would you put away your rudder over the smoke, and the fields worked by ox and sturdy mule would run to waste.

*(Contest of Homer and Hesiod,* Sect. 320–321)

Homer, then, having the advantage on every point, Hesiod was jealous and began again:

"Homer, son of Meles, if indeed the Muses, daughters of great Zeus the most high, honour you as it is said, tell me a standard that is both best and worst for mortal-men; for I long to know it." Homer replied: "Hesiod, son of Dius, I am willing to tell you what you command, and very readily will I answer you. For each man to be a standard to himself is most excellent for the good, but for the bad it is the worst of all things. And now ask me whatever else your heart desires."

HESIOD: "How would men best dwell in cities, and with what observances?"

HOMER: "By scorning to get unclean gain and if the good were honoured, but justice fell upon the unjust."

HESIOD: "What is the best thing of all for a man to ask of the gods in prayer?"

HOMER: "That he may be always at peace with himself continually."

HESIOD: "Can you tell me in briefest space what is best for all?"

HOMER: "A sound mind in a manly body, as I believe."

HESIOD: "Of what effect are righteousness and courage?"

HOMER: "To advance the common good by private pains."

HESIOD: "What is the mark of wisdom among men?"

HOMER: "To read aright the present, and to march with the occasion."

HESIOD: "In what kind of matter is it right to trust in men?"

HOMER: "Where danger itself follows the action close."

HESIOD: "What do men mean by happiness?"

HOMER: "Death after a life of least pain and greatest pleasure."

(Hesiod, *Works and Days*, l. 213–247)

But you, Perses, listen to right and do not foster violence; for violence is bad for a poor man. Even the prosperous cannot easily bear its burden, but is weighed down under it when he has fallen into delusion. The better path is to go by on the other side towards justice; for Justice beats Outrage when she comes at length to the end of the race. But only when he has suffered does the fool learn this. For Oath keeps pace with wrong judgments. There is a noise when Justice is being dragged in the way where those who devour bribes and give sentence with crooked judgments, take her. And she, wrapped in mist, follows to the city and haunts of the people, weeping, and bringing mischief to men, even to such as have driven her forth in that they did not deal straightly with her.

But they who give straight judgments to strangers and to the men of the land, and go not aside from what is just, their city flourishes, and the people prosper in it! Peace, the nurse of children, is abroad in their land, and all-seeing Zeus never decrees cruel war against them. Neither famine nor disaster ever haunt men who do true justice; but light-heartedly they tend the fields which are all their care. The earth bears them victual in plenty, and on the mountains the oak bears acorns upon the top and bees in the midst. Their wooly sheep are laden with fleeces; their women bear children like their parents. They flourish continually with good things, and do not travel on ships, for the grain-giving earth bears them fruit.

But for those who practise violence and cruel deeds far-seeing Zeus, the son of Cronos, ordains a punishment. Often even a whole city suffers for a bad man who sins and devises presumptuous deeds, and the son of Cronos lays great trouble upon the people, famine and plague together, so that the men perish away, and their women do not bear children, and their houses become few, through the contriving of Olympian Zeus. And again, at another time, the son of Cronos either destroys their wide army, or their walls, or else makes an end of their ships on the sea.

(Hesiod, *Works and Days*, 265–266)

He does mischief to himself who does mischief to another, and evil planned harms the plotter most.

(Hesiod, *Works and Days*, 275–285)

But you, Perses, lay up these things within your heart and listen now to right, ceasing altogether to think of violence. For the son of Cronos has ordained this law for men, that fishes and beasts and winged fowls should devour one another, for right is not in them; but to mankind he gave right which proves far the best. For whoever knows the right and is ready to speak it, far-seeing Zeus gives him prosperity; but whoever deliberately lies in his witness and forswears himself, and so hurts Justice and sins beyond repair, that man's generation is left obscure thereafter. But the generation of the man who swears truly is better thenceforward.

(Hesiod, *Works and Days*, 293–341)

That man is altogether best who considers all things himself and marks what will be better afterwards and at the end; and he, again, is good who listens to a good adviser; but whoever neither thinks for himself nor keeps in mind what another tells him, he is an unprofitable man. But do you at any rate, always remembering my charge, work, high-born Perses, that Hunger may hate you, and venerable Demeter richly crowned may love you and fill your barn with food; for Hunger is altogether a meet comrade for the sluggard. Both gods and men are angry with a man who lives idle, for in nature he is like the stingless drones who waste the labour of the bees, eating without working; but let it be your care to order your work properly, that in the right season your barns may be full of victual. Through work men grow rich in flocks and substance, and working they are much better loved by the immortals. Work is no disgrace: it is idleness which is a disgrace. But if you work, the idle will soon envy you as you grow rich, for fame and renown attend on wealth. And whatever be your lot, work is best for you, if you turn your misguided mind away from other men's property to your work and attend to your livelihood as I bid you. An evil shame is the needy man's companion, shame which both greatly harms and prospers men; shame is with poverty, but confidence with wealth.

Wealth should not be seized: god-given wealth is much better; for if a man take great wealth violently and perforce, or if he steal it through his tongue, as often happens when gain deceives men's sense and dishonour tramples down honour, the gods soon blot him out and make that man's house low, and wealth attends him only for a little while. Alike with him who does wrong to a suppliant or a guest, or who goes up to his brother's bed and commits unnatural sin in lying with his wife, or who infatuately offends against fatherless children, or who abuses his old father at the cheerless threshold of old age and attacks him with harsh words, truly Zeus himself is angry, and at the last lays on him a heavy requittal for his evil doing. But do you turn your foolish heart altogether away from these things, and as far as you are able, sacrifice to the deathless gods purely and cleanly, and burn rich meats also, and at other times propitiate them with libations and incense, both when you go to bed and when the holy light has come back, that they may be gracious to you in heart and spirit, and so you may buy another's holding and not another yours.

(Hesiod, *The Great Works*, I)

*The Great Works* was one of Hesiod's longer poems. Only the scantiest fragments of it survive.

"If a man sow evil, he shall reap evil increase; if men do to him as he has done, it will be true justice."

(Hesiod, *Fragments of Unknown Position*, 18)
(From Schol. on Theocritus, XI, 75)

H. G. Evelyn-White, whose translations of Hesiod are quoted here, classifies a number of fragments as "Fragments of Unknown Position." These fragments fail to fit into any of the extant titles of Hesiod's works.

Foolish the man who leaves what he has, and follows after what he has not.

(Hesiod, *Fragments of Unknown Position*, 20)

Howsoever the city does sacrifice, the ancient custom is best.

(Hesiod, *Works and Days*, l. 342–356)

Call your friend to a feast; but leave your enemy alone; and especially call him who lives near you: for if any mischief happen in the place, neighbours come ungirt, but kinsmen stay to gird themselves. A bad neighbour is as great a plague as a good one is a great blessing; he who enjoys a good neighbour, enjoys honour. Not even an ox would die but for a bad neighbour. Take fair measure from your neighbour and pay him back fairly with the same measure, or better, if you can; so that if you are in need afterwards, you may find him sure.

Do not get base gain: base gain is as bad as ruin. Be friends with the friendly, and visit him who visits you. Give to one who gives, but do not give to one who does not give. A man gives to the free-handed, but no one gives to the close-fisted.

## 6. THE DECLINE OF MAN

### (Hesiod, *Works and Days*, 109–201)

Hesiod stresses the descent of man from the viewpoint of a pre-existent "golden age."

First of all the deathless gods who dwell on Olympus made a golden race of mortal men who lived in the time of Cronos when he was reigning in heaven. And they lived like gods without sorrow of heart, remote and free from toil and grief: miserable age rested not on them; but with legs and arms never failing they made merry with feasting beyond the reach of all evils. When they died, it was as though they were overcome with sleep, and they had all good things; for the fruitful earth unforced bore them fruit abundantly and without stint. They dwelt in ease and peace upon their lands with many good things, rich in flocks and loved and blessed by the gods.

But after the earth had covered this generation—they are called pure spirits dwelling on the earth, and are kindly, delivering from harm, and guardians of mortal men; for they roam everywhere over the earth, clothed in mist and keep watch on judgments and cruel deeds, givers of wealth; for this royal right also they received;—then they who dwell on Olympus made a second generation which was of silver and less noble by far.  It was like the golden race neither in body nor in spirit.  A child was brought up at his good mother's side an hundred years, an utter simpleton, playing childishly in his own home.  But when they were full grown and were come to the full measure of their prime, they lived only a little time and that in sorrow because of their foolishness, for they could not keep from sinning and from wronging one another, nor would they serve the immortals, nor sacrifice on the holy altars of the blessed ones as it is right for men to do wherever they dwell.  Then Zeus the son of Cronos was angry and put them away, because they would not give honour to the blessed gods who live on Olympus.

But when earth had covered this generation also—they are called blessed spirits of the underworld by men, and though they are second order, yet honour attends them also—Zeus the Father made a third generation of mortal men, a brazen race, sprung from ash-trees; and it was in no way equal to the silver age, but was terrible and strong.  They loved the lamentable works of Ares and deeds of violence; they ate no bread, but were hard of heart like adamant, fearful men.  Great was their strength and unconquerable the arms which grew from their shoulders on their strong limbs.  Their armour was of bronze, and their houses of bronze, and of bronze were their implements: there was no black iron.  These were destroyed by their own hands and passed to the dark house of chill Hades, and left no name: terrible though they were, black Death seized them, and they left the bright light of the sun.

But when earth had covered this generation also, Zeus the son of Cronos made yet another, the fourth, upon the fruitful earth, which was nobler and more righteous, a god-like race of hero-men who are called demi-gods, the race before our own, throughout the boundless earth.  Grim war and dread battle destroyed a part of them, some in the land of Cadmus at seven-gated Thebe when they fought for the flocks of Oedipus, and some, when it had brought them in ships over the great sea gulf to Troy for rich-haired Helen's sake: there death's end enshrouded a part of them.  But to the others father Zeus the son of Cronos gave a living and an abode apart from men, and made them dwell at the ends of earth.  And they lived untouched by sorrow—in the islands of the blessed along the shore of the deep swirling Ocean, happy heroes for whom the grain-giving earth bears honey-sweet fruit flourishing thrice a year, far from the deathless gods, and Cronos rules over them; for the father of men and gods released him from his bonds.  And these last equally have honour and glory.

And again far-seeing Zeus made yet another generation, the fifth, of men who are upon the bounteous earth.

Thereafter, would that I were not among the men of the fifth generation, but either had died before or been born afterwards.  For now truly is a race of iron, and men never rest from labour and sorrow by day, and from perishing by night; and the gods shall lay sore trouble upon them.  But, notwithstanding, even these shall have some good mingled with their evils.  And Zeus will destroy this race of mortal men also when they come to have grey hair on the temples at their birth. The father will not agree with his children, nor the children with their father, nor guest with his host, nor comrade with comrade; nor will brother be dear to brother as aforetime. Men will dishonour their parents as they grow quickly old, and will carp at them chiding them with bitter words, hard-hearted they, not knowing the fear of the gods.  They will not repay their aged parents the cost of their nurture, for might shall be their right: and one man will sack another's city.  There will be no favour for the man who keeps his oath or for the just or for the good; but rather men will praise the evil-doer and his violent dealing.   Strength will be right and reverence will cease to be; and the wicked will hurt the worthy man, speaking false words against him; and will swear an oath upon them.   Envy, foul-mouthed, delighting in evil, scowling face, will go along with wretched men one and all.   And then Aidôs and Nemesis, with their sweet forms wrapped in white robes, will go from the wide-pathed earth and forsake mankind to join the company of the deathless gods: and bitter sorrows will be left for mortal men, and there will be no help against evil.

## 7. Principles of Economy and Rural Economy

### (Hesiod, *Works and Days,* 370–382)

Let the wage promised to a friend be fixed; even with your brother smile—and get a witness; for trust and mistrust, alike ruin men.

Do not let a flaunting woman coax and cozen and deceive you: she is after your barn.   The man who trusts womankind trusts deceivers.

There should be an only son, to feed his father's house, for so wealth will increase in the home; but if you leave a second son, you should die old.   Yet Zeus can easily give great wealth to a greater number.   More hands mean more work and more increase.

If your heart within you desires wealth, do these things and work with work upon work.

### (Hesiod, *Works and Days,* l. 383–617)

When the Pleiades, daughters of Atlas, are rising,[21] begin your harvest, and your ploughing when they are going to set.[22] Forty nights and days they are hidden and appear again as the year moves round, when first you sharpen your sickle.   This is the law of the plains, and of those who live near the sea, and who inhabit rich country, the glens and dingles far from the tossing sea,—strip to sow and strip to plough and strip to reap, if you wish to get in all Demeter's fruits in due season, and that each kind may grow in its season. Else, afterwards, you may chance to be in want, and go begging to other men's houses, but without avail; as you have already come to me. But I will give you no more nor give you further measure. Foolish Perses! Work the work which the gods ordained for men, lest in bitter anguish of spirit you and your wife and children seek your livelihood amongst your neighbours, and they do not heed you. Two or three times, may be, you will succeed, but if you trouble them further, it will not avail you, and all your talk will be in vain, and your word-play unprofitable. Nay, I bid you find a way to pay your debts and avoid hunger.

First of all, get a house, and a woman and an ox for the plough—a slave woman and not a wife, to follow the ox as well, —and make everything ready at home, so that you may not have to ask of another, and he refuse you, and so, because you are in lack, the season pass by and your work come to nothing. Do not put your work off till to-morrow and the day after; for a sluggish worker does not fill his barn, nor one who puts off his work: industry makes work go well, but a man who puts off work is always at hand-grips with ruin.

When the piercing power and sultry heat of the sun abate, and almighty Zeus sends the autumn rains, and men's flesh comes to feel far easier,—for then the star of Sirius passes over the heads of men, who are born to misery, only a little while by day and take greater share of night—then, when it showers its leaves to the ground and stops sprouting, the wood you cut with your axe is least liable to worm. Then remember to hew your timber; it is the season for that work. Cut a mortar three feet wide and a pestle three cubits long, and an axle of seven feet, for it will do very well so; but if you make it eight feet long, you can cut a beetle from it as well. Cut a felloe three spans across for a waggon of ten palms' width. Hew also many bent timbers, and bring home a plough-tree when you have found it, and look out on the mountain or in the field for one of holm-oak; for this is the strongest for oxen to plough with when one of Athena's handmen has fixed in the share-beam and fastened it to the pole with dowels. Get two ploughs ready and work on them at home, one all of a piece, and the other jointed. It is far better to do this for if you should break one of them, you can put the oxen to the other. Poles of laurel or elm are most free from worms, and a share-beam of oak and a plough-tree of holm-oak. . . .

So soon as the time for ploughing is proclaimed to men, then make haste, you and your slaves alike, in wet and in dry, to plough in the season for ploughing, and bestir yourself early in the morning so that your fields may be full. Plough in the spring; but fallow broken up in the summer will not belie your hopes. Sow fallow land when the soil is still getting light; fallow land is a defender from harm and a soother of children. . . .

Pass by the smithy and its crowded lounge in winter time when cold keeps men from field work,—for then an industrious man can greatly prosper his house—lest bitter winter catch you helpless and poor and you chafe a swollen foot with a shrunk hand. The idle man who waits on empty hope, lacking a livelihood, lays to heart mischief-making; . . .

But when the House-carrier climbs up the plants from the earth to escape the Pleiades, then it is no longer the season for digging vineyards, but to whet your sickles and rouse up your slaves. Avoid shady seats and sleeping until dawn in the harvest season, when the sun scorches the body. Then be busy, and bring home your fruits, getting up early to make your livelihood sure. For dawn takes away a third part of your part of your work, dawn advances a man on his journey and advances him in his work,—dawn which appears and sets many men on their road, and puts yokes on many oxen. . . .

Set your slaves to winnow Demeter's holy grain, when strong Orion first appears, on a smooth threshing-floor in an airy place. Then measure it and store it in jars. And so soon as you have safely stored all your stuff indoors, I bid you put your bondman out of doors and look out a servant-girl with no children;—for a servant with a child to nurse is troublesome. And look after the dog with jagged teeth; do not grudge him his food, or some time the Day-sleeper may take your stuff. Bring in fodder and litter so as to have enough for your oxen and mules. After that, let your men rest their poor knees and unyoke your pair of oxen.

But when Orion and Sirius are come into mid-heaven, and rosy-fingered Dawn sees Arcturus, then cut off all the grape-clusters, Perses, and bring them home. Show them to the sun ten days and ten nights: then cover them over for five, and on the sixth day draw off into vessels the gifts of joyful Dionysus. But when Pleiades and Hyades and strong Orion begin to set, then remember to plough in season: and so the completed year will fitly pass beneath the earth.

# CHAPTER III

## THE LYRIC AGE

DURING the last century and a half of the age of Homer and Hesiod (850–700 B.C.), kings, as rulers, gradually declined and disappeared, being supplanted by the nobles who ruled in their stead. These nobles were a group who began as wealthy merchants but who, through union with other families in marriage, accumulation of lands, and various other means, formed a class of hereditary nobles called eupatrids. By 750 B.C. the king's office was merely a title in many Greek states. Although the king was violently displaced in some states, for the most part the change was peaceful. The nobles often established elective officers who took charge of matters formerly controlled by the king. In Athens one noble was appointed to lead in war, while one was chosen as "archon," or ruler, whose duty it was to assist the king in matters of state. Gradually the Athenian king was shorn of his powers, becoming little more than the religious head of the people. Sparta used other means to check the king's powers. The nobles appointed a second king and, following this plan, retained kings for some time. In the next hundred years (750–650 B.C.) kingship virtually disappeared, although kings were to be found in a few states long after this period. The victory of the nobles in this social and political struggle led to their control in many states.

The rule of the nobles was an oppressive rule. Because they controlled most of the land, the bitter impoverishment of the peasant ensued. Hesiod's writings constituted the first outcry against these conditions. The plight of the Greek farmers led them to seek new homes and new lands beyond the Aegean

world.  And so, before 600 B.C., this group was to be found in
towns and settlements all along the Black Sea.  Greek coloniza-
tion along the southern coasts of Asia Minor reached as far as
Cyprus in the east.  Greek colonies appeared in the west also.
Colonists settled in small communities from the southernmost
tip of Italy to a point north of Naples.  Those who moved south
found a kindly welcome in Egypt.  They were permitted to
establish a trading city at Naucratis in the Nile Delta, and
some time later founded Cyrene west of the Delta.  They were
also to be found in Sicily, where they pushed out the Phoenician
trading posts, leaving them only at the western end of the
island.  Syracuse, which became one of the most powerful as
well as one of the most highly cultured cities in the Greek world,
was established in the southeastern corner of Sicily.  A town
was also established on the coast of what later became France
and was called Massilia (Marseilles).  The inhabitants successfully controlled all the trade of the Rhone valley and even
reached over to the Mediterranean coasts of Spain.

Deep and lasting changes were wrought by this colonial expansion of the Greeks.  Because of the needs of the colonies
and their dealings with the inland, large portions of Europe
were opened up as markets for Greek products.  The home
communities led by the Ionian cities began to meet the demand
for all sorts of goods.  Corinth and then Athens began to take
part in the greatly enlarged trade.

The Greek craftsmen, in order to satisfy the new demands
of trade and to be able to meet Phoenician competition, raised
the standard of their work.  Up to 600 B.C. Greek industries
were inferior to those of the Orient but after that time the
pupils outdid their masters.  Their hollow-bronze castings
similar to those of the Egyptians were greatly improved, while
their pottery became more beautiful and truly Greek; for they
painted scenes of Greek life on them instead of the Egyptian
ones of former years.  Because of increased trade, the craftsman found it necessary to enlarge his small shop.  Since labor
was scarce, the man who could afford it bought slaves whom he

trained to do the work. This necessitated the erection of a factory with a number of workers. From this time on slave labor became an important factor in Greek life.

Coined money, which had entered Greece about this time, made for many changes. Soon after 750 B.C. the kings of Lydia in Asia Minor cut up silver into bars of fixed weight in convenient size, stamped them with the symbol of the State to show that the State guaranteed their value, and used them in business transactions. These were the earliest known forms of coins. The Ionian cities took over this convenient system and it quickly spread to the islands and the Greek mainland. Previously the wealth of the Greeks had lain in land and stock; now capital, in money, became the standard of wealth. Whereas the practice of loans and interest had largely been confined to the Orient, it now was to be found throughout Greece. Men who had previously been poor suddenly grew rich. Enlarged industries and new commercial ventures soon created vast fortunes among men who had been obscure a short time before. In consequence, a prosperous *middle class* of merchants and industrialists was formed, and they demanded a share in the government. It was not long before they became an influential and powerful group who forced the noble class to recognize their power. At the beginning of the sixth century B.C. Solon wrote that "Money makes the man."

Although the new prosperity created the capitalistic class, it did little for the peasant, for his lands were heavily mortgaged, rapidly foreclosed on, and the owners found themselves being sold into slavery. The nobles as a class did little to improve the peasants' distressing situation. Many of the peasants, fearing slavery, fled into foreign lands. Bitter hatred prevailed between the new commercial class and the nobles. And since improved industrial conditions made metals far cheaper and thus enabled the common man to buy weapons and armour, his worth as a soldier made him increasingly important to both classes.

The nobility itself was torn by dissension. Feuds between

noble families divided them into hostile camps. A leader of such a faction often showed sympathy for the dissatisfied people, and succeeded in rallying about himself both the peasant and the capitalist. With this support he could expel his enemies among the noble class and become the sole ruler of the state. Such a ruler was called by the Greeks a "tyrant."

The sixth century is usually referred to as the Age of the Tyrants, although rulers of this type made their appearance as early as 650 B.C. They arose primarily in those states in which the people had gained power through commercial ventures—the Ionian cities of Asia Minor, Euboea, Athens, Corinth, and the colonies of Sicily. Their rise can be traced directly to the new power exerted by the people. Men like Pisistratus of Athens and Periander of Corinth accomplished a great deal. They defended the rights of the people, curbed the malpractices of the nobles, and built great public works such as state buildings, temples, and harbor improvements. They also fostered the cultivation of the arts—music, painting, sculpture, and literature. It was during this same century that the laws of Athens were codified by Draco (624 B.C.).

Toward the close of the seventh century B.C. Athens was faced with serious difficulties caused by neighboring states. Megara seized the island of Salamis and the nobles of Athens did nothing to recover it. This situation aroused intense anger among the Athenian population. Solon, who had gained great wealth in commercial enterprises, played upon this indignation of the people, exhorting them with fiery verse to wipe out the shame of this loss. In consequence, Salamis was recovered and Solon became the popular hero of the entire people of Athens. This popularity led to his election as archon in 594 B.C. with full power to change the conditions of the peasant. His reforms were vast and important: all mortgages on land were declared void, and creditors' claims which jeopardized the liberty of a citizen were cancelled; a limit was set on the amount of land a noble could hold; a case might be appealed to a jury of citizens who were chosen by lot. He also instituted a new constitution in Athens which gave all citizens a voice in the government. It took cognizance of four classes of citizens and graded them according to their wealth. Nobles, however, were the only ones permitted to hold the highest offices. The prosperous commercial group was barred from these positions, and therefore continued its struggle for greater political power.

After Solon's rule, a new group of tyrants continued to govern. Pisistratus, and after him his sons Hipparchus and Hippias, governed Athens until the close of the sixth century.

From the eighth to the sixth century B.C. that characteristically Greek institution, the city-state, was slowly evolved. It is true that some parts of Greece retained the old clan system of government for many years, but for the most part the Greek communities step by step developed this urban institution. Its essential feature was that political life was concentrated in one place. The city was the economic, religious and political center of the surrounding territory. All the members of this territory were citizens, with the exception of foreigners and slaves, and shared in the government. The city had no rivals in any particular territory, although large units of population might be found in various places outside the city proper. In these states rule by clan had been slowly broken down, but in private life it was still maintained. Each man was a member of a brotherhood (*phratria*), a family, and a subdivision of a clan (*phyle*). Often within one clan several city-states formed an alliance which had certain cults in common. These alliances were called *amphictyonies*.

During the seventh and sixth centuries B.C. a new form of political organization and social thinking was brought into being. An essential characteristic of this period was its individualism, boldness, and complete hardihood. H. P. Becker points out that this individualism might be accounted for by the frontier nature of the life of the Greek colonists.[1] Paralleling this form of individualism was the recognition of a common bond between Greek communities. It was the tie not only of a common language and a common religion, but also of almost identical culture. This bond was heightened by Greek expansion and trade. Greece and her colonies always maintained a mother-daughter relationship.

Religion among the Greeks of this age took on a moral hue. A reaction to the beliefs of the Homeric period which depicted the evil lives of the gods set in. A belief in moral righteousness for both gods and men became popular. The concept of punishment for sin in the world of the dead was developed. In Hades there was a place where the sinners were tortured and they were guarded by the monstrous dog Cerberus. On the other hand, the good were rewarded in the next world. Men looked to the gods for a revelation of the future, believing that the oracle could foretell every unseen event. Of greater consequence was the recognition that even the gods suffered punishment for their evil deeds. Apollo does penance for killing Python, and feeds the flocks of Admetus. In his shrine at Delphi he helped murderers free themselves from their crimes. Through repentance and purification their sins could be absolved. The one unforgivable crime was matricide.

Numerous temples were erected; some of the more influential were the Temple of Zeus at Olympia, and the temples of Apollo at Delphi, at Delos, and near Miletus. Competitions in honor of the gods were instituted in athletics, music, and poetry. Those who triumphed received a crown of twigs and were publicly acclaimed throughout Greece as national heroes.

The Greeks were greatly influenced in science, art, and technical skills by the East. In Asia Minor there was a close tie with the East and they learned much from their contact. Although their store of knowledge in the beginning came from others, they themselves were highly creative. Each problem was thoroughly investigated. If a satisfactory solution was reached, that solution became a starting point for new research. Unhampered by tradition, they were given to free inquiry on all subjects—nature, the world, and man. A law in nature was felt to exist and their chief interest was in the "why" rather than in the "how." In this manner, they gradually became the creators of geography, astronomy and cosmology.

The achievements of seventh-century Greece in architecture are well known.  It was in this epoch that the style of the Greek temple was evolved.  The general plan was the rectangular hall surrounded by a colonnade and covered by a gabled roof.  Variations in design were manifold.  The adornments were usually sculptured relief figures of the gods, grouped in scenes suggesting incidents of the myths.

Much progress was also made by the painters during this period.  In the paintings on vases they did not confine themselves to religious scenes, but depicted the everyday life about them.  Their figure drawings attained a more life-like form than any group of artists had been able to achieve prior to this time.

Poetry, too, came of age in this period.  In the changing scene, where political factions of all kinds arose, partisanship and local patriotism burst into flame.  Men were moved by what they saw about them and their experiences led them to self-expression.  During the Homeric period, a man was simply one of a mass and had little individuality.  Our present period (700–500 B.C.) saw the emergence of the private citizen as an individual and a political power.  His influence was more important than before, his work better, his pleasures improved, his knowledge broadened.  Science was about to be born and literature was about to blossom forth.  The epic poetry of an earlier time was found unsuitable for the expression of the emotions and thoughts of the individual.  A new form was invented in answer to the new need—the lyric poem (the elegy and the iambic) emerged.  For this reason the period has been called the Lyric Age.  The lyric was as characteristic of this period as the epic was of the age of Homer and Hesiod.

The lyric poets reflected in their poetry all the stirring, adventurous, and varied life of their time.  All were active men taking part vigorously in the revolutions, the feasts, the quarrels, the joys, that life laid before them.  Alcaeus of Lesbos was a trader and active politician; Archilochus of Paros, a warrior and a lover.  Anacreon of Teos sang songs of love and wine in the court of a tyrant, while Solon exhorted his fellow-citizens to reform Athens; and Theognis of Lesbos upheld the rights of the aristocracy. Stesichorus of Sicily, Simonides of Ceos, and Terpander of Lesbos, on the other hand, created magnificent songs to honor the gods.

Prose too came into its own. Travellers in foreign lands arrived home to tell of the strange sights they had seen. Slowly their tales emerged as descriptive and half scientific treatises on history, geography, and anthropology. The Ionian philosophers Anaximander and Anaximenes used the prose form, while Xenophanes, Parmenides, and Empedocles clung to the verse form.

Such was Greece in the 7th and 6th centuries B.C. In an unprecedented burst of genius in every field of endeavor she created a highly civilized culture which is clearly intelligible to the modern mind. The spirit of this work strikes an answering chord in our own thinking.

The material illustrating the social thought of the Lyric Age has been classified into the following categories: (1) *The Nature of Human Nature;* (2) *Gods, Fate: Their Relation to Man;* (3) *Man and Morals;* (4) *Social Attitudes: Attitudes of Man to Man;* (5) *Political Theory;* (6) *Position of Women;* (7) *Attitudes toward War: Patriotism and Valour;* (8) *Wealth and Riches;* (9) *Attitudes toward Old Age.*

Under each heading the excerpts are arranged chronologically, according to authorship. A short biography of each author can be found in the notes to this chapter. Reference to this biographical sketch is made the first time the author is presented in the text. Here, as in the previous chapter, the categories are self-explanatory.

## 1. THE NATURE OF HUMAN NATURE

### (Alcman, 55) [3]

Alcman [2] suggests that human motives are often concealed and therefore difficult to ascertain. In this respect he recognizes the modern methodological problem of subjectivity in social phenomena.

And prithee, who may read with ease the mind of another?

(Alcman, 67)

In the following fragment Alcman recognizes the fact that intelligence and wisdom are not innate, but are rather the result of human experiences.

Trial surely is the beginning of wisdom.

(Semonides of Samos, 4) [4]

No man is altogether without blame nor without harm.

(Semonides of Samos, 1)

Thundering Zeus, lad, hath the ends of all things there be, and doeth with them what he will.  There's no mind in us men, but we live each day as it cometh like grazing cattle, knowing no whit how God shall end it.  Yet Hope and Trust keep us all a-pondering the impracticable; some abide till a day come, others for the turning of years.  There's none alive but thinketh he will come home winged with wealth and good things next year; yet one of us ere he reach his goal is taken with un-envied Age, another's mind is wasted by miserable Disease, or Death sendeth him below dark earth whelmed by War.  Some die at sea when they have a laden ship with their substance, confounded by storm and the many waves of the purple brine; others tie a noose about their miserable neck and leave the sunlight of their free choice.  So true is it that nothing is with-out ills, nay, ten thousand the Dooms of men, and their woes and sorrows past reckoning.  If they would be advised by me, we should not set our hearts on good things, nor yet do our-selves despite by letting our minds dwell upon evil troubles.

(Alcaeus, 67) [5]

'Tis said that wrath is the last thing in a man to grow old.

(Alcaeus, 146)

We learn from our fathers.

(Solon, *Fragment* 13, l. 33–42) [6]

Solon [7] points out that the actual self differs from one's view of himself.

We mortal men, alike good and bad, are minded thus:—each of us keepeth the opinion he hath ever had till he suffer ill, and then forthwith he grieveth; albeit ere that, we rejoice open-mouthed in vain expectations, and whosoever be oppressed with sore disease bethinketh himself he will be whole; another that is a coward thinketh he be a brave man; or he that hath no comeliness seemeth to himself goodly to look upon; and if one be needy, and constrained by the works of Penury, he reckoneth always to win much wealth.

(Solon, *Fragment* 6)

So best will the people follow their leaders, neither too little restrained nor yet perforce; for excess breedeth outrage when much prosperity followeth those whose mind is not perfect.

(Solon, *Fragment* 27)

Solon enumerates the stages in the development of man as a person.

In seven years the half-grown boy casteth the first teeth he cut as a child; when God hath accomplished him seven years more he showeth signs that his youthful prime is nigh; in the third seven, when his limbs are still a-waxing, his chin groweth downy with the bloom of changing skin; in the fourth every man is at his best in the strength which men bear for a token of virture and valour; in the fifth 'tis time for a man to bethink him of marriage and to seek offspring to come after him; in the sixth a man's mind is trained in all things, and he wisheth not so much now for what may not be done; in seven sevens and in eight he is at his best in mind and tongue, to wit fourteen years of both; in the ninth age he is still an able man, but his tongue and his lore have less might unto great virtue; and if a man come to the full measure of the tenth, he will not meet the fate of Death untimely.

(Anaximander, from Hipp. *Ref.* i. 6)

Anaximander [8] appears as the first evolutionist when he deals with the origin of man.

Living creatures arose from the moist element as it was evaporated from the sun.  Man was like another animal, namely, a fish, in the beginning.[9]

(Anaximander, from Aet. v. 19, 4)

The first animals were produced in the moisture, each enclosed in a prickly bark.  As they advanced in age, they came out upon the drier part.  When the bark broke off, they survived for a short time.

(Anaximander, from Ps.-Plut. *Strom.* fr. 2)

Anaximander antedates John Fiske (1842–1890) by suggesting that man differs from the lower animals because of his prolonged infancy.

Further, he says that originally man was born from animals of another species.  His reason is that while other animals quickly find food by themselves, man alone requires a lengthy period of suckling.  Hence had he been originally as he is now, he would never have survived.

(Xenophanes, frag. 34) [11]

Xenophanes [10] indicates the imperfectability of man.

And in truth no man hath been or ever will be that knoweth about the Gods and all I speak of; for even though he chance to say the fullest truth, yet he knoweth it not himself; there is fancy in all things.

(Theognis, 183–192) [12]

Theognis applies the idea of eugenics to the perfection of the human race.  The author begins with the question of breeding, believing that nothing can be good of its kind, whether man or animal, unless its progenitors are good.  He would treat man like any other species of animals; viz., compulsorily breed the good with the good.

In rams and asses and horses, Cyrus, we seek the thorough-
bred, and a man is concerned therein to get him offspring of
good stock; yet in marriage a good man thinketh not twice of
wedding the bad daughter of a bad sire if the father give him
many possessions, nor doth the wife of a bad man disdain the
bed of a wealthy, but is fain rather to be rich than to be good.
For 'tis possessions they prize; and a good man weddeth of
bad stock and a bad man of good; race is confounded of riches.
In like manner, son of Polypaüs, marvel thou not that the race
of thy townsmen is made obscure; 'tis because bad things are
mingled with good.

(Theognis, 429–438)

To beget and breed a man is easier than to put into him
good wits; none hath ever devised means whereby he hath
made a fool wise and a bad man good.  If God had given the
children of Asclepius the art of healing a man's evil nature and
infatuate wit, they would receive wages much and great; and
if thought could be made and put into us, the son of a good
father would never become bad, because he would be persuaded by good counsel.  But by teaching never shalt thou
make the bad man good.

(Theognis, 901–902)

At each and every thing one man is better and another
worse; no man alive is skilled in all things.

(Theognis, 119–128)

Like Alcman, Theognis recognizes the difficulty in getting to know and
understand human behavior.

The loss of counterfeit gold or silver, Cyrnus, is easily endured, nor hard is it for a man of skill to find them out; but
if the mind of a friend be false within him unbeknown, and the
heart in his breast deceitful, this hath God made most counterfeit for mankind, this is most grievous hard of all things to
discover; for mind of man nor yet of woman shalt thou know

till thou hast made trial of it like a beast of burden, nor shalt thou ever guess it as when thou comest to buy, because outward shapes do so often cheat the understanding.

(Theognis, 117–118)

Nothing is harder to know, Cyrnus, than a counterfeit man, nor is aught worth more heed.

(Theognis, 895–896)

There is nothing a man possesseth of himself better than understanding, Cyrnus, nor bitterer than lack of understanding.

(Theognis, 305–308)

Theognis recognizes that culture and social surroundings are the casual factors in the development of the personality.

The bad are not all bad from the womb, but have learnt base works and unholy words and wanton outrage from friendship with the bad because they thought all they said was true.

(Simonides of Ceos,[13] 95) [14]

The city is the teacher of the man.

(Simonides of Ceos, 93)

For he that would live completely happy must before all things belong to a country that is of fair report.

(Simonides of Ceos, 22)

If thou be'st a mortal man, never say what To-morrow will bring, nor when thou seest a man happy, how long he shall be happy.  For swift is change—nay, not so swift the changing course of the wide-winged fly.

(Heracleitus, *Fragments*) [15]

91. Understanding is common to all.  It is necessary for those who speak with intelligence to hold fast to the common

element of all, as a city holds fast to law, and much more strongly.  For all human laws are nourished by one which is divine, and it has power so much as it will; and it suffices for all things and more than suffices.

96. For human nature has not wisdom, but divine nature has.

97. Man is called a baby by God, even as a child is by man.

98. And does not Herakleitos, whom you bring forward, say this very thing, that the wisest of men will appear as an ape before God, both in wisdom and beauty and in all other respects?

61. (God, ordering things as they ought to be, perfects all things in the harmony of the whole, as Herakleitos says that) for god all things are fair and good and just, but men suppose that some are just and others unjust.

62. Men should know that war is general and that justice is strife; all things arise and (pass away) through strife.

63. For they are all absolutely destined. . . .

67. Gods are mortals, men are immortals, each living in the others' death and dying in the others' life.

(Heracleitus, *Fragments*) [16]

Heracleitus considers opposition the cause for human association and contact.

8. Opposition brings men together, and out of discord comes the fairest harmony, and all things have their birth in strife.

51. Men do not understand how that which is torn in different directions comes into accord with itself,—harmony contrariety, as in the case of the bow and the lyre.

(Other Anonymous Fragments, 4) [17]

In time of discord even the villain receiveth honor.

(Other Anonymous Fragments, 18)

But a good man is sometimes bad and sometimes good.

## 2. Gods, Fate: Their Relation to Man

### (Solon, 13, l. 63–70) [6]

Aye, surely Fate it is that bringeth mankind both good and
ill, and the gifts immortal Gods offer must needs be accepted;
surely too there's danger in every sort of business; nor know
we at the beginning of a matter how it is to end; nay, sometimes
he that striveth to do a good thing falleth unawares into ruin
great and sore, whereas God giveth good hap in all things to
one that doeth ill, to be his deliverance from folly.

### (Theognis, 133–142) [6]

No man is himself the cause of loss and gain, Cyrnus; the
Gods are the givers of them both: nor doth any that laboureth
know in his heart whether he moveth to a good end or a bad.
For often when he thinketh he will make bad he maketh good,
and maketh bad when he thinketh he will make good.  Nor
doth any man get what he wisheth; for his desires hold the
ends of sore perplexity.  We men practise vain things, knowing
naught, while the Gods accomplish all to their mind.

### (Theognis, 373–392)

Dear Zeus!  I marvel at Thee.  Thou art lord of all, alone
having honour and great power; well knowest Thou the heart
and mind of every man alive; and Thy might, O King, is above
all things.  How then is it, Son of Cronus, that Thy mind can
bear to hold the wicked and the righteous in the same esteem,
whether a man's mind be turned to temperateness, or, unrighteous works persuading, to wanton outrage?  Nor is aught
fixed for us men by Fortune, nor the way a man must go to
please the Immortals.  Yet the wicked enjoy untroubled prosperity, whereas such as keep their hearts from base deeds,
nevertheless, for all they may love what is righteous, receive
Penury the mother of perplexity, Penury that misleadeth a
man's heart to evil-doing, corrupting his wits by strong necessity, till perforce he endureth much shame and yieldeth to want

who teacheth all evil, both lies and deceits and baleful conten-
tions, even to him that will not and to whom no ill is fitting;
for hard is the perplexity that cometh of her.

(Theognis, 1162A–1162F)

Nobody is all-happy in all things; rather doth the good
endure to have evil albeit men know it not, whereas the bad
man knoweth not how to mingle his heart either with good
hap or with bad; of all sorts are the gifts that come of the
Gods to man, yet must we endure to keep the gifts They send,
of whatsoever sort they be.

(Simonides of Ceos, *Fragments,* 29) [14]

Little is man's strength and his cares unavailing, and 'tis
toil upon toil for him in a life that is short; for all he can
do, there's a death hangs over him that will not be escaped,
in which both good men and bad must share alike.

(Simonides of Ceos, 32)

None getteth achievement without the Gods, neither man
nor city. He that can devise all is a God, and there's nothing
to be got among men without toil.

(Simonides of Ceos, 33)

There's no ill that a man must not expect, and 'tis not long
ere God turneth all things upside down.

(Simonides of Ceos, 65)

There's a tale that Virtue dwelleth on a rock hard to climb
and with a pure band of Godesses to watch over it, nor may
she ever be seen by eye of mortal, unless heart-devouring sweat
come out of one and he reach unto the very top of manliness.

(Simonides of Ceos, 90)

To incur no guilt and accomplish all things is the mark of
a God.

(Other Anonymous Fragments, 10) [17]

The Gods have not granted to all men to possess all things.

(Anonymous Inscriptions, 36) [17]

Far from their country these drew sword and put to rout the pride of the foe; aye, standing their trial for valour or cowardice, hoarded not their lives but made Death their impartial umpire, that the Greeks might not wear the yoke of slavery and have hated tyranny on either hand. But the bones of those that have borne the brunt lie in the bosom of their country; for it is the judgement of Zeus unto men that to make no slip in life and accomplish all things is for Gods, and He hath not granted unto man to escape destiny.

(Heracleitus, *Fragments*, 5) [16]

Men seek in vain to purify themselves from blood-guiltiness by defiling themselves with blood; as if, when one has stepped into the mud he should try to wash himself with mud. And I should deem him mad who should pay heed to any man who does such things. And, forsooth, they offer prayers to these statues here! It is as if one should try to converse with houses. They know nothing of the real nature of Gods and heroes.

## 3. MAN AND MORALS

(Mimnermus, 12) [6]

Mimnermus' remarks on social morality are closely connected with his observations on the nature of man.[18]

Harming neither sojourner nor citizens with deeds of mischief, but living a righteous man, rejoice your own heart; of your pitiless fellow-townsman assuredly some will speak ill of you and some good.

(Alcaeus, *Drinking Songs*, 164) [5]

In the following selection from Alcaeus traces of hedonism can be noted.

Over my long-suffering head, over my hoary breast, pour
me the unguent.  If any man be in pain, then let him drink.
[To all men soon or late the Olympians] give misfortune, [and
this woe of mine I share] with other men.  And as for him
that [says there is] no [good in drinking], you may say to
him 'Be hanged with you! [you know not good from bad.']

(Solon, 14) [3,7]

Nor is any mortal happy, but all men are unfortunate that
the Sun can see.

(Anacreon, 7) [19]

In Anacreon, we find a strong strain of hedonism.

### 7.

'You're old, Anacreon,'
    The ladies say; 'Look on
'Your forehead in the glass, and see
    'How thin your love-locks be.'

    As for my hair, I wot
    Not whe'r 'tis thin or not;
But this I know, the nigher Death's day
    The more should old men play.

(Anacreon, 8)

Give me not Gyges' Sardian gold;
Kings may keep their wealth untold
    But give me nard
    Upon my beard,
And roses round my brow.  My care's to-day;
    To-morrow tell who may.

So while the days are calm and fine,
    Come and toast the God of Wine;
        Let cups be tost,
        Stakes won and lost,

Lest sickness come and say 'The time is up;
    Put down the festive cup.'

(Anacreon, 32)

On lotus-leaves and myrtles fine
    I'll lean, and the Love-lad
        In apron clad
    Shall stand and serve me wine.

Like wheels our running lives are sped,
    And lie we shall and must
        A little dust
    Of bones uncemented.
Why at my grave your unguents pour?
    Why vain anoilment give?
        While yet I live
    Embalm my forehead o'er.
Bring roses, and some maiden fair;
    For ere to join I go
        The rout below,
    I fain would banish care.

(Anacreon, 38)

Let's drink then, me and you,
And give our thoughts relief;
    From pain and grief
What profit doth accrue?
No mortal man may see
    Futurity;
I'll e'en put cup to lip
    And measures trip,
Pour balm and play my fill
With pretty girls or boys;
    With all annoys
Concern himself who will
Let's quaff the cheering wine
And praise its Lord divine.

(Anacreon, 40)

Since I am mortal made
    Life's path to tread,
    What's past I know,
But not what's yet to go.

Cares, let me be; with you
    I've naught to do.
    With wine I'll play,
Laugh, dance, till end of day.

(Anacreon, 45)

When'er the wine I drink
My cares to sleep do sink,
What then of cares or tears reck I,
    What reck I then of toils
        And coils?

If willy-nilly I must die,
    Wherefore
Over life's riddle pore?
Let's drink fair Bacchus' best
For then our cares find rest.

(Phocylides, 10) [20]

Seek a living and when thou hast a living, virtue.

(Phocylides, 13)

We should learn noble deeds when we are yet children.

(Phocylides, 16)

Righteousness containeth the sum of all virtues.

(Xenophanes, 1) [11]

Xenophanes linked religion and morals. A similar tendency prevailed in the Homeric age.

What is good, is ever to have respect unto the Gods.

(Theognis, 315-318) [12]

Many bad men, for sure, are rich, and many good men poor: yet we will not change our virtue for these men's wealth, seeing that virtue endureth but possessions belong now to this man and now to that.


(Theognis, 635-636)

Judgement and respect for right are the portion of the good, and of such there are now but few, truth to tell, among many.


(Theognis, *Elegies*, 591-592)

We ought to put up with that which the Gods give to man, and bear in patience either lot.


(Simonides of Ceos, *To Scopas*, 19) [14,13]

It is hard to quit you like a truly good man fashioned without flaw in hand, foot, or mind, foursquare. . . . And though it come of a wise man, I hold not with the saying of Pittacus, ' 'Tis hard to be good.' Such is the lot of a God alone; as for a man, he cannot but be evil if he be overtaken by hopeless calamity; for any man is good in good fortune and bad in bad, and take it all in all, they are best who are loved by the Gods. Therefore never will I cast my portion of life profitless away upon a hope unaccomplishable, by going in quest of what cannot be, to wit a man without spot or blemish among all of us who win the fruit of the wide-set earth, but if so be I should come upon him I will send you word of it. My praise and friendship is for all them that of themselves earn no disgrace; even Gods fight not against necessity . . . I am no faultfinder; enough for me is he that is not good nor yet too exceeding wicked, that knoweth that Right which aideth cities, a sound man. Him will I never blame. For the generation of the worthless is without number, and surely all is fair wherein is mixed nothing foul.

(Simonides of Ceos, 71)

For what human life, nay, what throne, is desirable without pleasure?  Without her the life of a very God is not to be envied.

(Heracleitus, *Fragments*) [16]

Heracleitus condemns pleasure as an end in life.

4. If happiness consisted in the pleasures of the body, we should call cattle happy when they find grass to eat.

22. They who seek after gold dig up a lot of earth and find little.

23. Were there no injustice men would never have known the name of justice.

116. It is in the power of all men to know themselves and to practice temperance.

119. A man's character is his fate.

(Anonymous, Fragments, 122) [21]

Not glorious gold so rare in this mortal life of disappointment, nor diamonds, nor silver couches, shine in the eyes in comparison of a man, nor are the rich-laden self-sufficient fields of the wide-set earth of such account as the unanimous thinking of good men and true.

## 4. SOCIAL ATTITUDES:  ATTITUDES OF MAN TO MAN

(Alcman, 51) [2,3]

Neighbor is a great thing unto neighbor.

(Archilochus, 65)[22]

One thing I know, how to recompense with evil reproaches him that doeth me evil.

(Solon, *Scolia of the Seven Wise Men*, 30) [21]

Against every man be thou on thy guard, lest in his heart he hold a secret sword though he accost thee with a smiling face, lest his tongue speak all double-worded from a heart that is black.

(Stesichorus, 54) [23]

When a man dies, all his glory among men dies also.

(Ibycus, 27) [24]

There may well be one with a mouth greedy of strife who shall rouse battle against me.

(Ibycus, 45)

Contests allow no excuses, no more do friendships.

(Phocylides, 6) [20]

Thus also spake Phocylides—Comrade should consider with comrade what their fellow-townsmen mutter in their ears.

(Theognis, 29–38) [12]

This then I would have thee to know, nor to consort with the bad but ever to cleave unto the good, and at their tables to eat and to drink, and with them to sit, and them to please, for their power is great.  Of good men shalt thou learn good, but if thou mingle with the bad, thou shalt e'en lose the wit thou hast already.  Consort therefore with the good, and some-day thou'lt say that I counsel my friends aright.

(Theognis, 69–72)

Never take confident counsel, Cyrnus, with a bad man when thou wouldst accomplish a grave matter, but seek the counsel of the good, Cyrnus, even if it mean much labor and a long journey.

(Theognis, 73–74)

Share not thy device wholly with all thy friends; few among many, for sure, have a mind that may be trusted.

(Theognis, 77–78)

In sore dissension, Cyrnus, a trusty man is to be reckoned against gold and silver.

(Theognis, 79–82)

Few comrades, son of Polypaüs, wilt thou find worthy thy trust in difficulties, such, to wit, as would be of one mind with thee and suffer to share evenpoise in thy good fortune and thy bad.

(Theognis, 87–92)

If thou lovest me and the heart within thee is loyal, be not my friend but in word, with heart and mind turned contrary; either love with a whole heart, or disown me and hate me in open quarrel. Whosoever is in two minds with one tongue, he, Cyrnus, is a dangerous comrade, better as foe than friend.

(Theognis, 93–100)

If one praise thee so long as he see thee, and speak ill of thee behind thy back, such a comrade, for sure, is no very good friend—the man, to wit, whose tongue speaks fair and his mind thinks ill. But I would be friends with him that seeketh to know his comrade's temper and beareth with him like a brother. And thou, friend, consider this well, and someday hereafter thou'lt remember me.

(Theognis, 101–104)

May no mortal man persuade thee, Cyrnus, to love a bad man; what advantage is a friend from among the baser sort? He would neither save thee from sore trouble and ruin, nor wish to share with thee any good thing he had.

(Theognis, 105–112)

He that doeth good to the baser sort getteth him little thanks; as well might he sow the waters of the hoary brine. Thou wouldst no more receive good again if thou didst good unto the bad, than reap long straw if thou sowedst the waters. For the mind of the bad is insatiable; make thou but one mistake, and the friendship is poured out and lost from all the past. But the good are fain to blot out the worst of wrongs when they suffer it, whereas they keep remembrance afterward of good that is done them and abide grateful for it.

(Theognis, 219–220)

When thy fellow-townsmen are confounded, Cyrnus, be not thou too much vexed at aught they do, but walk the road, like me, in the middle.

(Theognis, 221–226)

Surely he that thinketh his neighbour knoweth nought and he alone hath subtle arts, he is a fool and his good wits attainted; truth to tell, we all alike have our wiles, but one is loath to follow base gain, while another taketh pleasure rather in false cozenings.

(Theognis, 271–278)

'Tis sure that the Gods have given mortal man fair share of all else, given them both Youth and baleful Age; but the worst of all their gifts, worse than death and any disease, is when thou hast brought up children and supplied all their need, and with much labour and trouble laid up possessions for them, and they hate their father and curse him, loathe him as they might a beggarman that came among them.

(Theognis, 697–698)

When I am in good plight my friends are many; if aught ill befall, there's but few whose hearts are true.

(Theognis, 801–804)

No man ever was or ever will be, who leaveth all men content when he goeth below, seeing that not even Cronus' Son, the Ruler of both Gods and men, can please all mankind.

(Theognis, 933–936)

Virtue and beauty fall to but few; happy he that hath share of both. He is honored of all; alike younger and elder yield him place, and the men of his age; when he groweth old he is conspicuous among his townsmen, and no man will do him harm either in honour or in right.

(Theognis, 963–970)

Never praise a man ere thou know him for certain, what he is in disposition, in feeling, and in character. Many, for sure, that are of a tricksy counterfeit turn of mind, hide it, putting into themselves a temper that is ordinary; yet Time exposeth the nature of each and all of them. I too, it seems, have gone far beyond good sense; I praised thee ere I knew all thy ways; and now I give thee a wide berth.

(Heracleitus, 107) [16]

Heracleitus calls for what might be considered "insight" as a mode of getting at a knowledge of human experience. He distrusts external observation and knowledge.

Eyes and ears are bad witnesses to men who have not an understanding heart.

(Heracleitus, 49)

One to me is as good as ten thousand if he be but the best.

## 5. POLITICAL THEORY

(Alcaeus, *Fragments*) [5]

### 28.

Not houses finely roofed or the stones of walls well-builded, nay nor canals and dockyards, make the city, but men able to use their opportunity.

### 29.

Not stone and timber, nor the craft of the joiner, makes the city; but wheresoever are men who know how to keep themselves safe, there are walls and there a city.

37, 38, 39.

Alcaeus likens the disturbances caused by the tyrants to stormy weather at sea.

I cannot tell the lie of the wind; one wave rolls from this quarter, another from that, and we are carried in the midst with the black ship, labouring in an exceeding great storm. The water is up to the mast-hole, the sail lets daylight through with the great rents that are in it, and the halyards are working loose.

(Solon, 4) [6,7]

But Athens, albeit she will never perish by the destiny of Zeus or the will of the happy Gods immortal—for of such power is the great-hearted Guardian, Daughter of a Mighty Sire, that holdeth Her hands over us—, Her own people, for lucre's sake, are fain to make ruin of this great city by their folly. Unrighteous is the mind of the leaders of the commons, and their pride goeth before a fall; for they know not how to hold them from excess, nor to direct in peace the jollity of their present feasting . . . but grow rich through the suasion of unrighteous deeds . . . and steal right and left with no respect for possession sacred or profane, nor have heed of the awful foundations of Justice, who is so well aware in her silence of what is and what hath been, and soon or late cometh always to avenge.  This is a wound that cometh inevitable and forthwith to every city, and she falleth quickly into an evil servitude, which arouseth discord and waketh slumbering War that destroyeth the lovely prime of so many men.  For in gatherings dear to the unrighteous a delightful city is quickly brought low at the hands of them that are her enemies.  Such are the evils which then are rife among the common folk, and many of the poor go slaves into a foreign land, bound with unseemly fetters, there to bear perforce the evil works of servitude.  So cometh the common evil into every house, and the street-doors will no longer keep it out; it leapeth the high hedge and findeth every

man, for all he may go hide himself in his chamber. This it is
that my heart biddeth me tell the Athenians, and how that even
as ill-government giveth a city much trouble, so good rule
maketh all things orderly and perfect, and often putteth fetters
upon the unrighteous; aye, she maketh the rough smooth,
checketh excess, confuseth outrage; she withereth the springing
weeds of ruin, she straighteneth crooked judgments, she mol-
lifieth proud deeds; she stoppeth the works of faction, she
stilleth the wrath of baneful strife; and of her all is made wise
and perfect in the world of men.

(Solon, 7)

Solon often suggests a recognition of classes in society.

In great matters it is hard to please all.

(Solon, 13, l. 43–56)

In the following excerpt Solon attributes social position to fate. Implicit in the passage is also the recognition of a division of labor in society.

Each hath his own quest; one for to bring home gain,
rangeth the fishy deep a-shipboard, tossed by grievous winds,
sparing his life no whit, another serveth them whose business
lieth with the curved ploughshare, ploughing the well-planted
land for them throughout the year; one getteth his living by
the skill of his hands in the works of Athena and the master
of many crafts, Hephaestus, another through his learning in
the gifts of Olympian Muses, cunning in the measure of lovely
art; others again as physicians, having the task of the Master
of Medicines, the Healer—for these men too there's no end
of their labors, for often cometh great pain of little and a man
cannot assuage it by soothing medicines, albeit at other times
him that is confounded by evil and grievous maladies maketh
he quickly whole by the laying on of hands; another again the
Far-Shooting Lord Apollo maketh a seer, and the mischief that
cometh on a man from afar is known to him that hath the Gods
with him, for no augury nor offering will ever ward off what is
destined to be.

(Solon, 9)

Solon warns his countrymen against the tyranny and despotism that he foresees.

The strength of snow and of hail is from a cloud, and thunder cometh of the bright lightning; a city is destroyed of great men, and the common folk fall into bondage unto a despot because of ignorance. For him that putteth out too far from land 'tis not easy to make haven afterward; all such things as these should be thought of ere it be too late.

(Solon, 10)

When Pisistratus became the ruling tyrant of Athens, Solon blamed the people themselves for allowing tyranny to gain power.

If ye suffer bitterly through your own fault, blame ye not the gods for it; for yourselves have ye exalted these men by giving them guards and therefore it is that ye enjoy foul servitude. Each one of you walketh with the steps of a fox, the mind of all of you is vain; for ye look to a man's tongue and shifty speech and never to the deed he doeth.

(Solon, 41)

Obey the lawful authorities, whether thou deem them right or no.

(Phocylides, 5) [20]

Thus also spake Phocylides—A little state living orderly in a high place is stronger than a block-headed Nineveh.

(Theognis, 535–538) [12]

Never is slavery straight of head, but ever crooked and keepeth her neck askew; for the child of a bond-woman is never free in spirit, any more than a rose or a hyacinth groweth upon a squill.

(Theognis, *Elegies*, 43–52)

Never yet, Cyrnus, have good men ruined a city; but when it pleases the bad to do the works of pride and corrupt the common folk and give judgment for the unrighteous for the sake of private gain and power, *then* expect not that city to be long quiet, for all she be now in great tranquility, ay, then when these things become dear to the bad—to wit, gains that bring with them public ill. For of such come discords and internecine slaughter, and of such come tyrants; which things I pray may never please this city.

(Heracleitus, *Fragments*) [15]

100. The people ought to fight for their law as for a wall.
110. It is law to obey the counsel of one.

### 6. Position of Women

(Semonides of Samos, 6) [4]

A man wins himself nothing whatsoever that is better than a good wife nor worse than a bad.

(Semonides of Samos, 7)

In the beginning God made woman's mind apart from man's.

One made He of a bristly Sow; all that is in her house lies disorderly, defiled with dirt, and rolling upon the floor, and she groweth fat a-sitting among the middens in garments as unwashed as herself.

Another did God make of a knavish Vixen, a woman knowing in all things, who taketh note of all, be it bad or good; for the bad often calleth she good and the good bad; and she hath now this mood and now that.

Another of a Bitch, a busybody like her mother, one that would fain hear all, know all, and peering and prying everywhere barketh e'en though she see nobody; a man cannot check her with threats, no, not if in danger he dash her teeth out with a stone, nor yet though he speak gently with her, even though she be sitting among strangers—she must needs keep up her idle baying.

Another the Olympians fashioned of Earth, and gave to her husband all wanting in wits; such a woman knoweth neither evil nor good; her only art is to eat; and never though God give a bad winter draweth her stool nigher the fire for the cold.

Another of the Sea, whose thoughts are in two minds; one day she laughs and is gay—a stranger seeing her within will praise her, saying 'There's no better wife in all the world, nay, nor comlier'; the next she is intolerable to behold or draw nigh to, for then she rageth unapproachably, like a bitch with young; implacable and nasty is she to all, alike foe and friend. Even as the sea in summer time often will stand calm and harmless, to the great joy of the mariners, yet often will rage and toss with roaring waves, most like unto it is such a woman in disposition, nor hath the ocean a nature of other sort than hers.

Another's made of a stubborn and belabored She-Ass; everything she doeth is hardly done, of necessity and after threats, and then 'tis left unfinished; meanwhile eateth she day in and day out in bower and in hall, and all men alike are welcome to her bed.

Another of a Cat, a woeful and miserable sort; for in her there's nought of fair or lovely or pleasant or desirable; she is wood for a love-mate, and yet when she hath him turneth his stomach; she doeth her neighbours much harm underhand, and often eateth up unaccepted offerings.

Another is the child of a dainty long-maned Mare; she refuseth menial tasks and toil; she'll neither set hand to mill nor take up sieve, nor cast forth the muck, nor, for that she shunneth the soot, will she sit beside the oven. She taketh a mate only of necessity. Every day will she wash herself twice, or even thrice, and anointeth her with unguents. She ever weareth her hair deep-combed and wreathed with flowers. Such a wife may be a fair sight for other men, but she's an ill to her husband if he be not a despot or king; such as take pride in adornments like to her.

Another cometh of an Ape; she is the greatest ill of all Zeus giveth man. Foul of face, such a woman maketh laughter for all men as she goeth through the town; short in neck, she moveth hardly, hipless, lean-shanked—alas for the wretched man that claspeth such a mischief! Like an ape she knoweth all arts and wiles, nor recketh of men's laughter. Neither will she do a man any kindness; all her care, all her considering, is how she shall do the greatest ill she may.

Another of a Bee; and happy he that getteth her; On her alone alighteth there no blame, and life doth flourish and increase because of her; loving and loved groweth she old with her husband, the mother of a fair and name-honoured progeny; she is pre-eminent among all the women, and a divine grace pervadeth her; neither taketh she delight in sitting among women where they tell tales of venery. Such wives are the best and wisest that Zeus bestoweth upon men; these other kinds thanks unto Him, both are and will ever be a mischief in the world.

For this is the greatest ill that Zeus hath made, woman. Even though they may seem to advantage us, a wife is more than all else a mischief to him that possesseth her; for who so dwelleth with a woman, he never passeth a whole day glad, nor quickly shall he thrust out of doors Hunger the hated housefellow and hostile deity. But when a man thinketh within doors to be gladdest at heart by grace of God or favor of man, then of all times will she find cause for blame and gird herself for battle. For where a woman is, they e'en cannot receive a stranger heartily. And she that most seemeth to be discreet, she is all the time doing the greatest harm; her husband is all agape for her, but the neighbors rejoice that yet another is deceived. And no man but will praise his own wife when he speaketh of her, and blame another's, yet we cannot see that we be all alike. Aye, this is the greatest ill that Zeus hath made, this hath he put about us as the bondage of a fetter irrefragable, ever since Death received them that went a-war-ring for a woman.

(Phocylides, 3) [20]

Thus also spake Phocylides—The tribes of women come of these four, the bitch, the bee, the savage-looking sow, and the long-maned mare; the mare's daughter sprightly, quick, gada-bout, and very comely, the savage-looking sow's neither bad, belike, nor good, the bitch's tetchy and ill-mannered; and the bee's a good house-wife who knows her work—and 'tis she, my friend, thou shouldst pray thou mayst get thee in delectable wedlock.

(Theognis, 1225-1226) [12]

Nothing, Cyrnus is more delightful than a good wife; To the truth of this I am a witness to thee and do thou become wit-ness to me . . . (by marrying one).

(Theognis, *Elegies*, 457-460)

A young wife is not proper to an old husband; she is a boat that answereth not the helm, nor do her anchors hold, but she slippeth her moorings often overnight to make another haven.

## 7. Attitudes Toward War: Patriotism and Valour

(Tyrtaeus, 10) [25]

For 'tis a fair thing for a good man to fall and die fighting in the van for his native land, whereas to leave his city and his rich fields and go a-begging is of all things the most miserable, wandering with mother dear and aged father, with little chil-dren and wedded wife. For hateful shall such an one be among all those to whom he shall come in bondage to Want and loathe-some Penury, and doth shame his lineage and belie his noble beauty, followed by all evil and dishonour. Now if so little thought be taken of a wanderer, and so little honour, respect, or pity, let us fight with a will for this land, and die for our chil-dren, and never spare our lives.

Abide then, O young men, shoulder to shoulder and fight; begin not foul flight nor yet be afraid, but make the heart in your breasts both great and stout, and never shrink, when you fight the foe. And the elder sort whose knees are no longer nimble, fly not ye to leave them fallen to earth. For 'tis a foul thing, in sooth, for an elder to fall in the van and lie before the younger, his head white and his beard hoary, breathing forth his stout soul in the dust, with his privities all bloody in his hands, a sight so foul to see and frought with such ill to the seer, and his flesh also all naked; yet to a young man all is seemly enough, so long as he have the noble bloom of lovely youth, aye a marvel he for men to behold, and desirable unto women, so long as ever he be alive, and fair in like manner when he be fallen in the vanguard. So let each man bite his lip with his teeth and abide firm-set astride upon the ground.

(Tyrtaeus, 11)

Ye are of the lineage of the invincible Heracles; so be ye of good cheer; not yet is the head of Zeus turned away. Fear ye not a multitude of men, nor flinch, but let every man hold his shield straight towards the van, making Life his enemy and the black Spirits of Death dear as the rays of the sun. For ye know the destroying deeds of lamentable Ares, and well have learnt the disposition of woeful War; ye have tasted both the fleeing and the pursuing, lads, and had more than your fill of either. Those who abiding shoulder to shoulder go with a will into the mellay and the van, of these are fewer slain, these save the people afterward; as for them that turn to fear, all their valour is lost—no man could tell in words each and all the ills that befall a man if he once come to dishonour. For pleasant it is in dreadful warfare to pierce the midriff of a flying man, and disgraced is the dead that dieth in the dust with a spear-point in his back. So let each man bite his lip and abide firm-set astride upon the ground, covering with the belly of his broad buckler thighs and legs below and breast and shoulders above; let him brandish the massy spear in his right hand, let him wave the dire crest upon his head; let him learn how to fight by doing doughty deeds, and not stand shield in hand beyond the missiles. Nay, let each man close the foe, and with his own long spear, or else with his sword, wound and take an enemy, and setting foot beside foot, resting shield against shield, crest beside crest, helm beside helm, fight his man breast to breast with sword or long spear in hand. And ye also, ye light-armed, crouch ye on either hand beneath the shield and fling your great hurlstones and throw against them your smooth javelins, in your place beside the man of heavier armament.

(Tyrtaeus, 12)

I would neither call a man to mind nor put him in my tale for prowess in the race or the wrestling, not even had he the stature and strength of a Cyclops and surpassed in swiftness the Thracian Northwind, nor were he a comelier man than Tithonus and a richer than Midas or Cinyras, nor though he were a greater king than Pelops son of Tantalus, and had Adrastus' suasiveness of tongue, nor yet though all fame were his save of warlike strength; for a man is not good in war if he have not endured the sight of bloody slaughter and stood nigh and reached forth to strike the foe. This is prowess, this is the noblest prize and the fairest for a lad to win in the world; a common good this both for the city and all the people, when a man standeth firm in the forefront without ceasing, and making heart and soul to abide, forgetteth foul flight altogether and hearteneth by his words him that he standeth by. Such a man is good in war; he quickly turneth the savage hosts of the enemy, and stemmeth the wave of battle, with a will; moreover he that falleth in the van and loseth dear life to the glory of his city and his countrymen and his father, with many a frontwise wound through breast and breastplate and through bossy shield, he is bewailed alike by young and old, and lamented with sore regret by all the city. His grave and his children are conspicuous among men, and his children's children and his line after them; nor ever doth his name and good fame perish, but though he be underground he liveth evermore, seeing that he was doing nobly and abiding in the fight for country's and children's sake when fierce Ares brought him low. But and if he escape the doom of outstretched Death and by victory make good the splendid boast of battle, he hath honour of all, alike young and old, and cometh to his death after happiness; as he groweth old he standeth out among his people, and there is none that will do him hurt either in honour or in right; and yield him place on the benches, alike the young and his peers and his elders. This is the prowess each man should this day aspire to, never relaxing from war.

(Callinus, 1) [26]

How long will ye be idle? When, young men, will ye show a stout heart? Have ye no shame of your sloth before them that dwell round about you? Purpose ye to sit in peace though the land is full of war? . . . and let every man cast his javelin once more as he dies. For 'tis an honourable thing and a glorious to a man to fight the foe for land and children and wedded wife; and death shall befall only when the Fates ordain it. Nay so soon as war is mingled let each go forward spear in poise and shield before stout heart; for by no means may a man escape death, nay not if he come of immortal lineage. Oftentime, it may be, he returneth safe from the conflict of battle and the thud of spears, and the doom of death cometh upon him at home; yet such is not dear to the people, nor regretted, whereas if aught happen to the other sort he is bewailed of small and great. When a brave man dieth the whole people regretteth him and while he lives he is as good as a demigod; for in their eyes he is a tower, seeing that he doeth single-handed as good work as man together.

(Archilochus, 6) [22]

When the poet Archilochus visited Sparta he was driven out of the city because they discovered that he had said in a poem that it was better to throw away one's arms than be slain.

The shield I left because I must, poor blameless armament! beside a bush, gives joy now to some Saian, but myself I have saved. What care I for that shield? It shall go with a curse. I'll get me another e'en as good.

(Archilochus, 63)

No man getteth honour or glory of his countrymen once he be dead; rather do we pursue the favour of the living while we live; the dead getteth ever the worst part.

(Simonides of Ceos, 21) [14]

To them that fell at Thermopylae belong a glorious fortune and a noble lot; for grave they have an altar, for libation-ewers remembrance, and the wine that comes thereof is praise. Such burial neither shall Decay darken, nor Time the all-vanquisher bedim. This shrine of brave men hath taken for its keeper the fair fame of Greece, witness Leonidas the king of Sparta by token of the great ornament of valour and the everlasting glory that he hath left behind.

(Simonides of Ceos, 116)

We were slain in a glen of Dirphys, and the mound of our grave is made beside Euripus at our country's charge, and rightly so; for by abiding the onset of the cruel cloud of war we lost our lovely time of youth.

(Simonides of Ceos, 127)

If the greatest part of virtue is to die well, that hath Fortune given, of all men, unto us; we lie here in glory unaging because we strove to crown Greece with freedom.

(Alcaeus, 27) [5]

Now is our song of thee, thou great Nurse of all those tender youths who recking so little of themselves took the field in the first rank of our people; for they have done the allotted task of men with the same will as those who have grown to be men. Were I all-wise, were I like to a God in shrewdness of wit, even so would I not so much as pluck out a hair contrary to the decree of Zeus, and being grown men our lives are mingled with troubles befitting our estate; but for youths to rush into the deep tumult of the battle mellay—that is not for them. [Yet these, when a host ill-conquerable came up against our city, laid fear aside and took arms and . . . ]

(Anacreon, 87) [14]

Of all my gallant friends, Aristocleides, I pity thee the most; for in the defence of thy country from slavery thou hast lost thy youth.

(Theognis, 865–868) [12]

God giveth prosperity to many useless men such as being of no worth are of no service to themselves nor to their friends. But the great fame of valour will never perish, for a man-at-arms saveth both soil and city.

(Theognis, 885–886)

May Peace and Wealth possess the city, so that I may make merry with other men; I love not evil War.

(Theognis, 889–890)

But it would be dishonourable for me not to mount behind swift steeds and look lamentable War in the face.

(Heracleitus, *Fragments*) [16]

24. Gods and men alike honour those who fall in battle.
25. Greater deaths receive greater rewards.
53. War is the father of all and the king of all, and some he has made Gods and some men, some bond and some free.
80. We ought to know that war is the common lot, and that justice is strife, and that all things arise through strife and necessity.

## 8. WEALTH AND RICHES

### (Alcaeus, *To Poverty*, 18) [3]

O Poverty, thou grievous and resistless ill, who with thy sister Helplessness overwhelmest a great people . . .

### (Alcaeus, 81)

. . . For even as once on a day 'tis told Aristodemus said at Sparta—and 'twas no bad thing—, the money is the man and no poor man is either good or honourable.

### (Sappho, 100) [27]

Wealth without worth is no harmless housemate; but the blending of the two is the top of fortune.

### (Solon, 13 l. 70–75) [6,7]

And as for wealth, there's no end set clearly down; for such as have to-day the greatest riches among us, these have twice the eagerness that others have, and who can satisfy all? 'Tis sure the Gods give us men possessions, yet a ruin is revealed thereout, which one man hath now and another then, whensoever Zeus sendeth it in retribution.

### (Solon, 15)

Many bad men are rich, many good men poor; but we, we will not exchange virtue for wealth, for the one endureth whereas the other belongeth now to this man and now to that.

### (Solon, 24)

Surely equal is the wealth of him that hath much silver and gold and fields of wheatland and horses and mules, to that of him that hath but this—comfort in belly and sides and feet. This is abundance unto men, seeing that no man taketh with him the many things he hath above this when he goeth below, nor shall he for a price escape death nor yet sore disease nor the evil approach of Age.

(Anacreon, *The Wounded Cupid*, 36) [19]

If wealth of gold
    Gave mortals breath,
Then I should hold
    It, that if Death
Should come to me,
    Then I might say
'Take your fee
    'And go away.'
But if his years
    No mortal buys,
Then wherefore tears,
    And wherefore sighs?
If we must die
    Doth gold avail?
Rather may I
    Drink good brown ale.


(Anacreon, 58)

When truant Gold away doth wing,
Swift as the wind ('tis no rare thing)
I go not after him; for who
Game he hateth will pursue?
I go within, fling care to th' breeze,
Take lute and troll love-melodies.
But when my pride takes heart of grace,
Then lo! the truant's in his place,
And drugs my wayward wit till I
Forget the dulcet quill to ply.
Fie, faithless Gold! your cozenings fail;
The strings afford me more regale
Love of envy and deceit,
That's what you give man for meat;
The lute doth mix him happier cheer,
Desire of bowers and kisses dear,

Play me truant when you will;
My lyre shall be my comrade still
Your wiles on those you're free to use
Who be no neighbors of Muse;
With sweepers of the string like me
The Muse keeps ever company
If you would stir a leaky pot, you may,
Or take a taper to the light of day.

(Phocylides, 7) [20]

If thou desirest riches, see that thou hast a fertile farm; for a farm, they say, is a horn of Amalthea.

(Theognis, *Elegies*, 1117–1118) [12]

Wealth, fairest and most desirable of all the Gods, with thee a man becometh good even if he be bad.

(1157–1160)

Riches and skill are ever the most irresistible of things to man; for thou canst not surfeit thy heart with riches, and in like manner he that is most skilled shunneth not skill, but desireth it and cannot have his fill.

(557–560)

Beware, the chances, for sure, are balanced very fine; one day thou shalt have much and another little; it behoveth thee, then, neither to become too rich nor to ride into great want.

(523–524)

With good reason, O Wealth, doth man honour thee above all, for how easily dost thou tolerate badness!

(525–526)

'Tis sure that it becometh the good to have riches, and 'tis proper to a bad man to suffer penury.

## 9. ATTITUDES TOWARD OLD AGE

(Archilochus, 48) [22]

An idle life is good for the aged, the more so if they be simple in their ways or be like to be stupid or to speak nought but foolishness, as old men will.

(Mimnermus, 2) [6]

Mimnermus adopts a pessimistic attitude toward life by considering life short, of little account, and full of care.

But we, like the leaves that come in the flowery Springtime when they wax so quickly beneath the sunbeams, like them we enjoy the blossoms of youth for a season but an ell long, the Gods giving us knowledge, neither of evil nor of good; for here beside us stand the black Death-spirits, the one with the end that is grievous Eld, the other that which is Death; and the harvest of youth is as quickly come as the rising sun spreadeth his light abroad. And when the end of maturity be past, then to be dead is better than to live; for many be the sorrows that rise in the heart; sometimes our house is wasted and Poverty's dolorous deeds are to do; or a man lacketh children and goeth down to Death desiring them more than all else; again he is possessed by heart-destroying Disease—there's no man in the world to whom Zeus giveth not manifold woe.

(Mimnermus, 3)

However fair he may once have been, when the season is overpast he is neither honoured nor loved, nay, not by his own children.

(Mimnermus, 5)

But precious Youth is short-lived as a dream, and woeful and ugly Eld hangeth plumb over our heads, Eld hateful alike and unhonoured, which maketh a man unknown and doeth him hurt by the overwhelming of eyes and wits.

# CHAPTER IV

## ATTIC AGE

THERE is little question that in the Hellas of the sixth century B.C. the leading role in the economic and highly civilized life was played by the Greek colonies in Asia Minor and to some extent those of Italy and Sicily, rather than by Greece proper.

Just as the Greeks at home were divided into independent states, each having her own traditions and policies, so was it with the Greeks of Asia Minor. Hatred and jealousy of their neighbors loomed large on their horizon. This situation led them to overlook the power of the Eastern empires. Consequently, when Lydia and later Persia attacked them, these Anatolian Greeks were easily conquered.

Because of these conquests in Asia Minor, Persia found herself embroiled in European politics. It became her policy to conquer all of Greece. The revolt of the Ionian Greeks (499 B.C.) prevented this conquest. The Asiatic Greeks, led by Miletus and aided by a small Athenian fleet, were at first successful against Persia. Since there was internal dissension among the Greeks, however, the Persians were able to reconquer all they had lost, and succeeded in destroying Miletus and other leading cities. Athens was the next city on the Persian list. The Athenians, the Spartans, and other Greek allies battled the invaders at Plataea and were victorious in 479 B.C. The Greek navy, too, was successful in defeating the Persian fleet at the battle of Mycale in the same year.

Among other consequences, the Persian wars made possible the rise of Athens to a position of material and cultural supremacy. For this reason, this period has been designated as the *Attic Age*.

Fifty years elapsed between the battle of Plataea and the beginning of the Peloponnesian War. It is a period about which little is known. Such information as we have refers, in the main, to the internal affairs of Greece. As Athens rose in political importance the friction between her and the neighboring states increased greatly. Motivating this hostility was Sparta, which constantly turned a jealous eye on the increased wealth and prominence of Athens.

In order to protect their kinsfolk in Asia Minor from a recurrence of the conquest by Persia, the Athenians organized the *Delian League,* which was a confederation of states for mutual protection. Its capital was on the island of Delos. Each state was to contribute to the upkeep of the League, the larger states furnishing their quota of ships and men while the smaller ones gave money. As time passed the larger states began to make their contributions in money also, finding it more convenient than their former mode of contribution. Thus the League was transformed into an empire with Athens supplying the navy and with other states giving money to maintain it. Athens, in her role of leader, refused to allow any member to withdraw, and crushed rebellion ruthlessly. Soon the treasury was moved from Delos to Athens, and the voluntary contributions now became taxes. Sparta was greatly aroused by these events. To circumvent any conflict with Sparta, Themistocles, leader of the anti-Sparta group in Athens, had built walls surrounding Athens and the seaport of Pireaus. Afterwards, long walls were built connecting Athens with Pireaus. This completed the fortifications which made Athens secure from invasion either by land or by sea.

Pericles was the head of the Athenian state during much of this time (461–429 B.C.). He was the exponent of Athenian democracy and believed in Athens' destiny as an imperial power. An excellent orator as well as a wise statesman, he influenced the life of Athens greatly. There is little wonder that

the period between 461 B.C. and 429 B.C. is called the age of
Pericles.  The imperialism of Athens was deemed necessary because she needed desperately the foodstuffs and raw materials
from Italy, Sicily, and Egypt.   Corinth, however, with her
western colonies, succeeded in excluding Athens from the great
grain markets of Sicily and Italy.  Hence, for commercial reasons, Athens went to War against Corinth as well as Aegina
and Boeotia.  Athens' desire to extend her sphere of influence
caused her to collide with Sparta, which sought to maintain the
neutrality of the Isthmus, since she was dependent upon the
importation of corn and raw materials from Italy and Sicily.
The war dragged tediously on and Athens was finally defeated.
A peace was made, but it did not settle permanently the question of leadership in Greece.

These events greatly influenced the internal affairs in
Athens.  Government changed its form to some extent in that
the lower classes exerted more and more influence.  In former
days the Council of Five Hundred, which consisted for the most
part of nobles, had been the powerful determinant in policies;
now the popular assembly ruled.  Once every thirty-six days
the assembly *(prytany)* reviewed the work of the magistrates
and if it discovered any irregularity brought them to trial.
This custom led to the magistrates' carrying out the decisions
of the assembly, while the council simply discussed matters
which the assembly later decided upon.  A new law was voted
upon by special committee, and if it did not pass its initiator
was fined or, in some cases, put to death.  At about the same
time a board of ten generals, called *strategi*, became increasingly influential.  All foreign and domestic policies were formu-
lated by them, and if their policies succeeded they were re-
elected many times.  On the other hand, if they failed they
were either condemned to death or exiled.

The *Heliaea*, which was composed of Athenian citizens
paid for their duties as jurists, was another very important
group.  It was composed of six thousand members and divided
into groups of five hundred, although the number varied, being

sometimes greater and sometimes smaller. The magistrates prepared the case, but took no part in the decision. Simple majority decided the verdict.

Dissension between Athens and Sparta steadily increased with the allies of Athens supporting her in the quarrel and with Sparta's allies favoring the Spartan cause. The wars of 500–450 B.C. seemingly did little to adjust their difficulties. Athens' growing trade menaced the security of Corinth, Megara, and Sparta, which were dependent upon Italy and Sicily for their food supply and raw materials, which Athens was diverting for her own use. When Pericles, provoked by continual friction with Megara, decided to blockade that city, Sparta was called upon to make a decision. The question was, in effect, whether Athens was to be permitted to gain complete control of the western trade routes, as well as political supremacy over all the Greek states. Sparta's answer was war. It began in 431 B.C. and lasted twenty-eight years.

The war, cruel and brutal in the extreme, sapped the energies of both sides. A *Great Plague* broke out in Athens during the course of the war and wiped out a large portion of the population. The most famous of the victims was Pericles, who died in 429 B.C. In 421 B.C. a truce was called.

Shortly after the truce had been made, a leader arose in Athens who, in an attempt to gain considerable power, advocated a resumption of hostilities. This was Alcibiades, and he succeeded in sending a strong expedition against Syracuse, the chief city in Sicily. This led to a war with Sparta. Persia now entered the conflict in an attempt to regain her former territory in Asia Minor. The expedition ended in disaster for Athens, with both her fleet and army so severely crushed that they never recovered. Spartan troops waged war incessantly upon Attica, while Persia aided the Peloponnesians to build an effective fleet which easily overcame the Athenian navy. At last, completely demoralized, Athens was forced to surrender in 404 B.C. The peace terms dictated by Sparta were (1) surrender of all war vessels; (2) destruction of the Long Walls;

(3) recognition of Spartan leadership in war and peace. This marked the end of Athens' political greatness.

Life for the citizens of fifth-century Athens was almost similar for all men. Although some men possessed great wealth, it was little in evidence. Simple living was the standard for the men of this epoch. Most of the time was spent by the men at the market place, the Pnyx (meeting place of the assembly), and the courts of law and council chambers. Gymnastics were a part of the life of all classes. A number of gymnasiums, wrestling schools, and paddocks were built in the suburbs. There all participated in such sports as running, wrestling, javelin-throwing and ball-playing. This was the place where the compulsory training of the young Athenian was given. This training consisted of learning to take part in local and Pan-Hellenic games, preparation for war, reading and writing, music, and declamation of great literary works.

Women were excluded from all these activities. With the growth of democracy women were more closely confined to their homes than before. During the years of aristocratic rule many women took part in political life as well as in literature. They still maintained some influence in public affairs in Sparta, but in Athens their sphere was limited to the home.

This period saw, too, an increased number of resident aliens and slaves. These *metoeci*, or resident aliens, were attracted to Athens by the political leaders. Since Athenian citizens were constantly occupied with public affairs and with war, it was necessary to have a group interested in commercial matters. The resident aliens came to control all the financial and industrial affairs of Athens, and were largely responsible for her wealth and power. Although they were not permitted to own land in Attica their social life was not restricted in any way.

Another important group arose in Athens—the slaves. Although they had no legal status, the entire economic life of the city was dependent upon them. They lived much as other men; the more ambitious among them eventually won freedom.

The greatest change of all took place in the intellectual life in this century. The most prominent thinkers and writers were almost all either Athenians by birth or residents of Athens. In Asia Minor philosophy still flourished under the guidance of Heracleitus, the first man to recognize the importance of motion in the universe. On the other hand, Anaxagoras, a native of Asia Minor, lived and worked in Athens, as did Empedocles of Acragas, Leucippus, and Democritus.

Religious changes were not so great in Athens, for the citizens were conservative in religious matters. Although men were permitted to speak and think freely, religious traditions were guarded jealously and resentment among the conservative element was felt when any of their beliefs were called into question. Thus it was that Socrates fell victim to this group's prejudices. Religion consisted for the most part in the practice of ancient rites, and was regarded with great respect. After a time, however, attempts were made to spiritualize religion, and this effort met with the approval of the population. The trend was toward monotheism, and Aeschylus in his tragedies was clearly pointing the way to this new idea.

Tragedy probably reached its peak in this period, and Aeschylus has been called the father of Greek Tragedy. Most of his plots have their roots in mythology but the characters are combined in endless variety. It was usual to write plays in trilogies, each of which consisted of three complete plays dealing with one subject. Each play was independent of the others but had the same characters. Only seven of Aeschylus' tragedies have been preserved. Sophocles, who was younger than Aeschylus, wrote prodigiously, but we have only seven and one half of his plays. Euripides, last of the great tragedians and a rival of Sophocles, left us nineteen of his plays. The influence of all these tragedies on the Greek mind is inestimable. For the citizens of Athens they meant a broadening of horizons never before perceived. Each man carried away with him new concepts that most certainly motivated his thoughts and his deeds.

Comedy, too, exerted great influence. It developed later than tragedy and owed a great deal to it. Its three most famous exponents were Eupolis, Cratinus, and Aristophanes. Only Aristophanes' works are known to us. Unlike tragedy, comedy chose as its subject matter the passing events and daily lives of the Athenians of that time. Aristophanes used all public matters as grist for his mill, and so we find in his plays discussions of emancipation for women, war and peace, education, and social theories. His great gift of high spirits and ironic nuances make his work highly contemporaneous and entertaining as well as informative.

The growth and influence of the sophists may be traced to the daily needs of the Athenian citizen, who was constantly occupied in voting on important political issues as well as having to defend himself from all sorts of charges. Hence the Sophists, whose interests lay in political and social questions, taught men how to decide on issues, what arguments to use, and so on. The Sophists have often been referred to as the fathers of political science.

Such was the nature of Greek civilization in the fifth century, when Athens was at the peak of her glory. Before this century was over, however, Sparta succeeded in capturing the political leadership. Sparta maintained this supremacy for more than thirty years. Sparta's rule seemed less happy than Athens' to the Greek cities. The garrisons of Sparta often kept in power oligarchies which were extremely offensive to the people. They were guilty of extreme cruelty, and time after time revolts broke out. At last Thebes, a city northwest of Athens, succeeded in crushing Sparta's power (371 B.C.). Thebes, too, was unsuccessful in keeping the Greek city-states united. Thus it was that Hellas was easy prey for foreign conquerors. In 338 B.C. Philip of Macedon defeated the Greek forces after a long and bitter struggle. After Philip's death, his son Alexander succeeded to his rule, and by military genius created a world-empire for himself. Alexander was imbued with a passion for Greek civilization (Aristotle having been his tutor) and his conquests served to spread Greek art, literature, language, and ideas throughout the Orient. His death came in 323 B.C.

In the fourth century B.C. Athens was still first in the march of civilization, even though her political power had been shorn from her. The Attic dialect became the accepted mode of speech of the educated throughout the Greek world.

It was in this last century that philosophy and rhetoric reached brilliant heights. In Plato and in Aristotle Greek philosophy had its greatest geniuses. The modern world recognizes their position among the creative thinkers of all time, and little need be said about them here.

A large number of fine orators and publicists flourished in this period. Their speeches were often published during their lifetimes and used as models for the following generation. Two types of speeches were written—the forensic and the political. The political speech was usually made by the orator himself before the popular assembly, while the forensic speech was written for other people to deliver because the Athenian courts required a defendant to give his own defence. Some political speeches were never delivered, but were published as pamphlets. Isocrates was one of the first great orators of Athens, and was followed by Lysias, Isaeus, Demosthenes and Aeschines. Their speeches enable the reader to see clearly the political and social scene of Athens in that age. Many excerpts from these works will be found in the text.

In general, it may be said that the fourth century saw no diminution of the Greek creative power. Greek law was developed in Athens and later was adopted by almost all the Greeks. This epoch also claims the important historian Xenophon, whose works include *Hellenica, Anabasis, The Education of Cyrus,* and *Recollections.*

As in previous chapters, the social thought of the Attic Age is classified under several headings. Many excerpts from the drama have been included. In order to facilitate the understanding of these excerpts, synopses of the plays are given in the notes and are referred to the first time an excerpt from any play appears in the text. The categories are as follows: (1) *The Gods And Their Relation To Man;* (2) *The Nature Of Human Nature;* (3) *The Beginnings Of Anthropological Thought;* (4) *The Relation Of The Physical Environment To Human Life;* (5) *The Idea Of The Economic Factor In Society;* (6) *Economic Thought And Theory;* (7) *Social Control: Tradition As A Basis Of Human Action;* (8) *Social Control: Mass Control Induced Through Propaganda, Public Opinion, and Leadership;* (9) *The Conception Of Social Competition;* (10) *Ideas On Law And Justice;* (11) *Comparative Government;* (12) *The Nature Of The State;* (13) *Ideas On War And Peace.* The reader will find these categories self-explanatory after reading the material under each of them.

## 1. THE GODS AND THEIR RELATION TO MAN

### (Aeschylus, *The Persians*, l. 800–834) [1]

The spirit of Darius speaks to the chorus, condemning Xerxes for destroying Grecian temples and predicting utter disaster as punishment for his deeds.[2]

DARIUS: Few indeed out of many, if, having beheld what has now been brought to pass, it is right to put any faith in the oracles of Heaven; for they have fulfilment—not some only, while others fail. And if this be truth, it is through persuasion of vain hopes that he is leaving behind a body of picked troops. They are now tarrying where the plain is watered by the stream of Asopus that gives kindly enrichment to Boeotia's fields. Here it awaits them to suffer their crowning disaster in requital for their presumptuous pride and impious thoughts. For, on reaching the land of Hellas, restrained by no religious awe, they ravaged the images of the gods and gave their temples to the flames. Altars have been destroyed, statues of the gods have been overthrown from their bases in utter ruin and confusion. Wherefore having evil wrought, evil they suffer in no less measure, and other evils are still in store: nor yet quenched is the spring of their woes, but it still wells forth. For so great shall be the mass of clotted gore spilled by the Dorian lance upon Plataean soil that heaps of dead shall make known, even to the third generation, a voiceless record for the eyes of men that mortal man needs must not vaunt him overmuch. For presumptuous pride, when it has burgeoned, bears as its fruit a crop of calamity, whence it reaps a plenteous harvest of tears.

Mark that such are the penalties for deeds like these and hold Athens and Hellas in your memory. Let no one of you, through disdain of present fortune and lust for more, squander his abundant wealth. Zeus, of a truth, is a chastiser of overweening pride and corrects with heavy hand. Therefore, now that my son has been warned to prudence by the voice of God, do ye instruct him by admonitions of reason to cease from drawing on himself the punishment of Heaven by his vaunting rashness.

(Aeschylus, *Agamemnon*,[3] l. 365–396)

The chorus speaks thus after hearing the news from Clytaemnestra that Troy has been conquered and that the army is returning home.

CHORUS: "The stroke of Zeus" they may call it; 'tis his hand that can be traced therein. As he determines, so he acts. It hath been said by some one that the gods deign not to be mindful of mortals who trample underfoot the grace of inviolable sanctities. But that man knew not the fear of God!

Now standeth revealed how ruin is the penalty for reckless crime when men breathe a spirit of pride above just measure for that their mansions teem with abundance o'erpassing their best good. But let there be such portion of wealth as bringeth no distress, so that he who hath a goodly share of sound sense may have a sufficiency therewith. For riches are no bulwark to the man who in wantonness hath spurned from his sight the mighty altar of Righteousness.

No, he is driven on by perverse Temptation, the overmastering child of designing Destruction; and remedy is utterly in vain. His evil is not hidden; it shineth forth, a baleful gleam. Like base metal beneath the touchstone's rub, when tested he showeth the blackness of his grain (for he is like a child that chaseth a winged bird) and upon his people he bringeth a taint not to be removed. To his prayers all gods are deaf, and the man who is conversant with such deeds, him they destroy in his unrighteousness.

(Aeschylus, Agamemnon, l. 456–470)

CHORUS: Dangerous is a people's voice charged with wrath —it hath the office of a curse of public doom. In anxious fear I bide to hear some tidings shrouded still in gloom; for Heaven is not unmindful of men of blood. In the end the black Spirits of Vengeance bring to obscurity him who hath prospered in unrighteousness and wear down his fortunes by reverse; and once he hath passed among them that are brought to naught, there is no more help for him. Glory in excess is fraught with peril; 'tis the lofty peak that is smitten by heaven's thunderbolt. Prosperity unassailed by envy is my choice. Let me not be a destroyer of cities, no, nor let me be despoiled and live to see my own life in another's power!

(Sophocles, Aias,[4] l. 127–133)

After driving Aias to madness in order to protect Odysseus from his jealousy, the goddess Athena speaks thus to Odysseus. In this way Sophocles expresses his belief in the omnipotence of the gods.[5]

ATHENA: Thou then, considering this, beware thou say
No arrogant word thyself against the Gods,
Nor be at all puffed up, if thou excell
Thy neighbor, or in prowess or in wealth.
One day brings low, one day again uplifts
All human greatness. Men of temperate soul
The Gods love, and abhor the wicked ones.

(Sophocles, Aias, l. 384)

In this one-line excerpt Sophocles shows how all-powerful the Gods are. When Aias, coming to his senses, realizes that he is subject to spells of madness, and rails against his fate, the chorus speaks out in this wise.

CHORUS: Men laugh, men mourn, only as God ordains.

(Sophocles, *Aias*, l. 1417–1419)

Here again is the recurrent theme of fate and its unpredictability in man's life. As the play *Aias* closes, the chorus repeats these lines as the moral of the story.

CHORUS: Full many a thing do men by seeing learn;
But, ere he see, no prophet may discern
What lot for him shall leap from fate's dark urn.

(Sophocles, *Oedipus The King*, l. 711–714)

Kreon has accused Oedipus of murdering Laius. Oedipus, full of anger, tells this to his wife Iokasta. She answers him that she knows that it is not true because of the oracle's prediction that Laius was to be murdered by his son whose identity is unknown to both Iokasta and Oedipus. (See synopsis in Note 6).

IOKASTA: An oracle came to Laius—I say not
From Phoebus' self, but from his ministers—
That death's doom should o'ertake him from the son
Even whoso should of me and him be born.

(Sophocles, *Oedipus The King*,[6] l. 1170–1177)

Here the tale unfolds and Oedipus learns from the Herdman the startling information that Laius was indeed his father and Iokasta his mother.

OEDIPUS: And I to hear. Howbeit, hear I must.
HERDMAN: Even his the child was called. But she within,
Thy wife, can tell thee best how these things are.
OEDIPUS: Ha! *she* gave to thee?—
HERDMAN:                                            Even so, O King.
OEDIPUS: And to what end?
HERDMAN:                                      That I might murder it.
OEDIPUS: Its mother—wretch!
HERDMAN:                                        By evil oracles scared.
OEDIPUS: Their purport?
HERDMAN:                              That he should his father slay.

(Sophocles, *Oedipus at Kolonus*,[7] l. 969–976)

Here Oedipus defends his past life by showing that Fate had planned it and he had no choice in the matter.

OEDIPUS:  Tell me—if to my sire came prophecy
Saying that he should by his son be slain,
Canst thou with this reproach me righteously,
Who neither was begotten nor conceived
As yet, but then was wholly uncreate?
And if, to misery born, as I was born,
I grappled with my sire, and struck him dead,
And what I did perceived not, nor to whom,
How canst thou rightly blame the unwitting deed?

(Sophocles, Antigone,[8] l. 1335–1336)

The following remarks close the Antigone.

CHORUS:  Nay, pray for naught, seeing escape is none
For mortals from the doom predestinate.

## 2. THE NATURE OF HUMAN NATURE

(Pindar,[9] Fragment 214) [10]

With him liveth sweet Hope, the nurse of eld, the fosterer of his heart,—Hope, who chiefly ruleth the changeful mind of man.

(Aeschylus, The Persians, l. 597–604)

Atossa comes to Darius' tomb to bring propitiatory sacrifices in the hope of arousing his dead spirit.

ATOSSA:  My friends, whosoever has experience of misery knows that when a sea of troubles comes upon mortal men, they are wont to view all things with alarm; but when fortune flows with prosperous tide, to trust that the selfsame fortune will waft them success for aye.

(Aeschylus, Agamemnon, l. 1331)

The chorus makes the following remark after Agamemnon has been escorted to his palace by Clytaemnestra.

CHORUS:  'Tis the nature of all human kind to be unsatisfied with prosperity.

(Bacchylides, 16) [11]

Hope robbeth men of their understanding.

(Bacchylides, 30–53)

Various are the paths men seek that shall lead them to conspicuous fame, and ten thousand the knowledges of man; for one thriveth in golden hope because he hath skill or hath honours of the Graces or is versed in divination, another bendeth a wily bow at pelf, others again exalt their spirits upon works of the field and with herds of kine. The future brings forth issues inscrutable; we know not on which side Fortune's scale will sink. The fairest of things is, that a good man be envied much of many, albeit I know the great power also of wealth, which turneth to account even the unprofitable.

(Bacchylides, 57)

No mortal man is for all time happy.

(Sophocles, *Trachinian Maidens*, l. 1–3) [12]

The following lines open the *Trachinian Maidens,* and are probably a proverb familiar to the audience of Sophocles' time. They are followed by Deianeira's recollection of what a strange life she has led and wonder as to what is in store for her. Sophocles suggests the unpredictability and indeterminacy of human events.

DEIANEIRA: There is an old law current among men—
*Thou canst not know a man's life ere he die,*
*Whether his days be evil days or good.*

(Sophocles, *Antigone,* l. 332–372)

After the messenger brings the news that someone has dared to bury Polyneikes, the chorus speaks the following lines. We find, in this excerpt, a recognition of man as a cultural being.

CHORUS: Many a wonder walks the earth, but wondrous
None is as Man: across the sea-foam-white
Driven by the storm-beast, plunging through the thund'rous
Chasms of surge, he wings his aweless flight;

Layeth his grasp on Earth, supreme, undying
Mother of Gods, and ever year by year
To and fro pass his ploughs; the steed's sons plying
Ever her stubborn strength, outweary her.

Yea, and the airy-hearted birds he snareth,
Trappeth the savage prowlers of the world,
Takes the brine-haunters whom the deep sea beareth
In his net-meshes—Man the cunning-souled;
Quelleth the forest-couching, mountain-roaming
Monsters by his devices masterful,
Bridles the stormy-maned, indignant-foaming
Horses, and yokes the tireless mountain bull.

Speech hath he taught himself, and thought swift flying
Windlike, all instincts which the state maintain;
Shelter from frost he hath found, from cheerless lying
Under the bleak sky, and from arrowy rain.
Ever resourceful, found in nought resourceless,
Dauntless he meets the future's mysteries:
Helpless against Death only, the remorseless,
His cunning foileth desperate maladies.

Crafty inventions, subtle past believing,
Now unto evil bring him, now to good.
When he hath honoured Law, by oath receiving
Justice's yoke, proudly his state hath stood.
He is an outcast, whose presumptuous daring
Moves him to be with sin confederate bound;
Never abiding by my hearth, nor sharing
Thoughts of my soul, be such transgressor found!

(Euripides,[13] *Medea*, l. 85–88)

The servants are here condemning Jason for his plan to remarry, and banish Medea, his first wife.[14]

CHILDREN'S GUARDIAN: Hast learned this only now,
That no man loves his neighbour as himself?

Good cause have some, with most 'tis greed of gain—
As here: their sire for a bride's sake loves not these.

(Euripides, *Hecuba,* l. 591–598) [15]

Hecuba, after hearing how bravely her daughter has died, repeats these lines proudly. That poverty and slavery do not affect the truly noble character seems evident to her.

HECUBA: Yet hast thou barred the worst, proclaimed to me
So noble. Lo, how strange, that evil soil
Heaven-blest with seasons fair, bears goodly crops,
While the good, if it faileth of its dues,
Gives evil fruit: but always among men
The caitiff nothing else than evil is,
The noble, noble, nor 'neath fortunes stress
Marreth his nature, but is good alway.

(Aristophanes, *The Birds,*[16] l. 1280–1307)

Aristophanes recognizes imitation as a factor in social life. In his play *The Birds,* which is a parody on life in Athens, men are subject to spells of imitation in their daily life. Thus we see a prototype in Greek drama of Tarde's "Laws of Imitation." [17]

HERMIT: O thou who hast built the ethereal glorious city,
Dost thou not know how men revere thy name,
And burn with ardour for this realm of thine?
Why, till ye built this city in the air,
All men had gone Laconian-mad; they went
Long-haired, half-starved, unwashed, Socratified,
With scytales in their hands; but O the change!
They are all bird-mad now, and imitate
The birds, and joy to do whate'er birds do.
Soon as they rise from bed at early dawn,
They settle down on laws, as ye on lawns,
And then they brood upon their leaves and leaflets,
And feed their fill upon a crop of statutes.
So undisguised their madness, that full oft
The names of birds are fastened on to men.

One limping tradesman now is known as "Partridge";
They dub Menippus "Swallow"; and Opuntius
"Blind Raven"; Philocles is "Crested Lark,"
Theagenes is nicknamed "Sheldrake" now;
Lycurgus "Ibis"; Chaerephon the "Vampire";
And Syracosius "Joy"; whilst Meidias there
Is called the "Quail"; aye and he's like a quail
Flipped on the head by some quail-filliper.
So fond they are of birds that all are singing
Songs where a swallow figures in the verse,
Or goose, or may-be widgeon, or ring-dove,
Or wings, or even the scantiest shred of feather.
So much from earth.  And let me tell you this;
More than ten thousand men will soon be here,
All wanting wings and taloned modes of life.
Somehow or other you must find them wings.

(Isocrates, To Nicocles, 45–48) [18]

This speech is actually a compendium of advice on how a ruler ought
to act and how he ought to treat his subjects.  It was written by Isocrates
and addressed to Nicocles, the young king of Cyprus, who probably had
been a student of Isocrates.  Actually, the speech is an ethical discourse
interspersed with worldly wisdom and containing much interesting material.

For if we are willing to survey human nature as a whole,
we shall find that the majority of men do not take pleasure in
the food that is the most wholesome, nor in the pursuits that
are the most honourable, nor in the actions that are the noblest,
nor in the creatures that are the most useful, but that they have
tastes which are in every way contrary to their best interests,
while they view those who have some regard for their duty as
men of austere and laborious lives.  How, then, can one advise
or teach or say anything of profit and yet please such people?
For, besides what I have said of them, they look upon men of
wisdom with suspicion, while they regard men of no understanding as open and sincere; and they so shun the verities of

life that they do not even know their own interests: nay, it irks them to take account of their own business and it delights them to discuss the business of others; and they would rather be ill in body than exert the soul and give thought to anything in the line of duty. Observe them when they are in each other's company, and you will find them giving and taking abuse; observe them when they are by themselves, and you will find them occupied, not with plans, but with idle dreams. I am, however, speaking now not of all, but of those only who are open to the charges I have made.

(Isocrates, *Nicocles, or The Cyprians*, 5–8)

For in the other powers which we possess we are in no respect superior to other living creatures; nay, we are inferior to many in swiftness and in strength and in other resources; but, because there has been implanted in us the power to persuade each other and to make clear to each other whatever we desire, not only have we escaped the life of wild beasts, but we have come together and founded cities and made laws and invented arts; and, generally speaking, there is no institution devised by man which the power of speech has not helped us to establish. For this it is which has laid down laws concerning things just and unjust, and things base and honourable; and if it were not for these ordinances we should not be able to live with one another. It is by this also that we confute the bad and extol the good.

(Isocrates, *Archidamus*, 91) [19]

Isocrates wrote to Archidamus, urging him to take steps to end civil strife in Greece. This was an idea dear to Isocrates' heart.

For not every people can adopt the same measures in the same situation, but each must follow the principles which from the very first they have made the foundation of their lives.

(Isocrates, *On The Peace*, 106–107) [20]

In *On The Peace*, Isocrates' main theme was the need for peace between Athens and the rest of the world. He also severely condemned the war-party in Athens,

For you will find that the great majority of mankind go astray in choosing a course of action and, being possessed of more desires for things evil than for things good, take counsel more in the interest of their foes than of themselves. You can observe this in matters of the greatest importance.

(Isocrates, *Areopagiticus*, 4–6) [21]

This speech was devoted to a contrast between the fine government in Athens under the constitutions of Solon and Cleisthenes, and the unsatisfactory state of affairs in Isocrates' time.

Nothing of either good or of evil visits mankind unmixed but that riches and power are attended and followed by folly, and folly in turn by licence; whereas poverty and lowliness are attended by sobriety and great moderation; so that it is hard to decide which of these lots one should prefer to bequeath to one's own children. For we shall find that from a lot which seems to be inferior men's fortunes generally advance to a better condition, whereas from one which appears to be superior they are wont to change to a worse. Of this truth I might cite examples without number from the lives of individual men, since these are subject to the most frequent vicissitudes; but instances which are more important and better known to my hearers may be drawn from the experiences of our city and of the Lacedaemonians.

(Isocrates, *Antidosis*, 207–215) [22]

This speech was written by Isocrates in defense of his life and his profession. It sets forth his theories on education, which have a close kinship with numerous modern ideas on education. Another idea that is expressed, is that human nature is achieved and not inherited.

Again, every one of you could name many of your schoolfellows who when they were boys seemed to be the dullest among their companions, but who, growing older, outstripped them farther in intelligence and in speech than they had lagged behind them when they were boys. From this fact you can best judge what training can do; for it is evident that when they were young they all possessed such mental powers as they were born with, but as they grew to be men, these outstripped the others and changed places with them in intelligence, because their companions lived dissolutely and softly, while they gave heed to their own opportunities and to their own welfare. But when people succeed in making progress through their own diligence alone, how can they fail to improve in a much greater degree both over themselves and over others if they put themselves under a master who is mature, of great experience, and learned not only in what has been handed down to him but in what he has discovered for himself? . . .

For, in the first place, they know that pains and industry give proficiency in all other activities and arts, yet deny that they have any such power in the training of the intellect; secondly, they admit that no physical weakness is so hopeless that it cannot be improved by exercise and effort, but they do not believe that our minds, which are naturally superior to our bodies, can be made more serviceable through education and suitable training; again, they observe that some people possess the art of training horses and dogs and most other animals by which they make them more spirited, gentle or intelligent, as the case may be, yet they do not think that any education has been discovered for training human nature, such as can improve men in any of those respects in which we improve the beasts. Nay, so great is the misfortune which they impute to us all, that while they would acknowledge that it is by our mental powers that every creature is improved and made more useful, yet they have the hardihood to claim that we ourselves, who are endowed with an intelligence through which we render all creatures of greater worth, cannot help each other to advance in excellence. But most absurd of all, they behold in the shows which are held year after year lions which are more gentle toward their trainers than some people are toward their benefactors, and bears which dance about and wrestle and imitate our skill, and yet they are not able to judge even from these instances the power which education and training have, nor can they see that human nature will respond more promptly than the animals to the benefits of education.

(Demosthenes,[24] *On The Embassy*, 215–216) [23]

In this speech, Demosthenes has accused his enemy Aeschines of having made a dishonorable peace for Athens. He describes Aeschines' activities with malice and skill and calls upon the jury to punish him as an example for all men.

For you doubtless know well that ever since the human race began and trials were instituted, no one was ever convicted admitting his crime: they brazen it out, they deny it, they lie, they make up excuses, they take every means to escape paying the penalty.

(Aeschines,[25] *On The Embassy*, 152–153) [26]

In the excerpt below, we note Aeschines' denial of the formative influences of culture on man's personality. How strikingly similar is his notion to that of the nineteenth century, which held to the same inborn, naturalistic approach to the study of man.

It is not Macedon that makes men good or bad, but their own inborn nature; and we have not come back from the embassy changed men, but the same men that you yourselves sent out.

(Anonymous, *Later Poets*, 113) [27]

One man is moved by disposition, another by thought.

(Xenophon, *Oeconomicus*, Chapter XIII, 6–12) [28]

It is exceedingly interesting to note the modernity of some of Xenophon's ideas regarding the psychological nature of animal and of man.

SOCRATES: The matter, I protest, is hardly one for laughter. The man who can make another capable of rule, clearly can teach him how to play the master; and if he can make him play the master, he can make him what is grander still, a kingly being. Once more, therefore, I protest: A man possessed of such creative power is worthy, not of ridicule, far from it, but of the highest praise.

Thus, then, I reason, Socrates (he answered): The lower animals are taught obedience by two methods chiefly, partly through being punished when they make attempts to disobey, partly by experiencing some kindness when they cheerfully submit. This is the principle at any rate adopted in the breaking of young horses. The animal obeys its trainer, and something sweet is sure to follow; or it disobeys, and in place of something sweet it finds a peck of trouble; and so on, until it comes at last to yield obedience to the trainer's every wish. Or to take another instance: Young dogs however far inferior to man in thought and language, can still be taught to run on errands and turn somersaults, and do a host of other clever things, precisely on this same principle of training. Every time the animal obeys it gets something or other which it wanted, and every time it misbehaves it gets a whipping. But when it comes to human beings: in man you have a creature still more open to persuasion through appeals to reason; only make it plain to him "it is his interest to obey." Or if they happen to be slaves, the more ignoble training of wild animals tamed to the lure will serve to teach obedience. Only gratify their bellies in the matter of appetite, and you will succeed in winning much from them. But ambitious, emulous natures feel the spur of praise, since some natures hunger after praise no less than others crave for meats and drinks. My practice then is to instruct those whom I desire to appoint as my bailiffs in the various methods which I have found myself to be successful in gaining the obedience of my fellows. To take an instance: There are clothes and shoes and so forth, with which I must provide my workfolk. Well, then, I see to it that these are not all alike in make; but some will be of better, some of less good quality: my object being that these articles for use shall vary with the service of the wearer; the worse man will receive the worse things as a gift, the better man the better as a mark of honour. For I ask you, Socrates, how can the good avoid despondency seeing that the work is wrought by their own hands alone, in spite of which these villains who will neither labour nor face danger when occasion calls are to receive an equal guerdon with themselves?  And just as I cannot bring myself in any sort of way to look upon the better sort as worthy to receive no greater honour than the baser, so, too, I praise my bailiffs when I know they have apportioned the best things among the most deserving.  And if I see that some one is receiving preference by dint of flatteries or like unworthy means, I do not let the matter pass; I reprimand my bailiff roundly, and so teach him that such conduct is not even to his interest.

### 3. The Beginnings of Anthropological Thought

(Aeschylus, *Prometheus Bound*, 439–516) [29]

In this excerpt we find an interpretation of the origin of civilization which is remarkable in its resemblance to the truth established by anthropology many centuries later.  Aeschylus indicates what the most important elements in civilization are, with great emphasis upon the religious factor.

PROMETHEUS: But hearken to the miseries that beset mankind—how that they were witless erst and I made them to have sense and be endowed with reason.  Nor will I speak to upbraid mankind, but to set forth the friendly purpose that inspired my boons.

First of all, though they had eyes to see, they saw to no avail; they had ears but understood not; but, like to shapes in dreams, throughout their length of days, without purpose they wrought all things in confusion.  Knowledge had they neither of houses built of bricks and turned to face the sun, nor yet of work in wood; but dwelt beneath the ground like swarming ants, in sunless caves.  They had no sign either of winter or of flowery spring or of fruitful summer, whereon they could depend, but in everything they wrought without judgment, until such time as I taught them to discern the risings of the stars and their settings, ere this ill distinguishable.

Aye, and numbers, too, chiefest of sciences, I invented for them, and the combining of letters, creative mother of the muses' arts, wherewith to hold all things in memory. I, too, first brought brute beasts beneath the yoke to be subject to the collar and the pack-saddle that they might bear in men's stead their heaviest burdens; and to the chariot I harnessed horses and made them obedient to the rein, to be an adornment of wealth and luxury. 'Twas I and no one else that contrived the mariner's flaxen-winged car to roam the sea.

Wretched that I am—such are the inventions I devised for mankind, yet have myself no cunning wherewith to rid me of my present suffering. . . . Hear but the rest and thou shalt wonder the more at the arts and resources I devised. This first and foremost: if ever man fell ill, there was no defence— no healing food, no ointment, nor any draught—but for lack of medicine they wasted away, until I showed them how to mix soothing remedies wherewith they now ward off all their disorders. And I marked out many ways whereby they might read the future, and among dreams I first discerned which are destined to come true; and voices baffling interpretation I explained to them, and signs from meetings by the way. The flight of crook-taloned birds I distinguished clearly—which by nature are auspicious, which sinister—their various modes of life, their mutual feuds and loves, and their consortings; and the smoothness of their entrails, and what colour the gall must have to please the gods, and the speckled symmetry of the liver-lobe; and the thigh-bones, enwrapped in fat, and the long chine I burned and initiated mankind into an occult art. Also I cleared their vision to discern signs from flames erstwhile obscure. So much then touching these arts. Now as to the benefits to men that lay concealed beneath the earth—bronze, iron, silver, and gold—who would claim to have discovered them before me? No one, I know full well, unless he were fain to babble idly. Hear the sum of the whole matter in the compass of one brief word—every art possessed by man comes from Prometheus.

CHORUS: Do not then benefit mortals beyond due measure and yet be heedless of thine own distress; forasmuch as I am of good hope that thou shalt yet be loosed from these bonds and have power no wise inferior to Zeus.

PROMETHEUS: Not thus, not yet, is fulfilling Fate destined to bring this end to pass. When I have been bent by pangs and tortures infinite, thus only am I to escape my bondage. Art is feebler far than necessity.

CHORUS: Who then is the steersman of necessity?

PROMETHEUS: The triform Fates and mindful Furies.

(Herodotus, *History,* Book IV, 110–117) [30]

The following passage illustrates the ability of Herodotus as an anthropologist. Though his views are more or less pre-scientific, it is interesting to note again the beginnings of anthropological thought.

About the Sauromatai the following tale is told:—When the Hellenes had fought with the Amazons,—now the Amazons are called by the Scythians *Oiorpata,* which name means in the Hellenic tongue "slayers of men," for "man" they call *oior,* and *pata* means "to slay,"—then, as the story goes, the Hellenes, having conquered them in the battle at the Thermodon, were sailing away and conveying with them in three ships as many Amazons as they were able to take prisoners. These in the open sea set upon the men and cast them out of the ships; but they knew nothing about ships, nor how to use rudders or sails or oars, and after they had cast out the men they were driven about by wave and wind and came to that part of the Maiotian lake where Cremnoi stands; now Cremnoi is in the land of the free Scythians. There the Amazons disembarked from their ships and made their way into the country, and having met first with a troop of horses feeding they seized them, and mounted upon these they plundered the property of the Scythians. The Scythians meanwhile were not able to understand the matter, for they did not know either their speech or their dress or the race to which they belonged, but were in wonder as to whence they had come and thought that they

were men, of an age corresponding to their appearance: and
finally they fought a battle against them, and after the battle
the Scythians got possession of the bodies of the dead, and thus
they discovered that they were women.  They took counsel
therefore and resolved by no means to go on trying to kill
them, but to send against them the youngest men from among
themselves, making conjecture of the number so as to send
just as many men as there were women.  These were told to
encamp near them, and do whatsoever they should do; if
however the women should come after them, they were not
to fight but to retire before them, and when the women stopped,
they were to approach and encamp.  This plan was adopted
by the Scythians because they desired to have children born
from them.  The young men accordingly were sent out and
did that which had been commanded them: and when the
Amazons perceived that they had not come to do them any
harm, they let them alone; and the two camps approached
nearer to one another every day: and the young men, like the
Amazons, had nothing except their arms and their horses, and
got their living as the Amazons did, by hunting and by taking
booty.  Now the Amazons at midday used to scatter abroad
either one by one or by two together, dispersing to a distance
from one another to ease themselves; and the Scythians also
having perceived this did the same thing: and one of the
Scythians came near to one of those Amazons who were apart
by themselves and she did not repulse him but allowed him to
lie with her: and she could not speak to him, for they did not
understand one another's speech, but she made signs to him
with her hand to come on the following day to the same place
and to bring another with him, signifying to him that there
should be two of them, and that she would bring another with
her.  The young man therefore, when he returned, reported
this to the others; and on the next day he came himself to the
place and also brought another, and he found the Amazon
awaiting him with another in her company.  Then hearing this
the rest of the young men also in their turn tamed for them-

selves the remainder of the Amazons; and after this they joined their camps and lived together, each man having for his wife her with whom he had had dealings at first; and the men were not able to learn the speech of the women, but the women came to comprehend that of the men. So when they understood one another, the men spoke to the Amazons as follows: "We have parents and we have possessions; now therefore let us no longer lead a life of this kind, but let us go away to the main body of our people and dwell with them; and we will have you for wives and no others." They however spoke thus in reply: "We should not be able to live with your women, for we and they have not the same customs. We shoot with bows and hurl javelins and ride horses, but the works of women we never learnt; whereas your women do none of these things which we said, but stay in the waggons and work at the works of women, neither going out to the chase nor anywhither else. We therefore should not be able to live in agreement with them; but if ye desire to keep us for your wives and to be thought honest men, go to your parents and obtain from them your share of the goods, and then let us go and dwell by ourselves." The young men agreed and did this, and when they had obtained the share of the goods which belonged to them and had returned to the Amazons, the women spoke to them as follows: "We are possessed by fear and trembling to think that we must dwell in this place, having not only separated you from your fathers, but also done great damage to your land. Since then ye think it right to have us as your wives, do this together with us,—come and let us remove from this land and pass over the river Tanais and there dwell." The young men agreed to this also, and they crossed over the Tanais and made their way towards the rising sun for three days' journey from the Tanais, and also towards the North Wind for three days' journey from the Maiotian lake: and having arrived at the place where they are now settled, they took up their abode there: and from thenceforward the women of the Sauromatai practice their ancient way of living, going

out regularly on horseback to the chase both in company with
the men and apart from them, and going regularly to war, and
wearing the same dress as the men.  And the Sauromatai make
use of the Scythian tongue, speaking it barbarously however
from the first, since the Amazons did not learn it thoroughly
well.

(Herodotus, *History*, Book I, 56–58)

Below we find Herodotus' interpretation of the origins of the Hellenic
race.

By these lines when they came to him Croesus was pleased
more than by all the rest, for he supposed that a mule would
never be ruler of the Medes instead of a man, and accordingly
that he himself and his heirs would never cease from their
rule.  Then after this he gave thought to inquire which people
of the Hellenes he should esteem the most powerful and gain
over to himself as friends.  And inquiring he found that the
Lacedemonians and the Athenians had the preeminence, the
first of the Dorian and the others of the Ionian race.  For these
were the most eminent races in ancient time, the second being
a Pelasgian and the first a Hellenic race; and the one never
migrated from its place in any direction, while the other was
very exceedingly given to wanderings; for in the reign of
Deucalion this race dwelt in Pthiotis, and in the time of Doros
the son of Hellen in the land lying below Ossa and Olympos,
which is called Histiaiotis; and when it was driven from
Histiaiotis by the sons of Cadmos, it dwelt in Pindos and was
called Makednian; and thence it moved afterwards to Dryopis,
and from Dryopis it finally came to Peloponnesus, and began
to be called Dorian.

What language however the Pelasgians used to speak I am
not able with certainty to say.  But if one must pronounce
judging by those that still remain of the Pelasgians who dwelt
in the city of Creston above the Tyrsenians, and who were
once neighbours of the race now called Dorian, dwelling then
in the land which is now called Thessaliotis, and also by those

that remain of the Pelasgians who settled at Plakia and Sky-lakē in the region of the Hellespont, who before that had been settlers with the Athenians, and of the natives of the various other towns which are really Pelasgian, though they have lost the name,—if one must pronounce judging by these, the Pelasgians used to speak a Barbarian language.  If therefore all the Pelasgian race was such as these, then the Attic race, being Pelasgian, at the same time when it changed and became Hellenic, unlearnt also its language.  For the people of Creston do not speak the same language with any of those who dwell about them, nor yet do the people of Plakia, but they speak the same language one as the other: and by this it is proved that they still keep unchanged the form of language which they brought with them when they migrated to these places.  As for the Hellenic race, it has used ever the same language, as I clearly perceive, since it first took its rise; but since the time when it parted off feeble at first from the Pelasgian race, setting forth from a small beginning it has increased to that great number of races which we see, and chiefly because many Barbarian races have been added to it besides.  Moreover it is true, as I think, of the Pelasgian race also, that so far as it remained Barbarian it never made any great increase.

(Herodotus, History, Book V, 58–59)

Herodotus, here, discusses the transmission of the alphabet, indicating his recognition of the principle of cultural diffusion.

Now these Phenicians who came with Cadmos, of whom were the Gephyraians, brought in among the Hellenes many arts when they settled in this land of Boeotia, and especially letters, which did not exist, as it appears to me, among the Hellenes before this time; and at first they brought in those which are used by the Phenician race generally, but afterwards, as time went on, they changed with their speech the form of the letters also.  During this time the Ionians were the race of Hellenes who dwelt near them in most of the places where they were; and these, having received letters by instruc-

tion of the Phenicians, changed their form slightly and so made
use of them, and in doing so they declared them to be called
"phenicians," as was just, seeing that the Phenicians had intro-
duced them into Hellas.  Also the Ionians from ancient time
call paper "skins," because formerly, paper being scarce, they
used skins of goats and sheep; nay, even in my own time many
of the Barbarians write on such skins.  I myself too once saw
Cadmeian characters in the temple of Ismenian Apollo at
Thebes of the Boeotians, engraved on certain tripods, and in
most respects resembling the Ionic letters. . . .

(Herodotus, History, Book III, 38)

Herodotus shows a recognition of the existence of ethnocentrism.

It is clear to me therefore by every kind of proof that
Cambyses was mad exceedingly; for otherwise he would not
have attempted to deride religious rites and customary observances.  For if one should propose to all men a choice,
bidding them select the best customs from all customs there
are, each race of men, after examining them all, would select
those of their own people; thus all think that their own customs
are by far the best: and so it is not likely that any but a mad-
man would make jest of such things.  Now of the fact that all
men are thus wont to think about their customs, we may judge
by many other proofs and more especially by this which follows:—Darieos in the course of his reign summoned those of
the Hellenes who were present in his land, and asked them for
what price they would consent to eat up their fathers when
they died; and they answered that for no price would they
do this.  After this Darieos summoned those Indians who are
called Callatians, who eat their parents, and asked them in the
presence of the Hellenes, who understood what was said by
help of an interpreter, for what payment they would consent
to consume with fire the bodies of their fathers when they died;
and they cried out loud and bade him keep silence from such
words.  Thus then these things are established by usage, and

I think Pindar spoke rightly in his verse, when he said that "of all things law is king."

(Thucydides, Book I, Sect. 2–3) [31]

The country which is now called Hellas was not regularly settled in ancient times. The people were migratory, and readily left their homes whenever they were overpowered by numbers. There was no commerce, and they could not safely hold intercourse with one another either by land or by sea. The several tribes cultivated their own soil just enough to obtain a maintenance from it. But they had no accumulations of wealth, and did not plant the ground; for, being without walls, they were never sure that an invader might not come and despoil them. Living in this manner and knowing that they could anywhere obtain a bare subsistence, they were always ready to migrate; so that they had neither great cities nor any considerable resources. The richest districts were most constantly changing their inhabitants; for example, the countries which are now called Thessaly and Boeotia, the greater part of the Peloponnesus with the exception of Arcadia, and all the best parts of Hellas. For the productiveness of the land increased the power of the individuals; this in turn was a source of quarrels by which communities were ruined, while at the same time they were more exposed to attacks from without. Certainly, Attica, of which the soil was poor and thin, enjoyed a long freedom from civil strife, and therefore retained its original inhabitants. And a striking confirmation of my argument is afforded by the fact that Attica through immigration increased in population more than any other region. For the leading men of Hellas, when driven out of their own country by war or revolution, sought an asylum at Athens; and from the very earliest times, being admitted to rights of citizenship, so greatly increased the number of inhabitants that Attica became incapable of containing them, and was at last obliged to send out colonies to Ionia.

## 4. The Relation of Physical Environment to Human Life

(Hippocrates: *Influences of Atmosphere, Water, and Situation,* Chapter 16) [32]

In the following excerpt Hippocrates appears as one of the earliest forerunners of the geographical determinists—Montesquieu, Ratzel, Buckle, Semple, and others—who have insisted, in varying degrees, that the conditions of the physical environment are the dominant factors in controlling and shaping human events.

We have now discussed the organic and structural differences between the populations of Asia and Europe, but we have still to consider the problem why the Asiatics are of a less warlike and a more tame disposition than the Europeans. The deficiency of spirit and courage observable in the human inhabitants of Asia has for its principal cause the low margin of seasonal variability in the temperature of that continent, which is approximately stable throughout the year. Such a climate does not produce those mental shocks and violent bodily dislocations which would naturally render the temperament ferocious and introduce a stronger current of irrationality and passion than would be the case under stable conditions. It is invariably changes that stimulate the human mind and that prevent it from remaining passive. These, in my view, are the reasons why the Asiatic race is unmilitary, but I must not omit the factor of institutions. The greater part of Asia is under monarchical government; and wherever men are not their own masters and not free agents, but are under despotic rule, they are not concerned to make themselves militarily efficient but, on the contrary, to avoid being regarded as good military material—the reason being that they are not playing for equal stakes. It is theirs, presumably, to serve and struggle and die under compulsion from their masters and far from the sight of their wives and children and friends. Whenever they acquit themselves like men, it is their masters who are exalted and aggrandised by their achievements, while their own share of the profits is the risking and the losing of their lives.  And not only this, but, in the case of the people so circumstanced, it is also inevitable that the inactivity consequent upon the absence of war should have a taming effect upon the temperament, so that even a naturally courageous and spirited individual would be inhibited on the intellectual side by the prevailing institutions.  A strong argument in favor of my contention is furnished by the fact that all the Hellenes and non-Hellenes in Asia who are under despotic rule, but are free agents and struggle for their own benefit, are as warlike as any populations in the world—the reason being that they stake their lives in their own cause and reap the rewards of their own valour (and the penalties of their own cowardice, into the bargain).  You will also find that the Asiatics differ among one another, some being finer and others poorer in quality, and these differences also have their cause in the seasonal climatic variations, as I have stated above.

(Hippocrates, *Influences of Atmosphere, Water and Situation*, Chapter 24)

In this selection, Hippocrates indicates the effect of the physical environment on racial characteristics.

Our comparative survey of Europe and Asia is now complete in general outline.  In Europe itself there are, however, a number of distinct stocks differentiated by physical structure and proportions and by moral qualities.  The differentiating factors are the same as those described in previous connections, but I will explain them again with greater precision.  Inhabitants of mountainous, rocky, well-watered country at a high altitude, where the margin of seasonal climatic variation is wide, will tend to have large-built bodies constitutionally adapted for courage and endurance, and in such natures there will be a considerable element of ferocity and brutality.  Inhabitants of sultry hollows covered with water-meadows, who are more commonly exposed to warm winds than to cold and who drink tepid water, will—in contrast—not be large-built or slim, but thick-set, fleshy and dark-haired, with swarthy rather than fair complexions and with less phlegm than bile in their constitutions. Courage and endurance will not be innate in their characters to the same degree, but will be capable of being produced in them by the coefficient of institutions. If there are rivers in the country which drain it of the stagnant water and the rainfall, the population will be healthy and in good condition; while, if there are no rivers and their drinking water comes from stagnant lakes and marshes, their bodies will run to spleen and will incline to be pot-bellied. Inhabitants of rolling, wind-swept, well-watered country at a high altitude will be large-built and un-individualised, with a vein of cowardice and tameness in their characters. Inhabitants of thin-soiled, waterless country without vegetation, where the seasonal climatic changes are abrupt and violent, will tend to have bony, muscular bodies, fair rather than swarthy complexions, and headstrong, self-willed characters and temperaments. Where seasonal changes are most frequent and show the widest margin of variability, there you will find the greatest differentiation in the human body, character and organism.

These are the most important varieties of organism, and then there is the effect of the country and the water which constitute the human environment. In the majority of cases, you will find that the human body and character vary in accordance with the nature of the country. Where the soil is rich and soft and well-watered, and where the water remains extremely near the surface, so that it is tepid in summer and chilly in winter, and where the climatic conditions are also favorable, the inhabitants will be fleshy, loose-jointed, flaccid, unenergetic and poor-spirited as a general rule. Laziness and sleepiness will be prominent among the characteristics, and they will be clumsy instead of being neat or quick at skilled occupations.  Where the country is rocky, waterless and without vegetation, and suffers from severe winters and from scorching suns, you will find the inhabitants bony and without spare flesh, with well-articulated joints and muscular, shaggy bodies.  Such constitutions are instinct with energy and alertness, and their possessors have headstrong, self-willed characters and temperaments, with a tendency towards ferocity instead of tameness, and with a superior quickness and intelligence in skilled occupations and a superior aptitude for war. You will further find that the non-human fauna and flora of a given soil likewise vary according to the quality of that soil. I have now described the extreme contrasts of type and organism; and if you work out the rest for yourself on the analogy of these, you will not go wrong.

### 5. The Idea of the Economic Factor in Society

(Timocreon, Book I, 8) [33]

Oh how I wish, blind God of Riches, you were to be seen neither ashore nor at sea nor on the mainland, but dwelt by Acheron's bank in Tartarus.  For you it is that are the cause of all the evil of the world.

(Sophocles, *Antigone*, l. 295–303)

The watchman comes to tell Kreon that someone has dared to bury Polyneikes.  Kreon is furious and forthwith accuses the guards of having been bribed.

KREON:  Nought current among men hath been devised
Accurst as gold.   By this are cities made
Desolate; men are banished from their homes.
This teacheth, this perverteth good men's hearts
To champion many a shameful enterprise,
Yea, hath taught men to harbor villainy,
And to know every deed of godlessness.
Ha! but they who for bribes brought this to pass
Shall reap at last the vengeance they have sown!

When Wealth protests his fear of Zeus, who has blinded him through
jealousy, Chremylus and his servant Carion carry on the following conversation. The excerpt shows clearly the power of wealth.

CHREMYLUS:   Come, what makes Zeus the Ruler of the
    Gods?
CARION:   His silver. He's the wealthiest of them.
CHREMYLUS:                                          Well,
Who gives him all his riches?
CARION:                    Our friend here.
CHREMYLUS:  And for whose sake do mortals sacrifice
To Zeus?
CARION:   For *his:*  And pray straight out for wealth.

(Aristophanes, *The Plutus,* 144–197)

Here again Chremylus and his servant seek to prove to Wealth how all-
powerful he is and what vast influence is his. For this reason, it is pointed
out, Wealth ought not to fear anyone.

CHREMYLUS:   And whatsoever in the world is bright,
And fair, and graceful, all is done for thee.
For every mortal thing subserves to Wealth.
CARION:   Hence for a little filthy lucre I'm
A slave, forsooth, because I've got no wealth.
CHREMYLUS:   And those Corinthian huzzies, so they say,
If he who sues them for their love is poor,
Turn up their noses at the man; but grant
A wealthy suitor more than he desires.
CARION:   So too the boy-loves: just to get some money,
And not at all because they love their lovers.
CHREMYLUS:   Those are the baser, not the nobler sort,
These never ask for money.
CARION:                    No?  What then?
CHREMYLUS:   O one a hunter, one a pack of hounds.
CARION:   Ah, they're ashamed, I warrant, of their vice,
And seek to crust it over with a name.

CHREMYLUS:   And every art existing in the world,
And every craft, was for thy sake invented—
For thee one sits and cobbles all the day,
One works in bronze, another works in wood,
One fuses gold—the gold derived from thee—
  CARION:   One plies the footpad's, one the burglar's trade,
  CHREMYLUS:   One is a fuller, one a sheepskin-washer,
One is a tanner, one an onion-seller,
Through thee the nabbed adulterer gets off plucked.
  WEALTH:   O, and all this I never knew before!
  CHREMYLUS:   Aye, 'tis on him the Great King plumes
      himself;
And our Assemblies all are held for him;
Dost thou not man our triremes?   Answer that.
Does he not feed the foreign troop at Corinth?
Won't Pamphilus be brought to grief for him?
  CARION:   Won't Pamphilus and the needle-seller too?
Does not Agyrrhius flout us all for him?
  CHREMYLUS:   Does not Philepsius tell his tales for thee?
Doest thou not make the Egyptian our allies?
And Lais love the uncouth Philonides?
  CARION:   Timotheus' tower—
  CHREMYLUS:          Pray Heaven it fall and crush you!
Aye, everything that's done is done for thee.
Thou art alone, thyself alone, the source
Of all our fortunes, good and bad alike.
'Tis so in war; wherever *he* alights,
That side is safe the victory to win.
  WEALTH:   Can I, unaided, do such feats as these?
  CHREMYLUS:   O yes, by Zeus, and many more than these.
So that none ever has enough of thee,
Of all things else a man may have too much,
Of love,
  CARION:   Of loaves,
  CHREMYLUS:          Of literature,
  CARION:                  Of sweets,

CHREMYLUS: Of honour,
CARION:                Cheesecakes,
CHREMYLUS:                    Manliness,
CARION:                         Dried figs,
CHREMYLUS: Ambition,
CARION:              Barley-meal,
CHREMYLUS:                Command,
CARION:                      Pea soup.
CHREMYLUS: But no man ever has enough of thee.
For give a man a sum of thirteen talents,
And all the more he hungers for sixteen;
Give him sixteen, and he must needs have forty,
Or life's not worth his living, so he says.

(Aristophanes, *The Plutus*, 228–231)

Chremylus invited Wealth to take up his abode in his house for evermore with these words.

CHREMYLUS: I'll see to that: You run away directly.
But thou, dear Wealth, the mightiest Power of all,
Come underneath my roof. Here stands the house,
Which thou art going evermore to fill
With wealth and plenty, by fair means or foul.

(Aristophanes, *The Plutus*, 352–362)

Chremylus, meeting his friend Blepsidemus tells him of the good that
has befallen him through his meeting with Wealth. Blepsidemus, however,
is suspicious of his friend and believes that his sudden riches are due to a
large theft. The power of wealth and its effects on men are again pointed
out by Aristophanes.

BLEPSIDEMUS: I like not this; there's something wrong
     behind,
Some evil venture. To become, off-hand,
So over-wealthy, and to fear such risks,
Smacks of a man who has done some rotten thing.
CHREMYLUS: Rotten! What mean you?

BLEPSIDEMUS:                              If you've stolen aught,
Or gold or silver, from the God out there,
And now perchance repent you of your sin,—
      CHREMYLUS:   Apollo shield us!   No, I've not done that.
BLEPSIDEMUS:   O don't tell *me*.   I see it plainly now.
CHREMYLUS:   Pray don't suspect me of such crimes.
BLEPSIDEMUS:                                        Alas!
There's nothing sound or honest in the world,
The love of money overcomes us all.


(Aristophanes, *The Plutus*, 506–516)

Here Poverty seeks to show Blepsidemus and Chremylus all the good
that she does.  She points out that if she were driven from the land, all
great enterprise would stop, for men would no longer attempt to achieve
anything.


POVERTY:   O men on the least provocation prepared
            to be crazy and out of your mind,
Men bearded and old, yet companions enrolled
            in the Order of zanies and fools,
O what is the gain that the world would obtain
            were it governed by you and your rules?
Why, if Wealth should allot himself equally out
            (assume that his sight ye restore),
The none would to science his talents devote
            or practice a craft any more.
Yet if science and art from the world should depart,
            pray whom would ye get for the future
To build you a ship, or your leather to snip
            or to make you a wheel or a suture?
Do ye think that a man will be likely to tan,
            or a smithy or laundry to keep,
Or to break up the soil with his ploughshare, and toil
            the fruits of Demeter to reap,
If regardless of these he can dwell at his ease,
            a life without labour enjoying?

(Aristophanes, *The Plutus*, 527–534)

Poverty continues the argument begun in the previous passage, pointing out how useful she is to men because she spurs them on to achievements through fear of her.

POVERTY:   No more on a bed will you pillow your head,
    for there won't be a bed in the land,
Nor carpets; for whom will you find at the loom,
    when he's plenty of money in hand?
Rich perfumes no more will ye sprinkle and pour
    as home ye are bringing the bride,
Or apparel the fair in habiliments rare
    so cunningly fashioned and dyed.
Yet of little avail is your wealth if it fail
    such enjoyments as these to procure you.
Ye fools, it is I who alone a supply
    of the goods which ye covet insure you.
I sit like a Mistress, by Poverty's lash
    constraining the needy mechanic;
When I raise it to earn his living he'll turn,
    and work in a terrible panic.

(Aristophanes, *The Plutus*, 563–570)

Chremylus shows Poverty that she brings evil to men, while Poverty protests that she is much better for men than Wealth.

POVERTY:   I can show you besides that Decorum abides
    with those whom I visit; that mine
Are the modest and orderly folk, and that Wealth's
    are "with insolence flushed and with wine."
CHREMYLUS:   'Tis an orderly job, then, to thieve and to
    rob and to break into houses by night.
BLEPSIDEMUS:   Such modesty too!   In whatever they do
    they are careful to keep out of sight.
POVERTY:   Behold in the cities the Orator tribe;
    when poor in their early career

How faithful and just to the popular trust,
     how true to the State they appear.
When wealth at the City's expense they have gained,
     they are worsened at once by the pelf,
Intriguing the popular cause to defeat,
     attacking the people itself.

(Aristophanes, *The Plutus*, 1106–1117)

Hermes tells Carion that since Wealth has come to good men, Zeus is no longer receiving sacrifices and he himself receives nothing. In a subsequent passage it is arranged that Hermes become a scullion in Chremylus' household.

HERMES:   . . . Zeus is going
To mix you up, you rascal, in one dish,
And hurl you all into the Deadman's Pit!
     CARION:   Now for this herald must the tongue be cut.
But what's the reason that he is going to do us
Such a bad turn?
     HERMES:     Because ye have done the basest
And worst of deeds.   Since Wealth began to see,
No laurel, meal-cake, victim, frankincense,
Has any man on any altar laid.
Or aught beside.
     CARION:     Or ever will, for scant
Your care for us in the evil days gone by.

## 6. ECONOMIC THOUGHT AND THEORY

(Aristophanes, *Ecclesiazusae*, l. 587–724) [35]

The extract below indicates Aristophanes' attitude on communism. Praxagora, the leader of the new commonwealth being run by women, suggests a plan of community ownership. Her husband Blepyros, and his friend Chremes, question her about various phases of the plan.

PRAXAGORA:   Then all to the speaker in silence attend,
And don't interrupt till I come to the end,
And weigh and perpend, till you quite comprehend,

The drift and intent of the scheme I present.
The rule which I dare to enact and declare,
Is that all shall be equal, and equally share
All wealth and enjoyments, no longer endure
That one should be rich, and another be poor,
That one should have acres, far-stretching and wide,
And another not enough to provide
Himself with a grave: that this at his call
Should have hundreds of servants, and that none at all.
All this I intend to correct and amend:
Now all of all blessings shall freely partake,
One life and one system for all men I make.

BLEPYROS:   And how will you manage it?

PRAXAGORA:                 First, I'll provide
That the silver, and land, and whatever beside
Each man shall possess, shall be common and free,
One fund for the public; then out of it we
Will feed and maintain you, like housekeepers true,
Dispensing, and sparing, and caring for you.

BLEPYROS:   With regard to the land, I can quite under-
stand
But how, if a man have his money in hand,
Not farms, which you see, and he cannot withhold,
But talents of silver and Darics of gold?

PRAXAGORA:   All this to the stores he must bring.

BLEPYROS:                But suppose
He choose to retain it, and nobody knows;
Rank perjury doubtless; but what if it be?
'Twas by that he acquired it at first.

PRAXAGORA:          I agree.
But now 'twill be useless; he'll need it no more.

BLEPYROS:   How mean you?

PRAXAGORA:         All pressure from want will be o'er.
Now each will have all that a man can desire,
Cakes, barley-leaves, chestnuts, abundant attire,
Wine, garlands, and fish; then why should he wish

The wealth he has gotten by fraud to retain?
If you know any reason, I hope you'll explain.

BLEPYROS:  'Tis those that have most of these goods, I
believe,
That are always the worst and the keenest to thieve.

PRAXAGORA:  I grant you, my friend, in the days that are
past,
In your old-fashioned system, abolished at last;
But what he's to gain, though his wealth he retain,
When all things are common, I'd have you explain.

BLEPYROS:  If a youth to a girl his devotion would show,
He surely must woo her with presents.

PRAXAGORA:                    O no.
All women and men will be common and free,
No marriage or other restraint there will be.

BLEPYROS:  But if all should aspire to the favours of one,
To the girl that is fairest, what then will be done?

PRAXAGORA:  By the side of the beauty, so stately and
grand,
The dwarf, the deformed, and the ugly will stand;
And before you're entitled the beauty to woo,
Your court you must pay to the hag and the shrew.

BLEPYROS:  For the ladies you've nicely provided no doubt;
No woman will now be a lover without.
But what of the men?  For the girls, I suspect,
The handsome will choose, and the ugly reject.

PRAXAGORA:  No girl will of course be permitted to mate
Except in accord with the rules of the State.
By the side of her lover, so handsome and tall,
Will be stationed the squat, the ungainly and small,
And before she's entitled the beau to obtain,
Her love she must grant to the awkward and plain.

BLEPYROS:  O then such a nose as Lysicrates shows
Will vie with the fairest and best, I suppose.

PRAXAGORA:  O yes 'tis a nice democratic device,
A popular system as ever was tried,

A jade on the swells with their rings and their pride.
*Now, fopling, away,* Gaffer Hobnail will say,
*Stand aside! it is I have precedence to-day.*

BLEPYROS: But how, may I ask, will the children be
known?
And how can a father distinguish his own?

PRAXAGORA: They will never be known: it can never be
told;
All youths will in common be sons of the old.

BLEPYROS: If in vain to distinguish our children we seek,
Pray what will become of the aged and weak?
At present I own, though a father be known,
Sons throttle and choke him with hearty goodwill;
But will they not do it more cheerily still,
When the sonship is doubtful?

PRAXAGORA: No, certainly not.
For now if a boy should a parent annoy,
The lads who are near will of course interfere;
For they may themselves be his children, I wot.

BLEPYROS: In much that you say there is much to ad-
mire;
But what if Leucolophus claim me for sire,
Or vile Epicurus? I think you'll agree
That a great and unbearable nuisance 'twould be.

CHREMES: A nuisance much greater than this might befall you.

BLEPYROS: How so?

CHREMES: If the skunk Aristyllus should call you
His father, and seize you, a kiss to imprint.

BLEPYROS: O hang him! Confound him! O how I would
sound him!

CHREMES: I fancy you soon would be smelling of mint.

PRAXAGORA: But this, sir, is nonsense; it never could be.
That whelp was begotten before the Decree.
His kiss, it is plain, you can never obtain.

BLEPYROS: The prospect I view with disgust and alarm.
But who will attend to the work of the farm?

PRAXAGORA:   All labour and toil to your slaves you will
        leave;
Your business 'twill be, when the shadows of eve
Ten feet on the face of the dial are cast,
To scurry away to your evening repast.
    BLEPYROS:   Our clothes, what of them?
    PRAXAGORA:                              You have plenty in store,
When these are worn out, we will weave you some more.
    BLEPYROS:   Just one other thing.  If an action they bring,
What funds will be mine for discharging the fine?
You won't pay it out of the stores, I opine.
    PRAXAGORA:   A fine to be paid when an action they bring!
Why bless you, our people won't know such a thing
As an action.
    BLEPYROS:   No actions!  I feel a misgiving.
Pray what are "our people" to do for a living?
    CHREMES:   You are right: there are many will rue it.
    PRAXAGORA:                              No doubt.
But what can one then bring an action about?
    BLEPYROS:   There are reasons in plenty; I'll just mention
        one.
If a debtor won't pay you, pray what's to be done?
    PRAXAGORA:   If a debtor won't pay!  Nay, but tell me, my
        friend,
How the creditor came by the money to lend?
All money, I thought, to the stores had been brought.
I've got a suspicion, I say it with grief,
Your creditor's surely a bit of a thief.
    BLEPYROS:   Now that is an answer acute and befitting.
But what if a man should be fined for committing
Some common assault, when elated with wine;
Pray what are his means for discharging that fine?
I have posed you, I think.
    PRAXAGORA:                Why his victuals and drink
Will be stopped by command for a while; and I guess

That he will not again in a hurry transgress,
When he pays with his stomach.

BLEPYROS:                    Will thieves be unknown?

PRAXAGORA:   Why?   How should they steal what is partly
their own?

BLEPYROS:   No chance then to meet at night in the street
Some highwayman coming our cloaks to abstract?

PRAXAGORA:   No, not if you're sleeping at home; nor, in
fact,
Though you choose to go out.   That trade, why pursue it?
There's plenty for all: but suppose him to do it,
Don't fight and resist him; what need of a pother?
You can get to the stores, and they'll give you another.

BLEPYROS:   Shall we gambling forsake?

PRAXAGORA:                    Why, what could you stake?

BLEPYROS:   But what is the style of our living to be?

PRAXAGORA:   One common to all, independent and free,
All bars and partitions for ever undone,
All private establishments fused into one.

BLEPYROS:   Then where, may I ask, will our dinners be
laid?

PRAXAGORA:   Each court and arcade of the law shall be
made
A banqueting hall for the citizens.

BLEPYROS:                    Right.
But what will you do with the desk for the speakers?

PRAXAGORA:   I'll make it stand for the cups and the
beakers;
And there shall the striplings be ranged to recite
The deeds of the brave, and the joys of the fight,
And the cowards' disgrace; till out of the place
Each coward shall slink with a very red face,
Not stopping to dine.

BLEPYROS:        O but that will be fine.
And what of the balloting booths?

PRAXAGORA: They shall go
To the head of the market place, all in a row,
And there by Harmodius taking my station,
I'll tickets dispense to the whole of the nation,
Till each one has got his particular lot.
And manfully bustles along to the sign
Of the letter whereat he's empanelled to dine.
The man who has A shall be ushered away
To the Royal Arcade; to the next will go B;
And C to the Cornmarket.

BLEPYROS: Merely to see?
PRAXAGORA: No, fool, but to dine.

BLEPYROS: 'Tis an excellent plan.
Then who gets never a letter, poor man,
Gets never a dinner.

PRAXAGORA: But 'twill not be so.
There'll be plenty for all, and to spare.
No stint and no grudging our system will know,
But each will away from the revelry go,
Elated and grand, with a torch in his hand
And a garland of flowers in his hair.
And then through the streets as they wander, a lot
Of women will round them be creeping,
"O come to my lodging," says one, "I have got
Such a beautiful girl in my keeping."
"But here is the sweetest and fairest, my boy,"
From a window another will say,
"But ere you're entitled her love to enjoy
Your toll to myself you must pay."
Then a sorry companion, flat-visaged and old,
Will shout to the youngster "Avast!
And where are *you* going, so gallant and bold,
And where are *you* hieing so fast?
'Tis in vain; you must yield to the laws of the State,
And I shall be courting the fair,
Whilst you must without the vestibule wait,

And strive to amuse yourself there, dear boy,
And strive to amuse yourself there."
There now, what think ye of my scheme?

BLEPYROS:                                    First-rate.

PRAXAGORA:   Then now I'll go to the market-place, and
   there,
Taking some clear-voiced girl as crieress,
Receive the goods as people bring them in.
This must I do, elected chieftainess
To rule the State and start the public feasts;
That so your banquets may commence to-day.

BLEPYROS:   What, shall we banquet now at once?

PRAXAGORA:                                    You shall
And next I'll make a thorough sweep of all
The flaunting harlots.

BLEPYROS:        Why?

PRAXAGORA:              That these free ladies
May have the the firstling manhood of our youths.
Those servile hussies shall no longer poach
Upon the true-love manors of the free.
No, let them herd with slaves, and lie with slaves,
In servile fashion, snipped and trimmed to match.

(Lysias, *Against the Corn Dealers*, 1–22) [86]

*Against the Corn Dealers* was written for a client, whose name is not
known, about 388 B.C.   Anytus, a corn inspector, seems to have given the
retail corn dealers permission to form a combine against the importers, in
order to keep down the prices, which, because of a bad harvest would
have gone up.   However, anything in the nature of a "ring" was not allowed by Athenian law and so the importers took legal action against the
corn-dealers.   The decision of the court is not known.   Lysias clearly
wrote this speech for the importers.

Many people have come to me, gentlemen of the jury, in
surprise of my accusing the corn-dealers in the Council, and
telling me that you, however sure you are of their guilt, none
the less regard those who deliver speeches about them as slan-

der-mongers. I therefore propose to speak first of the grounds on which I have found it necessary to accuse them.

When the Committee of the time brought up their case before the Council, the anger felt against them was such that some of the orators said that they ought to be handed over without trial to the Eleven, for the penalty of death. But I, thinking it monstrous that the Councils should get into the way of such practice, rose and said that in my opinion we ought to try the corn-dealers in accordance with the law; for I thought that if they had committed acts deserving of death you would be no less able than we to come to a just decision, while, if they were not guilty, they ought not to perish without trial. After the Council adopted this view, attempts were made to discredit me by saying that I hoped to save the corn-dealers by these remarks. Now before the Council, when the case came up for their hearing, I justified myself in a practical way: while the rest kept quiet, I rose and accused these men, and made it evident to all that my remarks were not made in their defence, but in support of the established laws. Well, these were my reasons for beginning my task, in fear of those incriminations; but I consider it would be disgraceful to leave off before you have given such verdict upon them as you may prefer.

So, first of all, go up on the dais. Tell me, sir, are you a resident alien? Yes. Do you reside as an alien to obey the city's laws, or to do just as you please? To obey. Must you not, then, expect to be put to death, if you have committed a breach of the laws for which death is the penalty? I must. Then answer me: do you acknowledge that you bought up corn in excess of the fifty measures which the law sets as the limit? I bought it up on an order from the magistrates.

Well, now, gentlemen, if he proves that there is a law which orders the corn dealers to buy up the corn on an order from the magistrates, acquit him; if not, it is just that you should condemn him. For we have produced to you the law which forbids anyone in the city to buy up corn in excess of fifty measures.

This accusation of mine should have sufficed, gentlemen of the jury, since this man acknowledges that he bought up the corn, while the law clearly forbids him to do so; and you have sworn to decide in accordance with the laws. Nevertheless, in order that you may be convinced that they are actually traducing the magistrates, it is necessary to speak of them at some greater length. For since these men shifted the blame on to them, we called the magistrates before us and questioned them. Two of them denied any knowledge of the matter; but Anytus stated that in the previous winter, as the corn was dear, and these men were outbidding each other and fighting amongst themselves, he had advised them to cease their competition, judging it beneficial to you, their customers, that they should purchase at as reasonable a price as possible: for they were bound, in selling, to add no more than an obol to the price. Now, that he did not order them to buy up the corn for holding in store, but only advised them not to buy against each other, I will produce to you Anytus himself as witness.

(Testimonies)

These statements were made by him in the time of the former Council, whereas these men evidently bought up the corn in the time of the present one.

So now you have heard that it was not on an order from the magistrates that they bought up the corn; yet, in my opinion, however true their statements may be on these points, they will not be clearing themselves, but only accusing the magistrates. For where we have laws expressly drafted for the case, surely punishment should fall alike on those who disobey them and on those who order an infringement of them.

But in fact, gentlemen of the jury, I believe they will not have recourse to this argument, but will repeat, perhaps, what they said before the Council,—that it was in kindness to the city that they bought up the corn so that they might sell it to you at as reasonable a price as possible.  But I will give you a very strong and signal proof that they are lying.  If they were doing this for your benefit, they ought to have been found selling it at the same price for a number of days, until the stock that they had bought up was exhausted.  But in fact they were selling at a profit of a drachma several times in the same day, as though they were buying by the medimnus at a time.  I adduce you as witnesses of this.  And it seems to me a strange thing that, when they have to contribute to a special levy of which everyone is to have knowledge, they refuse, making poverty their pretext; but illegal acts, for which death is the penalty, and in which secrecy was important to them,—these they assert that they committed in kindness to you.  Yet you are all aware that they are the last persons to whom such statements are appropriate.  For their interests are the opposite of other men's: they make most profit when, on some bad news reaching the city, they sell their corn at a high price.  And they are so delighted to see your disasters that they either get news of them in advance of anyone else, or fabricate the rumor themselves; now it is the loss of your ships in the Black Sea, now the capture of vessels on their outward voyage by the Lacedaemonians, now the blockade of your trading ports, or the impending rupture of the truce; and they have carried their enmity to such lengths that they choose the same critical moments as your foes to overreach you.  For, just when you find yourselves worst off for corn, these persons snap it up and refuse to sell it, in order to prevent our disputing about the price: we are to be glad enough if we come away from them with a purchase made at any price, however high.  And thus at times, although there is peace, we are besieged by these men.  So long is it now that the city has been convinced of their knavery and disaffection that, while for the sale of all other commodities, you have appointed the market-clerks as controllers, for this trade alone you elect special corn-controllers by lot; and often you have been known to inflict the extreme penalty on those officials, who were citizens, for having failed to defeat the villainy of these men. Now, what should be your treatment of the actual offenders, when you put to death even those who are unable to control them?

You should reflect that it is impossible for you to vote an acquittal. For if you reject the charge, when they admit that they are combining against the traders, you will be regarded as aiming a blow at the importers. If they were putting up some other defence, nobody would censure a verdict for acquittal; for it rests with you to choose which side you are to believe. But, as matters stand, your action cannot but be thought extraordinary, if you dismiss unpunished those who confess to breaking the law. Remember, gentlemen of the jury, that many in the past have met this charge with denial, and have produced witnesses; yet you have condemned them to death because you gave more credence to the statements of their accusers. But surely it would be astounding if, in passing judgement on the same offences, you are more eager to punish those who deny! And, moreover, gentlemen, I conceive it is obvious to you all that suits of this kind are of the closest concern to the people of our city; and hence they will inquire what view you take of such matters, in the belief that, if you condemn these men to death, the rest will be brought to better order; while if you dismiss them unpunished, you will have voted them full licence to do just as they please. You must chastise them, gentlemen, not only on account of the past, but also to give an example for the future: even so these people will be barely tolerable. Consider that great numbers in this business have been tried for their lives: so much profit do they make by it that they choose rather to risk death every day than to cease making illicit gain out of you. Nay, more, not even if they implore and beseech you, would you be justified in taking pity on them: far rather ought you to pity those of our citizens who perished by their villainy, and the traders against whom they have combined. These you will gratify and render more zealous by punishing the accused. Otherwise, what do you suppose their feelings will be, when they learn that you have acquitted the retailers who confessed to overreaching the importers?

I do not see what more there is to say: when suits against other malefactors are heard, you have to get your information from the accusers, whereas the villainy of these men is understood by you all. So, if you convict them, you will both do justice and buy your corn at a fairer price; otherwise, it will be dearer.

(Xenophon, *Oeconomicus*, Part I, Chapter I, 1–23) [28]

Socrates proceeds dialectically to point out six essentials, or first principles of economy. Socrates is represented by the author as repeating, for the benefit of Critobulus, certain conversations which he had once held with Ischomachus on the essentials of economy.

I once heard him discuss the topic of economy after the following manner. Addressing Critobulus, he said: Tell me, Critobulus, is "economy," like the words "medicine," "carpentry," "building," "smithying," "metal-working," and so forth, the name of a particular kind of knowledge or science?

CRITOBULUS:   Yes, I think so.

SOCRATES:   And as, in the case of the arts just named, we can state the proper work or function of each, can we (similarly) state the proper work and function of economy?

CRITOBULUS:   It must, I should think, be the business of the good economist at any rate to manage his own house or estate well.

SOCRATES:   And supposing another man's house to be entrusted to him, he would be able, if he chose, to manage it as skillfully as his own, would he not?   Since a man who is skilled in carpentry can work as well for another as for himself: and this ought to be equally true of the good economist?

CRITOBULUS:   Yes, I think so, Socrates.

SOCRATES:   Then there is no reason why a proficient in this art, even if he does not happen to possess wealth of his own, should not be paid a salary for managing a house, just as he might be paid for building one?

CRITOBULUS: None at all: and a large salary he would be entitled to earn if, after paying the necessary expenses of the estate entrusted to him, he can create a surplus and improve the property.

SOCRATES: Well! and this word "house," what are we to understand by it? the domicile merely? or are we to include all a man's possessions outside the actual dwelling-place?

CRITOBULUS: Certainly, in my opinion at any rate, everything which a man has got, even though some portion of it may lie in another part of the world from that in which he lives, forms part of his estate.

SOCRATES: "Has got?" but he may have got enemies?

CRITOBULUS: Yes, I am afraid some people have got a great many.

SOCRATES: Then shall we say that a man's enemies form part of his possessions?

CRITOBULUS: A comic notion indeed! that some one should be good enough to add to my stock of enemies, and that in addition he should be paid for his kind services.

SOCRATES: Because, you know, we agreed that a man's estate was identical with his possessions?

CRITOBULUS: Yes, certainly! the good part of his possessions; but the evil portion! no, I thank you, that I do not call part of a man's possessions.

SOCRATES: As I understand, *you* would limit the term to what we may call a man's useful or advantageous possessions?

CRITOBULUS: Precisely; if he has things that injure him, I should regard these rather as a loss than as wealth.

SOCRATES: It follows apparently that if a man purchases a horse and does not know how to handle him but each time he mounts he is thrown and sustains injuries, the horse is not part of his wealth?

CRITOBULUS: Not, if wealth implies weal, certainly.

SOCRATES:   And by the same token land itself is no wealth to a man who so works it that his tillage only brings him loss?

CRITOBULUS:   True; mother earth herself is not a source of wealth to us if, instead of helping us to live, she helps us to starve.

SOCRATES:   And by a parity of reasoning, sheep and cattle may fail of being wealth if, through want of knowledge how to treat them, their owner loses by them; to him at any rate the sheep and the cattle are not wealth?

CRITOBULUS:   That is the conclusion I draw.

SOCRATES:   It appears, *you* hold to the position that wealth consists of things which benefit, while things which injure are not wealth?

CRITOBULUS:   Just so.

SOCRATES:   The same things, in fact, are wealth or not wealth, according as a man knows or does not know the use to make of them?   To take an instance, a flute may be wealth to him who is sufficiently skilled to play upon it, but the same instrument is no better than the stones we tread under our feet to him who is not so skilled . . . unless indeed he chose to sell it?

CRITOBULUS:   That is precisely the conclusion we should come to.   To persons ignorant of their use flutes are wealth as salable, but as possessions not for sale they are no wealth at all; and see, Socrates, how smoothly and consistently the argument proceeds, since it is admitted that things which benefit are wealth.   The flutes in question unsold are not wealth, being good for nothing; to become wealth they must be sold.

SOCRATES:   Yes! (rejoined Socrates), presuming the owner knows how to sell them; since, supposing again he were to sell them for something which he does not know how to use, the mere selling will not transform them into wealth, according to your argument.

CRITOBULUS:   You seem to say, Socrates, that money itself in the pockets of a man who does not know how to use it is not wealth?

SOCRATES: And I understand *you* to concur in the truth of our proposition so far: wealth is that, and that only, whereby a man may be benefited. Obviously, if a man used his money to buy himself a mistress, to the grave detriment of his body and soul and whole estate, how is that particular money going to benefit him now? What good will he extract from it?

CRITOBULUS: None whatever, unless we are prepared to admit that hyoscyamus, as they call it, is wealth, a poison the property of which is to drive those who take it mad.

SOCRATES: Let money then, Critobulus, if a man does not know how to use it aright—let money, I say, be banished to the remote corners of the earth rather than be reckoned as wealth. But now, what shall we say of friends? If a man knows how to use his friends so as to be benefited by them, what of these?

CRITOBULUS: They are wealth indisputably and in a deeper sense than cattle are, if, as may be supposed, they are likely to prove of more benefit to a man than wealth of cattle.

SOCRATES: It would seem, according to your argument, that the foes of a man's own household after all may be wealth to him, if he knows how to turn them to good account?

CRITOBULUS: That is my opinion, at any rate.

SOCRATES: It would seem, it is the part of a good economist to know how to deal with his own or his employer's foes so as to get profit out of them?

CRITOBULUS: Most emphatically so.

SOCRATES: In fact, you need but use your eyes to see how many private persons, not to say crowned heads, do owe the increase of their estates to war.

CRITOBULUS: Well, Socrates, I do not think, so far, the argument could be improved on; but now comes a puzzle. What of people who have got the knowledge and the capital required to enhance their fortunes, if only they will put their shoulders to the wheel; and yet, if we are to believe our senses, that is just the one thing they will not do, and so their knowledge and accomplishments are of no profit to them? Surely in their case also there is but one conclusion to be drawn, which is, that neither their knowledge nor their possessions are wealth.

SOCRATES: Ah! I see, Critobulus, you wish to direct the discussion to the topic of slaves?

CRITOBULUS: No indeed, I have no such intention—quite the reverse. I want to talk about persons of high degree, of right noble family some of them, to do them justice. These are the people I have in my mind's eye, gifted with, it may be martial or, it may be, civil accomplishments, which, however, they refuse to exercise, for the very reason, as I take it, that they have no masters over them.

SOCRATES: No masters over them! but how can that be if, in spite of their prayers for prosperity and their desire to do what will bring them good, they are still so sorely hindered in the exercise of their wills by those that lord it over them?

CRITOBULUS: And who, pray, are these lords that rule them and yet remain unseen?

SOCRATES: Nay, not unseen; on the contrary, they are very visible. And what is more, they are the basest of the base, as you can hardly fail to note, if at least you believe idleness and effeminacy and reckless negligence to be baseness. Then, too, there are other treacherous beldames giving themselves out to be innocent pleasures, to wit, dicings and profitless associations among men. These in the fulness of time appear in all their nakedness even to them that are deceived, showing themselves that they are after all but pains tricked out and decked with pleasures. These are they who have the dominion over those you speak of and quite hinder them from every good and useful work.

CRITOBULUS: But there are others, Socrates, who are not hindered by these indolences—on the contrary, they have the most ardent disposition to exert themselves, and by every means to increase their revenues; but in spite of all, they wear out their substance and are involved in endless difficulties.

SOCRATES: Yes, for they too are slaves, and harsh enough are their taskmasters; slaves are they to luxury and lechery, intemperance and the wine-cup along with many a fond and ruinous ambition. These passions so cruelly belord it over the poor soul whom they have got under their thrall, that so long as he is in the heyday of health and strong to labour, they compel him to fetch and carry and lay at their feet the fruit of his toils, and to spend it on their own heart's lusts; but as soon as he is seen to be incapable of further labour through old age, they leave him to his gray hairs and misery, and turn to seize on other victims. Ah! Critobulus, against these must we wage ceaseless war, for very freedom's sake, no less than if they were armed warriors endeavouring to make us their slaves. Nay, foemen in war, it must be granted, especially when of fair and noble type, have many times ere now proved benefactors to those they have enslaved. By dint of chastening, they have forced the vanquished to become better men and to lead more tranquil lives in future. But these despotic queens never cease to plague and torment their victims in body and soul and substance till their sway is ended.

(Xenophon, *Oeconomicus*, Chapter III, 1–16)

Socrates holds the following conversation with Critobulus on economics.

CRITOBULUS: . . . Be sure, Socrates, I will not let you go now until you give the proofs which, in the presence of our friends, you undertook just now to give me.

SOCRATES: Well then, Critobulus, (Socrates replied) what if I begin by showing you two sorts of people, the one expending large sums of money in building useless houses, the other at far less cost erecting dwellings complete with all they need: will you admit that I have laid my finger here on one of the essentials of economy?

CRITOBULUS: An essential point most certainly.

SOCRATES: And suppose in connection with the same, I next point out to you two other sets of persons:—The first possessors of furniture of various kinds, which they cannot, however, lay their hands on when the need arises; indeed they hardly know if they have got all safe and sound or not: whereby they put themselves and their domestics to much mental torture.  The others are perhaps less amply, or at any rate not more amply supplied, but they have everything ready at the instant for immediate use.

CRITOBULUS:   Yes, Socrates, and is not the reason simply that in the first case everything is thrown down where it chanced, whereas those others have everything arranged, each in its appointed place?

SOCRATES:   Quite right, (he answered) and the phrase implies that everything is orderly arranged, not in the first chance place, but in that to which it naturally belongs.

CRITOBULUS:   Yes, the case is to the point, I think, and does involve another economic principle.

SOCRATES:   What, then, if I exhibit to you a third contrast, which bears on the condition of domestic slaves?  On the one side you shall see them fettered hard and fast, as I may say, and yet for ever breaking their chains and running away.  On the other side the slaves are loosed and free to move, but for all that, they choose to work, it seems; they are constant to their masters.  I think you will admit that I here point out another function of economy worth noting.

CRITOBULUS:   I do indeed—a feature most noteworthy.

SOCRATES:   Or take, again, the instance of two farmers engaged in cultivating farms as like as possible.  The one has never done asserting that agriculture has been his ruin, and is in the depth of despair; the other has all he needs in abundance and of the best, and how acquired?—by this same agriculture.

Yes (Critobulus answered), to be sure; perhaps the former spends both toil and money not simply on what he needs, but on things which cause an injury to house alike and owner.

SOCRATES:   That is a possible case, no doubt, but it is not the one that I refer to: I mean people pretending they are farmers, and yet they have not a penny to expend on the real needs of their business.

CRITOBULUS: And pray, what may be the reason of that, Socrates?

SOCRATES: You shall come with me and see these people also; and as you contemplate the scene, I presume you will lay to heart the lesson.

CRITOBULUS: I will, if possibly I can, I promise you.

SOCRATES: Yes, and while you contemplate, you must make trial of yourself and see if you have wit to understand. At present, I will bear you witness that if it is to go and see a party of players performing in a comedy, you will get up at cock-crow, and come trudging a long way, and ply me volubly with reasons why I should accompany you to see the play. But you have never once invited me to come and witness such an incident as those we were speaking of just now.

CRITOBULUS: And so I seem to you ridiculous?

SOCRATES: Far more ridiculous to yourself, I warrant. But now let me point out to you another contrast: between certain people whose dealing with horses has brought them to the brink of poverty, and certain others who have found in the same pursuit the road to affluence, and have a right besides to plume themselves upon their gains.

CRITOBULUS: Well, then, I may tell you, I see and know both characters as well as you do; but I do not find myself a whit the more included among those who gain.

SOCRATES: Because you look at them just as you might at the actors in a tragedy or comedy, and with the same intent —your object being to delight the ear and charm the eye, but not, I take it, to become yourself a poet. And there you are right enough, no doubt, since you have no desire to become a playwright. But, when circumstances compel you to concern yourself with horsemanship, does it not seem to you a little foolish not to consider how you are to escape being a mere amateur in the matter, especially as the same creatures which are good for use are profitable for sale?

CRITOBULUS: So you wish me set up as a breeder of young horses, do you, Socrates?

SOCRATES: Not so, no more than I would recommend you to purchase lads and train them up from boyhood as farm-labourers. But in my opinion there is a certain happy moment of growth which must be seized, alike in man and horse, rich in present service and in future promise. In further illustration, I can show you how some men treat their wedded wives in such a way that they find in them true helpmates to the joint increase of their estate, while others treat them in a way to bring upon themselves wholesale disaster.

CRITOBULUS: Ought the husband or the wife to bear the blame of that?

SOCRATES: If it goes ill with a sheep we blame the shepherd, as a rule, or if a horse shows vice we throw the blame in general upon the rider. But in the case of women, supposing the wife to have received instruction from her husband and yet she delights in wrong-doing, it may be that the wife is justly held to blame; but supposing he has never tried to teach her the first principles of "fair and noble" conduct, and finds her quite an ignoramus in these matters, surely the husband will be justly held to blame. But come now (he added), we are all friends here; make a clean breast of it, and tell us, Critobulus, the plain unvarnished truth: Is there any one to whom you are more in the habit of entrusting matters of importance than to your wife?

CRITOBULUS: There is no one.

SOCRATES: And is there any one with whom you are less in the habit of conversing than with your wife?

CRITOBULUS: Not many, I am forced to admit.

SOCRATES: And when you married her she was quite young, a mere girl—at an age when, as far as seeing and hearing go, she had the smallest acquaintance with the outer world?

CRITOBULUS: Certainly.

SOCRATES: Then would it not be more astonishing that she should have real knowledge how to speak and act than that she should go altogether astray?

CRITOBULUS: But let me ask you a question, Socrates: have those happy husbands, you tell us of, who are blessed with good wives educated them themselves?

SOCRATES: There is nothing like investigation. I will introduce you to Aspasia, who will explain these matters to you in a far more scientific way than I can. My belief is that a good wife, being as she is the partner in a common estate, must needs be her husband's counterpoise and counterpart for good; since, if it is through the transactions of the husband, as a rule, that goods of all sorts find their way into the house, yet it is by means of the wife's economy and thrift that the greater part of the expenditure is checked, and on the successful issue or the mishandling of the same depends the increase or impoverishment of a whole estate. And so with regard to the remaining arts and sciences, I think I can point out to you the ablest performers in each case, if you feel you have any further need of help.

(The dialogue called *"Eryxias,"* 399–405) [87]

The authorship of the dialogue called *Eryxias* is uncertain, for although it was found among the works of Plato, modern criticism does not credit this dialogue to him. Many of the ideas expressed are closely allied to those in Xenophon's *Oeconomicus*. The date of *Eryxias* has been placed about the end of the fourth century B.C. The dialogue itself is a skillful dissertation on the meaning and importance of wealth. The difference between wealth and money is clearly pointed out. The conclusion reached is that a possession becomes wealth only when it is of use to its owner.

Nevertheless, Sokrates, Erasistratos replied, even if you are speaking in jest, there is, clearly, in my opinion, a good deal in Kritias' statement.

I assure you, I am not jesting in the least, was my reply. But to revert, as you two have carried on the discussion so admirably, why do you not complete the rest of the argument? I think that part of your investigation is still wanting. You appear to be agreed on this point, that wealth is good for some and bad for others. It remains to investigate what wealth it-

self is; for unless you know this first, you cannot reach unanimity on the question whether it is bad or good. I, for my
part, am ready to join in your investigation to the best of my
ability. First, then, let him who asserts that wealth is good,
explain to us what he means by wealth.

Well, Sokrates, Erasistratos said, I do not claim greater
importance for wealth than the rest of mankind do. To have
money in abundance, that, men say, constitutes wealth. I
imagine that Kritias here too regards wealth in much the same
light.

Even so, I replied, it still remains for us to investigate
the nature of money in order that the two of us may not a
little later on again be seen to disagree. For example, the
Carthaginians use a currency of the following kind: something
approximately as large as a stater is tied up in a small strip of
leather, but no one but the maker knows what the object inside
is. Then, when a seal has been affixed thereto, it is used as
currency and any man owning a great number of these tokens
is thought to possess much money and to be very rich. But
amongst us, if anyone owned a great number of such pieces
he would be no richer than if he had a collection of mountain-
pebbles. In Lacedaemon iron by weight—and that, too, the
otherwise unserviceable part of the metal—is used, and the
man who owns a heavy load of such iron is esteemed rich;
elsewhere that possession would be valueless. In Aethiopia
engraved stones are employed, which a Lacedaemonian in his
own country could not use. Among the nomads of Scythia any
man who possessed Pulytions' mansion would be thought no
richer than a man owning Mount Lycabettas would with us.
Therefore obviously these various objects cannot all be possessions if some of the owners are no richer on their account. But,
I said each of these is regarded by some as money, and their
owners as rich; by others they are not looked on as money nor
are the owners esteemed wealthy, just in the same way as the
same things are not good or base in everyone's eyes, but different things are differently regarded by men. If we desire

to investigate why houses do not represent wealth to a Scythian, though they do with us, or why leather represents money to a Carthaginian or iron to a Lacedaemonian but in neither case does so with us, should we find a solution in some such way as this: if any Athenian were to own a thousand talents' weight of stones such as lie about here in the market-place, which we do not use for any purpose, would he for that reason be deemed to be richer?

I should certainly not so regard him.

But if he possessed a thousand talents' weight of fine white marble we should say he was very rich?

Undoubtedly.

Well, then, is your reason for this that the one is useful, the other useless to us?

Yes.

Thus, too, among the Scythians houses for this reason do not represent wealth, because they have no need for them. A Scythian would not prefer the most exquisite house to a leather wrap because, while the one is useful, the other is useless to him. Again, we do not regard the Carthaginian currency as money, for we could not purchase with it any of the things we need, as we can with silver coin; consequently it is useless to us.

That is reasonable enough.

Thus, what happens to be useful to us constitutes wealth, what is useless does not.

Eryxias interrupting said: How so, Sokrates? Do we not sometimes in our relations to others find a use for conversation, injurious treatment and so forth? Should we count these as wealth? Yet they clearly have their use.

Even now and so it is not clear to us what wealth is. That things, if they are to constitute wealth, must be useful; on that, everyone is more or less agreed. But what kind of useful thing is wealth, since it is not all? Come now, suppose we carried on our argument again thus, we may find some answer to our inquiry: What is the use of wealth and to what end has the acquisition of wealth been invented, as drugs have been discovered to counteract disease? Perhaps by this line of inquiry the question will become clearer to us. It appears to be essential that whatever happens to make up wealth must also be useful, and further, what we call wealth is a species of useful things. It remains to investigate for what service are the useful things, which make up wealth of use? Perhaps everything which is used for production is useful just as every creature which has life is an animal, but a species of the genus animal we call man. Suppose we were asked: What thing is that by whose removal we should have no need of medical science and of its instruments? We should be able to reply that this would happen if diseases were expelled from our bodies and did not occur at all, or else were expelled as soon as they appeared. Thus, it would appear, among the sciences medicine is the one useful for this purpose, namely, to expel disease. Again, if we were asked by the removal of what thing could we dispense with wealth should we have a reply ready? If not, let us consider the point in this way: If a man could exist without food and drink, and feel neither hunger nor thirst, would he require any of these commodities or silver coin or anything, to enable him to obtain victuals?

I think not.

Then the same will hold good of other articles (besides food). If we did not require for our physical well-being any of the things we now need, now yet warmth or coolness or any of the other conditions of which man feels the want, what we call wealth would be useless to us, supposing, that is, that no one required any of the things for whose sake we now desire to possess wealth, namely, to satisfy the desires and requirements of the body for which we severally crave. If the acquisition of wealth is an advantageous thing for this purpose, namely, attention to the requirements of the body, if this purpose were removed root and branch, we should not require wealth and may be wealth would not exist at all.

That is clear.

In that case, I imagine, it is clear to us that those things which are useful to this end constitute wealth. He agreed to this definition of wealth, not but what my little argument rather perturbed him. What is your answer to the following? Should we maintain that the same thing can at one time be useful, at another time useless, to bring about the same result?

I should not maintain more than that, if we need the same thing to bring about the same result, then it appears to me to be useful; if not, not.

In that case, if we could fashion a statue of bronze without fire, we should have no need of fire for its production, and fire would be useless to us if we did not need it? The same argument holds good in the other cases.

Obviously.

Then whatever is superfluous for the creation of a thing we should also regard as useless for that purpose?

Yes.

Then if it were obvious that without silver and gold and other such materials, which we do not themselves employ for our body as we do food, drink, clothing, bedding and houses, we could satisfy our bodily needs so that we should no longer require those metals, then we should not regard them as useful for that purpose, if we could carry on without them.

We should not.

In fact, we should not even look on them as wealth, being of no use. On the other hand, those things would constitute wealth in our eyes by means of which we could obtain what was useful.

Sokrates, I could never be convinced that gold, silver and similar materials are not wealth. However, I am firm in the belief that those things which are useless to us are not wealth, and that money which is useful to this end belongs to the most useful things; not that these things are not of service to us for life, if by their means we can obtain its necessaries.

Come now, what would you say of the following? Are there not men who teach music, grammar and other arts who, by charging fees for this, provide themselves with the needs of life?

There are.

These men, then, by means of this art of theirs and in exchange for their art, can obtain the necessaries of life, just as we can in exchange for gold and silver.

I agree.

If therefore they acquire what they use for their daily life by this means, the means itself will be of use for life. For we said that silver was serviceable on this account, because it enabled us to provide ourselves with bodily necessaries.

Quite so.

If, then, these arts are included among things useful for that purpose, clearly they constitute wealth for the same reason that gold and silver do. Obviously those, too, who possess them are richer thereby. But a little while ago we were reluctant to accept the statement that the wisest are richest. The inevitable conclusions, however, from the argument on which we are now agreed is that sometimes the more knowledge men have the wealthier they are. If we were asked whether we thought a horse useful for everybody, what would you say? Would you not reply that it would be useful to those who are skilled in the use of the horse, but not to those ignorant of this?

I should.

Then, I said, by the same argument a drug is not serviceable to everyone, but only to him who happens to have acquired the knowledge of its proper use?

I agree.

And thus it is in all other cases?

So I suppose.

Thus gold, silver and the other things that are considered to be wealth are only of use to the man who happens to know how they must be used.

Precisely.

Well now, a little earlier we thought it was the function of

the good and upright man to know where and how to use these
several things.

I agree.

Then to such men, and to them alone, these things will also
be useful, provided they are skilled in the use of them.  If
these things are only useful to them, then they alone will regard
them as wealth.  Nevertheless, I imagine, if a person unskilled
in riding, who possesses horses which are useless to him, is
taught by another to ride, the teacher has made him wealthier,
if he has made that which previously happened to be useless to
him useful; that is to say, by imparting knowledge to someone
you also make him wealthier.

So it would seem.

Still, I think I would take an oath on Kritias' behalf that
he has not been convinced by any of these arguments.

Bless me, no; I should be mad if I were convinced.  But
why have you not concluded that argument that those things
which seem to be wealth, to wit, gold and silver and so forth,
are not wealth?  For I have been greatly charmed to listen to
the statements which you have just been putting forward.

Thereupon I replied: I think, Kritias, that you had the
same pleasure in listening to me that you would have from the
minstrels who recite Homer's lays, seeing that none of my
arguments appears true to you.  Still, come now, what would
you say to this?  Would you admit that certain objects are
useful to builders towards the construction of a house?

I should.

Further, should we say that those materials which they use
for building are useful to them, that is to say, stones, bricks,
timber and so on?  Or again, the instruments with which they
construct the house and the things by which they procured
the stone and timber, and further the instruments by which
these were obtained?

All these, he said, are, I think, useful for the end in view.

Then, said I, in the case of the other industries also, not

only those things which we employ for the several works are useful, but the instruments with which we obtain these, without which nothing could be done?

Most decidedly.

Then again there are the instruments by which these instruments are obtained, and we can go back still farther so that we end by having an infinite number of such—all these must clearly be of use for the performance of the work?

There does not appear to be any objection to this view.

If then a man had food, drink, clothes and whatever else he is likely to use for his body, would he have any need of gold, silver or any other medium with which to provide himself with what he now has?

I think not.

Then there would appear to us to be no occasion when a man requires any of these for his bodily needs?

No.

Then if we regard these as useless for that purpose, we ought never again to consider them useful? For we postulated that the same thing cannot be at one time useful, at another useless, for the same purpose.

Thus, he answered, your contention and mine coincide. For if these things are useless for this purpose, they could never again become useful. Nor I maintain that for some purposes bad things are required, for others good.

But is it possible for an evil thing to be of use for producing something good?

I should hardly think so.

Should we describe those actions as good which a man performs for the sake of virtue?

Yes.

Can a man learn any of those subjects which are taught by word of mouth, if he has entirely lost the power of hearing?

Most emphatically not.

Then we should regard the power of hearing as one of those things useful for acquiring virtue, if virtue is taught by hearing and we employ this sense for receiving instruction.

So it seems.

If then medical science is able to arrest the sick man's disorder, we should regard it too at times as one of the things useful for virtue, if by its aid a man's hearing were restored?

That seems reasonable enough.

Again, if we procured medical science in exchange for wealth, we should look on wealth also as useful for virtue?

That also is true, he said.

Or again in the same way the instruments by which we acquire wealth?

Yes, every one of them.

So you consider that a man might make money by means of evil and shameful transactions and in exchange for it might acquire the services of medical science, thereby being enabled to hear, though he was previously unable to do so; and then could employ that same sense for the acquisition of virtue and other like qualities?

I think so certainly.

Can that which is evil be of use for the acquisition of virtue?

No.

Then it necessarily follows that the instruments by which we provide ourselves with things useful for various purposes, must also be useful for the same purposes; for it would seem that at times evil actions may be useful to attain something good. This point may become rather plainer in the light of the following questions: If these things are useful for acquiring the several objects without which the latter would not exist, assuming that the former were not pre-existent, tell me now, how would you describe them? Is it possible for ignorance to be of service for the acquisition of knowledge, or sickness for health, or vice for virtue?

I should say not.

And yet we should agree that the following is impossible, namely, that knowledge can reside in a subject in whom there has not previously been ignorance, or health in one who has not been sick, or virtue where there has been no vice?

He agreed, as I thought.

Then it would not necessarily follow that the antecedents essential to the existence of a thing are also of use to it; otherwise we should regard ignorance as useful for knowledge, sickness for health, and vice for virtue.

Kritias was very sceptical towards these arguments which proved that all these things did not constitute wealth. But I, realising that to convince him was much the same as "to boil a stone," as the saying is, continued: Let us bid farewell to these arguments since we cannot agree whether these things constitute wealth or not.

# CHAPTER IV (*Continued*)

## ATTIC AGE

### 7. SOCIAL CONTROL: TRADITION AS A BASIS OF HUMAN ACTION

(Aristophanes, *The Birds*, l. 155–186)

Euelpides and Peisthetaerus, elderly citizens of Athens, disgusted with the atmosphere in their own city, seek a new city. In the following excerpt we see that Aristophanes apparently recognized that habit and tradition were forces that lend stability to society and to the state. Thus in the conversation between Euelpides and Hoopoe, a bird, as to living conditions in birdland, Euelpides points out the necessity of stability in a city that is to be important.

EUELPIDES:    But this, this bird-life here, you know it well,
What is it like?
HOOPOE:    A pleasant life enough.
Foremost and first you don't require a purse.
EUELPIDES:    There goes a grand corrupter of our life!
HOOPOE:    Then in the gardens we enjoy the myrtles,
The cress, the poppy, the white sesame.
EUELPIDES:    Why then, ye live a bridegroom's jolly life.
PEISTHETAERUS:    Oh! Oh!
O the grand scheme I see in the birds' reach,
And power to grasp it, if ye'd trust to me!
HOOPOE:    Trust you in what?
PEISTHETAERUS:                What? First don't fly about
In all directions, with your mouths wide open.
That makes you quite despised. With *us,* for instance,
If you should ask the flighty people there,
*Who is that fellow?* Teleas would reply,
*The man's a bird, a flighty feckless bird,*
*Inconsequential, always on the move.*

HOOPOE: Well blamed, i' faith; but what we ought to do,
Tell us.

PEISTHETAERUS: Live all together: found one State.

HOOPOE: What sort of State are birds to found, I wonder.

PEISTHETAERUS: Aye, say you so? You who have made
    the most
Idiotic speech, look down.

HOOPOE:                 I do.

PEISTHETAERUS:           Look up.

HOOPOE: I do.

PEISTHETAERUS: Twirl round your head.

HOOPOE:                         Zeus! I shall be
A marvellous gainer, if I twist my neck!

PEISTHETAERUS: What did you see?

HOOPOE:                     I saw the clouds and sky.

PEISTHETAERUS: And is not that the Station of the Birds?

HOOPOE: Station?

PEISTHETAERUS:           As one should say, their habitation.
Here while the heavens revolve, and yon great dome
Is moving round, ye keep your Station still.
Make this your city, fence it round with walls,
And from your Station is evolved your State.
So ye'll be lords of men, as now of locusts,
And Melian famine shall destroy the Gods.

        (Aristophanes, *Ecclesiazusae*, l. 205–240)

    This is the speech Praxagora plans to make before the assembly which will turn the state over to the women. We can see Aristophanes' real bitterness as to the way the government has ruined the fine things of Athens in the line about "Things that worked well,"—and his belief that the old ways are the best ways.

PRAXAGORA: Ye are to blame for this, Athenian people,
Ye draw your wages from the public purse,
Yet each man seeks his private gain alone.
So the State reels, like any Aesimus.
Still, if ye trust me, ye shall yet be saved.
I move that now the womankind be asked

To rule the State.   In our own homes, ye know
They are the managers and rule the house.

> FIRST WOMAN:   O good, good, good! speak on, speak on,
>     dear man.

> PRAXAGORA:   That they are better in these ways than we
I'll soon convince you.   First, they dye their wools
With boiling tinctures, in the ancient style.
You won't find *them* I warrant, in a hurry
Trying new plans.   And would it not have saved
The Athenians' city had she let alone
Things that worked well, nor idly sought things new?
They roast their barley, sitting as of old;
They on their heads bear burdens, as of old:
They keep their Thesmophoria, as of old:
They bake their honied cheesecakes as of old;
They victimize their husbands, as of old:
They still secrete their lovers, as of old:
They buy themselves sly dainties, as of old:
They love their wine unwatered, as of old:
They like a woman's pleasures, as of old:
Then let us, gentlemen, give up to them
The helm of State, and not concern ourselves,
Nor pry, nor question what they mean to do;
But let them really govern, knowing this,
The statesman-mothers never will neglect
Their soldier-sons.   And then a soldier's ration,
Who will supply as well as she who bare him?
For ways and means none can excel a woman.
And there's no fear at all that they'll be cheated
When they're in power, for they're the cheats themselves.
Much I omit.   But if you pass my motion,
You'll lead the happiest lives that e'er you dreamed of.

(Demosthenes, *On The Crown*, 203–206) [38]

*On The Crown* has often been called Demosthenes' greatest speech. In it he identifies himself with Athens, pointing out that he has always submerged his own interests in those of the city.

From the beginning of time no one had ever yet succeeded in persuading the city to throw in her lot with those who were strong, but unrighteous in their dealings, and to enjoy the security of servitude.  Throughout all time she has maintained her perilous struggle for preeminence, honour, and glory.  And this policy you look upon as so lofty, so proper to your own national character, that, of your forefathers also, it is those who have acted thus that you praise most highly.   And naturally.  For who would not admire the courage of those men, who did not fear to leave their land and their city, and to embark upon their ships, that they might not do the bidding of another; who chose for their general Themistocles (who had counselled them thus), and stoned Cyrsilus to death, when he gave his voice for submission to a master's orders—and not him alone, for your wives stoned his wife also to death.  For the Athenians of that day did not look for an orator or a general who would enable them to live in happy servitude; they cared not to live at all, unless they might live in freedom! For every one of them felt that he had come into being, not for his father and his mother alone, but also for his country.  And wherein lies the difference?—He who thinks he was born for his parents alone awaits the death which destiny assigns him in the course of nature:  but he who thinks he was born for his country also will be willing to die, that he may not see her in bondage, and will look upon the outrages and the indignities that he must needs bear in a city that is in bondage as more to be dreaded than death.

(Demosthenes, On The Crown, 210–211)

Demosthenes points out that his policy has always been true to the spirit of Athenian history and in accordance with Athens' finest tradition and ideals.

For you too, men of Athens, ought not to judge private suits and public in the same spirit.  The business transactions of every-day life must be viewed in the light of the special law and practice associated with each; but the public policy of statesmen must be judged by the principles that your forefathers set before them. And if you believe that you should act worthily of them, then, whenever you come into court to try a public suit, each of you must imagine that with his staff and his ticket there is entrusted to him also the spirit of his country.

(Isocrates, *Panegyricus*, 32–34) [39]

In the *Panegyricus*, Isocrates calls upon the city-states of Greece to cease their dissensions and unite to overthrow Persia.

But apart from these considerations, if we waive all this and carry our inquiry back to the beginning, we shall find that those who first appeared upon the earth did not at the outset find the kind of life which we enjoy to-day, but that they procured it little by little through their own joint efforts. Whom, then, must we think the most likely either to have received this better life as a gift from the gods or to have hit upon it through their own search? Would it not be those who are admitted by all men to have been the first to exist, to be endowed with the greatest capacity for the arts, and to be the most devoted in the worship of the gods? And surely it is superfluous to attempt to show how high is the honour which the authors of such great blessings deserve; for no one could find a reward great enough to match the magnitude of their achievements.

8. SOCIAL CONTROL: MASS CONTROL INDUCED THROUGH PROPAGANDA, ORATORY, PUBLIC OPINION, AND LEADERSHIP

(Aeschylus, *Agamemnon*, l. 938–940)

Clytaemnestra tries to persuade Agamemnon to dismount and walk on the tapestries that she has laid down before the palace in his honor. He protests, but finally acquiesces.

CLYTAEMNESTRA: Then be not thou swayed by fear of men's cavillings.

AGAMEMNON: And yet a people's voice is a mighty power.

(Euripides, *Hippolytus*, l. 983–989) [40]

In this passage Hippolytus defends himself against his father's wrath and accusations.

HIPPOLYTUS:   Father, thy rage and strong-strained fury
        of soul
Are fearful: yet, fair-seeming though the charge,
If one unfold it, all unfair it is.
I have no skill to speak before a throng:
My tongue is loosed with equals, and those few.
And reason: they that are among the wise
Of none account, to mobs are eloquent.

                (Euripides, *Hippolytus*, l. 486–489)

Phaedra's nurse counsels her not to stifle her love, for it is God's will.
Phaedra answers her in this manner.

PHAEDRA:   This is it which doth ruin goodly towns
And homes of men, these speeches over-fair.
It needeth not to speak words sweet to ears,
But those whereby a good name shall be saved.

                (Euripides, *Orestes*, l. 902–913) [41]

In the two passages that follow, the messenger is relating the occurrences of the council meeting at which Orestes and Electra were condemned to die. Euripides again indicates the influence of the demagogue
and his oratorical propaganda on the masses.

MESSENGER:                        Thereafter rose up one
Of tongue unbridled, stout in impudence,
An Argive, yet no Argive, thrust on us,
In bluster and coarse-grained fluency confident,
Still plausible to trap the folk in mischief:
For when an evil heart with winning tongue
Persuades the crowd, ill is it for the state:
Whoso with understanding counsel well
Profit the state—ere long, if not straightway.
Thus ought we on each leader of men to look,
And so esteem: for both be in like case,
The orator, and the man in office set.

                (Euripides, *Orestes*, l. 915–920)

MESSENGER:   To plead against him then another rose.
No dainty presence, but a manful man,

In town and market-circle seldom found,
A yeoman—such as are the land's one stay,—
Yet shrewd in grapple of words, when this he would;
A stainless man, who lived a blameless life.

(Euripides, *Orestes*, l. 692–703)

Menelaus explains to Orestes that he is unable to help him, but points out that perhaps after a time the people's anger against him will subside. Menelaus describes crowd reaction and its workings.

MENELAUS:    If we might prevail
By soft words, this is our hope's utmost bound.
For with faint means how should a man achieve
Great things?  'Twere witless even to wish for this.
For, in the first rush of a people's rage,
'Twere even as one would quench a ravening fire.
But if one gently yield him to their stress,
Slacken the sheet, and watch the season due,
Their storm might spend its force.  When lulls the blast,
Lightly thou mightest win thy will of them.
In them is ruth, high spirit is in them—
A precious thing to whoso bides his time.

(Aristophanes, *The Knights*, l. 40–72) [42]

Aristophanes attacks Paphlagon's (Cleon's) ways of getting power by soliciting and flattering his way with Demus, the people.

DEMUS:    I'll tell them now.  We two have got a master,
Demus of Pnyx-borough, such a sour old man,
Quick tempered, country-minded, bean-consuming,
A trifle hard of hearing.  Last new moon
He bought a slave, a tanner, Paphlagon,
The greatest rogue and liar in the world.
This tanning-Paphlagon, he soon finds out
Master's weak points; and cringing down before him
Flatters, and fawns, and wheedles, and cajoles,
With little apish leather snippings, thus;
*O Demus, try one case, get the three-obol,*
*Then take your bath, gorge, guzzle, eat your fill.*

*Would you I set your supper?*  Then he'll seize
A dish some other servant has prepared,
And serve it up for master; and quite likely
I'd baked a rich Laconian cake at Pylus,
When in runs Paphlagon, and bags my cake,
And serves it up to Demus as his own.
But us he drives away, and none but he
Must wait on master; there he stands through dinner
With leathern flap, and flicks away the speakers,
And he chants oracles, till the dazed old man
Goes Sibyl-mad; then, when he sees him mooning,
He plies his trade.  He slanders those within
With downright lies, so then we're flogged, poor wretches,
And Paphlagon runs round, extorting, begging,
Upsetting every one; and *Mark,* says he
*There's Hylas flogged; that's all my doing; better*
*Make friends with me, or you'll be trounced today.*
So then we bribe him off, or if we don't
We're sure to catch it thrice as bad from master.
Now let's excogitate at once, good fellow,
Which way to turn our footsteps, and to whom.

(Aristophanes, The Knights, l. 1110–1150)

Below, Aristophanes shows how simple it is to sway a populace by force of oratory.  His reference is again to Cleon.

CHORUS:  Proud, O Demus, thy sway,
Thee, as Tyrant and King,
All men fear and obey,
Yet, O yet, 'tis a thing
Easy, to lead thee astray,
Empty fawning and praise
Pleased thou art to receive;
All each orator says
Sure at once to believe;
Wit thou hast, but 'tis roaming;
Ne'er we find it its home in.

DEMUS:   Wit there's none in your hair.
What, you think me a fool!
What, you know not I wear,
Wear my motely by rule.
Well all day do I fare,
Nursed and cockered by all;
Pleased to fatten and train
One prime thief in my stall.
When full gorged with his gain,
Up that instant I snatch him,
Strike one blow and dispatch him.

CHORUS:   Art thou really so deep?
Is such artfulness thine?
Well for all if thou keep
Firm to this thy design.
Well for all if, as sheep
Marked for victims, thou feed
These thy knaves in the Pnyx,
Then, if dainties thou need,
Haste on a victim to fix;
Slay the fattest and finest;
There's thy meal when thou dinest.

DEMUS:   Ah! they know not that I
Watch them plunder and thieve.
Oh! *'tis easy*, they cry,
*Him to gull and deceive*.
Comes *my* turn by and by!
Down their gullet, full quick,
Lo, my verdict-tube coils,
Turns them giddy and sick,
Up they vomit their spoils;
Such with rogues, is my dealing,
'Tis for *myself* they are stealing.

(Aristophanes, *The Acharnians*, l. 628–642) [43]

    The following speech, delivered by the leader of the chorus, is a direct reflection of Aristophanes' idea that public opinion and alertness to the pitfalls of propaganda are democracy's safeguard.

LEADER OF THE CHORUS:   Since first to exhibit his plays
he began,
      Our chorus-instructor has never
Come forth to confess in this public address
      How tactful he is and how clever.
But now that he knows he is slandered by foes
      before Athens so quick to assent,
Pretending he jeers our City and sneers
      at the people with evil intent,
He is ready and fain his cause to maintain
      before Athens so quick to repent.
Let honour and praise be the guerdon, he says,
      of the poet whose satire has stayed you
From believing the orators' novel conceits
      wherewith they cajoled and betrayed you;
Who bids you despise adulation and lies
      nor be citizens Vacant and Vain.
For before, when an embassy came from the states
      intriguing your favour to gain,
And called you the town of the Violet Crown,
      so grand and exalted ye grew,
That at once on your tiptails erect ye would sit,
      those Crowns were so pleasant to you.
And then, if they added the Shiny, they got
      whatever they asked for their praises,
Though apter, I ween, for an oily sardine
      than for you and your city the phrase is.
By this he's a true benefactor to you,
      and by showing with humour dramatic
The way that our wise democratic allies
      are ruled by our State democratic.

(Isocrates, *On The Peace*, 3–8)

I observe, however, that you do not hear with equal favor
the speakers who address you, but  that, while you give your
attention to some, in the case of others you do not even suffer

their voice to be heard. And it is not surprising that you do
this; for in the past you have formed the habit of driving all the
orators from the platform except those who support your desires. Wherefore one may justly take you to task because,
while you know well that many great houses have been ruined
by flatterers and while in your private affairs you abhor those
who practice this art, in your public affairs you are not so
minded towards them; on the contrary, while you denounce
those who welcome and enjoy the society of such men, you yourself make it manifest that you place greater confidence in them
than in the rest of your fellow-citizens.

Indeed, you have caused the orators to practise and study,
not what will be advantageous to the state, but how they may
discourse in a manner pleasing to you. And it is to this kind of
discourse that the majority of them have resorted also at the
present time, since it has become plain to all that you will be
better pleased with those who summon you to war than with
those who counsel peace; for the former put into our minds the
expectation both of regaining our possessions in the several
states and of recovering the power which we formerly enjoyed,
while the latter hold forth no such hope, insisting rather that
we must have peace and not crave great possessions contrary to
justice, but be content with those we have—and that for the
great majority of mankind is of all things the most difficult.
For we are so dependent on our hopes and so insatiate in seizing
what seems to be our advantage that not even those who possess the greatest fortunes are willing to rest satisfied with them
but are always grasping after more and so risking the loss of
what they have. Wherefore we may well be anxious lest on the
present occasion also we may be subject to this madness.

(Isocrates, *Antidosis*, 133–135)

"You observe," I would say to him, "the nature of the multitude, how susceptible they are to flattery; that they like those
who cultivate their favour better than those who seek their
good; and that they prefer those who cheat them with beaming

smiles and brotherly love to those who serve them with dignity and reserve.  You have paid no attention to these things, but are of the opinion that if you attend honestly to your enterprises abroad, the people at home also will think well of you. But this is not the case, and the very contrary is wont to happen.  For if you please the people in Athens, no matter what you do they will not judge your conduct by the facts but will construe it in a light favourable to you; and if you make mistakes, they will overlook them, while if you succeed, they will exalt your success to the high heaven.  For good will has this effect upon all men."

(Isocrates, *On The Peace*, 133–134)

The first way by which we can set right and improve the conditions of our city is to select as our advisers on affairs of state the kind of men whose advice we should desire on our private affairs, and to stop thinking of the sycophants as friends of democracy and of the good men and true among us as friends of oligarchy, realizing that no man is by nature either the one or the other but that all men desire, in each case, to establish that form of government in which they are held in honour.

(Aeschines, *Against Ctesiphon*, 248–250) [44]

*Against Ctesiphon* was written by Aeschines to show that Ctesiphon had been guilty of illegality when he had proposed that a crown should be awarded Demosthenes in the theater.  In reality, Aeschines attempts to deride all Demosthenes' achievements and blames him for all the evil that has befallen Athens.

[Man must guard] against those who arrogate to themselves the name of "patriot" and "benefactor," but are untrustworthy in character.  For loyalty and the name of a friend of the people are prizes which are offered to us all, but for the most part those persons are the first to take refuge in them in speech who are fartherest from them in conduct.  When, therefore, you find a politician coveting crowns and proclamations

in the presence of the Greeks, bid him bring his argument back
to the proof of a worthy life and a sound character, precisely
as the law commands a man to give security for property. But
if he has no testimony to this, do not confirm to him the praises
which he seeks; let your thought be for the democracy, which
is already slipping through your hands.

## 9. THE CONCEPTION OF SOCIAL COMPETITION
### (Sophocles, *Electra*, l. 945) [45]

Upon hearing of her brother's death, Electra decides to avenge her
father's death and asks Chrysothemis, her sister, to aid her in this dangerous enterprise. Realizing the terrific odds against the success of her venture, Electra makes the following remark to her sister. This is quite
clearly a part of the author's philosophy, since all the characters acquiesce
to its wisdom.

ELECTRA: Mark—without striving no success is won.

### (Euripides, *Suppliants,* l. 552–557) [46]

This is the answer that Theseus makes to Creon's warnings. He tells
the messenger to carry these words back to Creon.

THESEUS: O fools, learn ye the real ills of men:—
Our life is conflict all: Of mortals some
Succeed ere long, some late, and straightway some;
While Fortune sits a queen: worship and honour
The unblest gives her, so to see good days;
The prosperous extols her, lest her breeze
Fail him one day. Remembering this, should we
Meet wrong with calmness, not with fury of rage,
Neither on one whole nation visit wrong.

### (Xenophon, *Hiero,* Chapter IX, 5–11) [28]

Simonides here suggests that prizes be awarded in order to encourage
men to put forth their utmost effort in whatever work they do. He believes this method will act as an incentive to produce good work.

All states as units are divided into tribes, or regiments, or
companies, and there are officers appointed in command of each
division.

Well then, suppose that some one were to offer prizes to these political departments on the pattern of the choric prizes just described; prizes for excellence in arms, or skill in tactics, or for discipline and so forth, or for skill in horsemanship; prizes for prowess in the field of battle, bravery in war; prizes for uprightness in fulfillment of engagements, contracts, covenants. If so, I say it is to be expected that these several matters, thanks to emulous ambition, will one and all be vigorously cultivated. Vigorously! why, yes, upon my soul, and what a rush there would be! How in the pursuit of honor they would tear along where duty called: with what promptitude pour in their money contributions at a time of crisis.

And that which of all arts is the most remunerative, albeit the least accustomed hitherto to be conducted on the principle of competition—I mean agriculture—itself would make enormous strides, if some one were to offer prizes in the same way, "by farms and villages," to those who should perform the works of tillage in the fairest fashion. Whilst to those members of the state who should devote themselves with right and main to this pursuit, a thousand blessings would be the result. The revenues would be increased; and self-restraint be found far more than now, in close attendance on industrious habits. Nay further, crimes and villainies take root and spring less freely among busy workers.

Once more, if commerce is of any value to the state, then let the merchant who devotes himself to commerce on the greatest scale receive some high distinction, and his honours will draw on other traders in his wake.

Or were it made apparent that the genius who discovers a new source of revenue, which will not be vexatious, will be honoured by the state, a field of exploration will at once be opened, which will not long continue unproductive.

And to speak compendiously, if it were obvious in each department that the introducer of any salutary measure whatsoever will not remain unhonoured, that in itself will stimulate a host of people who will make it their business to discover some good thing or other for the state. Wherever matters of advantage to the state excite deep interest, of necessity discoveries are made more freely and more promptly perfected.

But if you are afraid, O mighty prince, that through the multitude of prizes offered under many heads, expenses also must be much increased, consider that no articles of commerce can be got more cheaply than those which people purchase in exchange for prizes. Note in the public contests (choral, equestrian, or gymnastic) how small the prizes are and yet what vast expenditures of wealth and toil, and painful supervision these elicit.

## 10. IDEAS ON LAW AND JUSTICE

### (Sophocles, *Aias*, l. 1071–1076)

After Aias' death Menelaus tries to punish him for his misdeeds by refusing to allow his burial. When Teucer, Aias' friend, reproaches him for his harshness, Menelaus defends himself with these words. We can see clearly that Sophocles believes in these words, because in a passage directly following this one the chorus refers to Menelaus' words as "wise saws." Although Odysseus shows himself to be kinder and nobler than Menelaus by seeing that Aias is buried, the beliefs expressed in the following passage are undoubtedly the beliefs of Sophocles in general, in regard to authority.

MENELAUS: Yet 'tis a knave's part when a citizen
Brooks not to hearken to authority.
For neither in a city shall the laws
Have fair course when there lives no fear of them,
Nor shall a host be wisely disciplined
Without these bulwarks, fear and reverence.

### (Sophocles, *Antigone*, l. 661–680)

Kreon gives the following advice to his son Haimon when he discloses that Haimon's betrothed, Antigone, is to be killed. Kreon here upholds the authority of the law.

KREON: For whoso ruleth justly his own house
Shall also in the state deal righteously.

But whoso doth transgress, and wrest the laws,
Or thinks to browbeat them that rule the state,
Never shall such an one win praise of me.
But whom the state appoints must we obey
In small and great things, just things—ay, unjust!
Who thus obeys, I fear not to maintain,
Hath learnt to rule and to submit to rule,
And in the storm of spears to hold the post
Appointed him, a comrade loyal and staunch.
But greater curse is none than scorn of rule.
Towns this destroyeth, this subverteth homes
In ruin:  this aids battling spears to shatter
Ranks on a stricken field:  such as abide
Unbroken, only obedience saves their lives.
So championed must the friends of order be,
And to a woman never must we yield.
Better be by a man dethroned, if this
Must be, so we be called not woman-cowed!

(Sophocles, *Antigone*, l. 872-875)

When Antigone bewails her fate, crying that she did what was just for
the sake of her family, the chorus answers her in this way.

CHORUS:  The claim of kin—to reverence this is just:
Yet may defiance of authority
Not be passed over of him who holds in trust
Its power.  Thine own self-will hath ruined thee.

(Euripides, *Suppliants*, l. 304-313)

Aethra pleads with her son Theseus to intercede in the quarrel and
uphold the righteous cause.

AETHRA:  Nay more—I had endured, and murmured not,
Wert thou not bound to champion the oppressed.
Lo, this is the foundation of thy fame;
Therefore I fear not to exhort thee, son,
That thou wouldst lay thy strong constraining hand

On men of violence which refuse the dead
The dues of burial and of funeral-rites,
And quell the folk that would confound all wont
Of Hellas: for the bond of all men's states
Is this, when they with honour hold by law.

(Hippias, from Xenophon's *Memorabilia,* Book 4, Chapter 4, 6–24) [47]

The following is a conversation between Socrates and Hippias, a sophist, on justice.

HIPPIAS: . . . However, to revert to justice (and uprightness), I flatter myself I can at present furnish you with some remarks which neither you nor any one else will be able to controvert.

By Hera! (he exclaimed), what a blessing to have discovered! Now we shall have no more divisions of opinion on points of right and wrong; judges will vote unanimously; citizens will cease wrangling; there will be no more litigation, no more party faction, states will reconcile their differences, and wars are ended. For my part I do not know how I can tear myself away from you, until I have heard from your own lips all about the grand discovery you have made.

You shall hear all in good time (Hippias answered), but not until you make a plain statement of your own belief. What is justice? We have had enough of your ridiculing all the rest of the world, questioning and cross-examining first one and then the other, but never a bit will you render an account to anyone yourself or state a plain opinion upon a single topic.

What, Hippias (Socrates retorted), have you not observed that I am in a chronic condition of proclaiming what I regard as just and upright?

HIPPIAS: And pray what is this theory of yours on the subject? Let us have it in words.

SOCRATES: If I fail to proclaim it in words, at any rate I do so in deed and in fact. Or do you not think that a fact is worth more as evidence than a word?

Worth far more, I should say (Hippias answered), for many

a man with justice and right on his lips commits injustice and wrong, but no doer of right ever was a misdoer or could possibly be.

SOCRATES: I ask then, have you ever heard or seen or otherwise perceived me bearing false witness or lodging malicious information, or stirring up strife among friends or political dissension in the city, or committing any other unjust and wrongful act?

No, I cannot say that I have (he answered).

SOCRATES: And do you not regard it as right and just to abstain from wrong?

HIPPIAS: Now you are caught, Socrates, plainly trying to escape from a plain statement. When asked what you believe justice to be, you keep telling us not what the just man does, but what he does not do.

Why, I thought for my part (answered Socrates) that the refusal to do wrong and injustice was a sufficient warrant in itself of righteousness and justice, but if you do not agree, see if this pleases you better: I assert what is "lawful" is "just and righteous."

Do you mean to assert (he asked) that lawful and just are synonymous terms?

SOCRATES: I do.

I ask (Hippias added), for I do not perceive what you mean by *lawful*, nor what you mean by *just*.

SOCRATES: You understand what is meant by *laws of a city or state?*

Yes (he answered).

SOCRATES: What do you take them to be?

HIPPIAS: The several enactments drawn up by the citizens or members of a state in agreement as to what things should be done or left undone.

Then I presume (Socrates continued) that a member of a state who regulates his life in accordance with these enactments will be law abiding, while the transgressor of the same will be lawless?

Certainly (he answered).

SOCRATES: And I presume the law-loving citizen will do what is just and right, while the lawless man will do what is unjust and wrong?

HIPPIAS: Certainly.

SOCRATES: It would appear, then, that the law-loving man is *just,* and the *lawless unjust?*

Then HIPPIAS: Well, but *laws,* Socrates, how should anyone regard as a serious matter either the laws themselves, or obedience to them, which laws the very people who made them are perpetually rejecting and altering?

Which is also true of war (Socrates replied); cities are perpetually undertaking war and then making peace again.

Most true (he answered).

SOCRATES: If so, what is the difference between depreciating obedience to law because laws will be repealed, and depreciating good discipline in war because peace will one day be made? But perhaps you object to enthusiasm displayed in defence of one's home and fatherland in war?

No, indeed I do not! I heartily approve of it (he answered).

SOCRATES: Then have you laid to heart the lesson taught by Lycurgus to the Lacedaemonians, and do you understand that if he succeeded in giving Sparta a distinction above other states, it was only by instilling into her, beyond all else, a spirit of obedience to the laws? And among magistrates and rulers in the different states, you would scarcely refuse the palm of superiority to those who best contribute to make their fellow citizens obedient to the laws? And you would admit that any particular state in which obedience to the laws is the paramount distinction of the citizens flourishes most in peace time, and in time of war is irresistible? But, indeed, of all the blessings which a state may enjoy, none stands higher than the blessing of unanimity. "Concord among citizens"—that is the constant theme of exhortation emphasized in the council of elders and by the choice spirits of the community; at all times and every-

where through the length and breadth of Hellas it is an established law that the citizens be bound together by an oath of
concord; everywhere they do actually swear this oath; not of
course as implying that citizens shall all vote for the same
choruses, or give their plaudits to the same flute-players, or
choose the same poets, or limit themselves to the same pleasures, but simply that they shall pay obedience to the laws,
since in the end that state will prove most powerful and most
prosperous in which the citizens abide by these; but without
concord neither can a state be well administered nor a household well organized.

And if we turn to private life, what better protection can a
man have than obedience to the laws?   This shall be his safe-
guard against penalties, his guarantee of honours at the hands
of the community; it shall be a clue to thread his way through
the mazes of the law courts unbewildered, secure against defeat, assured of victory.   It is to him, the law-loving citizen,
that men will turn in confidence when seeking a guardian of
the most sacred deposits, be it of money or be it their sons or
daughters.   He, in the eyes of the state collectively, is trust-
worthy—he and no other; who alone may be depended on to
render to all alike their dues—to parents and kinsmen and
servants, to friends and fellow-citizens and foreigners.   This is
he whom the enemy will soonest trust to arrange an armistice,
or a truce, or a treaty of peace.   They would like to become the
allies of this man, and to fight on his side.   This is he to whom
the allies of his country will most confidently entrust the command of their forces, or of a garrison, or their states themselves.
This, again, is he who may be counted on to recompense kindness with gratitude, and who, therefore, is more sure of kindly
treatment than another whose sense of gratitude is duller.   The
most desirable among friends, the enemy of all others to be
avoided, clearly he is not the person whom a foreign state would
choose to go to war with; encompassed by a host of friends and
exempt from foes, his very character has a charm to compel

friendship and alliance, and before him hatred and hostility melt away.

And now, Hippias, I have done my part; that is my proof and demonstration that the *"lawful"* and *"law-observant"* are synonymous with the *"upright"* and the *"just"*; do you, if you hold a contrary view, instruct us.

Then HIPPIAS: Nay, upon my soul, Socrates, I am not aware of holding any contrary opinion to what you have uttered on the theme of justice.

SOCRATES: But now, are you aware, Hippias, of certain unwritten laws?

Yes (he answered), these held in every part of the world, and in the same sense.

Can you then assert (asked Socrates) of these unwritten laws that men made them?

Nay, how (he answered) should that be, for how could they all have come together from the ends of the earth? and even if they had so done, men are not all of one speech?

SOCRATES: Whom then do you believe to have been the makers of these laws?

HIPPIAS: For my part I think that the gods must have made these laws for men, and I take it as a proof that first and foremost it is a law and custom everywhere to worship and reverence the gods.

SOCRATES: And, I presume, to honor parents is also customary everywhere.

Yes, that too (he answered).

SOCRATES: And, I presume, also the prohibition of intermarriage between parents and children?

HIPPIAS: No; at that point I stop, Socrates. That does not seem to me to be a law of God.

Now, why? (he asked)

Because I perceive it is not infrequently transgressed (he answered).

SOCRATES: Well, but there are a good many other things

which people do contrary to law; only the penalty, I take it, affixed to the transgression of the divine code is certain; there is no escape for the offender after the manner in which a man may transgress the laws of man with impunity, slipping through the fingers of justice by stealth, or avoiding it by violence.

HIPPIAS: And what is the inevitable penalty paid by those who, being related as parents and children, intermingle in marriage?

SOCRATES: The greatest of all penalties; for what worse calamity can human beings suffer in the production of offspring than to misbeget?

HIPPIAS: But how or why should they breed them ill where nothing hinders them, being a good stock themselves and producing from stock as good?

SOCRATES: Because, forsooth, in order to produce good children, it is not simply necessary that the parents should be good and of a good stock, but that both should be equally in the prime and vigour of their bodies. Do you suppose that the seed of those who are at their prime is like theirs who either have not yet reached their prime, or whose prime is passed?

HIPPIAS: No, it is reasonable to expect that the seed will differ.

SOCRATES: And for the better—which?

HIPPIAS: Theirs clearly who are at their prime.

SOCRATES: It would seem that the seed of those who are not yet in their prime or have passed their prime is not good?

HIPPIAS: It seems most improbable it should be.

SOCRATES: Then the right way to produce children is not that way?

HIPPIAS: No, that is not the right way.

SOCRATES: Then children so produced are produced not as they ought to be?

HIPPIAS: So it appears to me.

What offspring then (he asked) will be ill produced, ill begotten, and ill born, if not these?

I subscribe to that opinion also (replied Hippias).

SOCRATES: Well, it is a custom universally respected, is it not, to return good for good, and kindness for kindness?

HIPPIAS: Yes, a custom, but one which again is apt to be transgressed.

SOCRATES: Then he that so transgresses it pays penalty in finding himself isolated; bereft of friends who are good, and driven to seek after those who love him not. Or is it not so that he who does me kindness in my intercourse with him is my good friend, but if I requite not this kindness to my benefactor, I am hated by him for my ingratitude, and yet I must needs pursue after him and cling to him because of the great gain to me of his society?

HIPPIAS: Yes, Socrates. In all these cases, I admit, there is an implication of divine authority; that a law should in itself be loaded with the penalty of its transgression does suggest to my mind a higher than human type of legislator.

SOCRATES: And in your opinion, Hippias, is the legislation of the gods just and righteous, or the reverse of what is just and righteous?

HIPPIAS: Not the reverse of what is just and righteous, Socrates, God forbid! for scarcely could any other legislate aright, if not God himself.

SOCRATES: It would seem then, Hippias, the gods themselves are well pleased that "the lawful" and "the just" should be synonymous?

(Thrasymachus, from Plato, *Republic*, I, 338) [48]

The following is a conversation between Socrates and Thrasymachus, the sophist.

Listen, then, he said; I proclaim that justice is nothing else than the interest of the stronger. And now why do you not praise me? But of course you won't.

Let me first understand you, I replied. Justice, as you say, is the interest of the stronger. What, Thrasymachus, is the meaning of this? You cannot mean to say that because Polydamas, the pancratiast, is stronger than we are, and finds the eating of beef conducive to his bodily strength, that to eat beef is therefore equally for our good who are weaker than he is, and right and just for us?

That's abominable of you, Socrates; you take the word in the sense which is most damaging to the argument.

Not at all, my good sir, I said: I am trying to understand them; and I wish that you would be a little clearer.

Well, he said, have you never heard that forms of government differ; there are tyrannies, and there are democracies, and there are aristocracies?

Yes, I know.

And the government is the ruling power in each state?

Certainly.

And the different forms of government make laws democratical, aristocratical, tyrannical, with a view to their several interests; and those laws, which are made by them for their own interests, are the justice which they deliver to their subjects, and him who transgresses them they punish as a breaker of the law, and unjust. And that is what I mean when I say that in all states there is the same principle of justice, which is the interest of the government; and as the government must be supposed to have power, the only reasonable conclusion is, that everywhere there is one principle of justice, which is the interest of the stronger.

(Thrasymachus, from Plato, *Republic,* Book I, 343–344)

Because you fancy that the shepherd or neatherd fattens or tends the sheep or oxen with a view to their own good and not the good of himself or his master; and you further imagine that the rulers of states, if they are true rulers, never think of their subjects as sheep, and that they are not studying their own advantage day and night. Oh, no; and so entirely astray are you in your ideas about the just and unjust as not even to know that justice and the just are in reality another's good; that is to say, the interest of the ruler and stronger, and the loss of the subject and servant; and injustice the opposite; for the unjust is lord over the truly simple and just: he is the stronger, and his subjects do what is for his interest, and minister to his happiness, which is very far from being their own.  Consider further, most foolish Socrates, that the just is always a loser in comparison with the unjust.  First of all, in private contracts: Wherever the unjust is the partner of the just you will find that, when the partnership is dissolved the unjust man has always more and the just less.  Secondly, in their dealings with the State: when there is an income-tax, the just man will pay more and the unjust less on the same amount of income; and when there is anything to be received the one gains nothing and the other much.  Observe also what happens when they take an office; there is the just man neglecting his affairs and perhaps suffering other losses, and getting nothing out of the public, because he is just; moreover he is hated by his friends and acquaintance for refusing to serve them in unlawful ways.  But all this is reversed in the case of the unjust man.  I am speaking, as before, of injustice on a large scale in which the advantage of the unjust is most apparent; and my meaning will be most clearly seen if we turn to that highest form of injustice in which the criminal is the happiest of men, and the sufferers or those who refuse to do injustice are the most miserable— that is to say tyranny, which by fraud and force takes away the property of others, not little by little but wholesale; comprehending in one, things sacred as well as profane, private and public; for which acts of wrong, if he were detected perpetrating any one of them singly, he would be punished and incur great disgrace—they who do such wrong in particular cases are called robbers of temples, and man-stealers and burglars and swindlers and thieves.  But when a man besides taking away the money of the citizens has made slaves of them, then, instead of these names of reproach, he is termed happy and blessed, not only by the citizens but by all who hear of his having achieved the consummation of injustice.  For mankind censure injustice, fearing that they may be the victims of it and not because they shrink from committing it.  And thus, as I have shown, Socrates, injustice, when on a sufficient scale, has more strength and freedom and mastery than justice; and, as I said at first, justice is the interest of the stronger, whereas injustice is a man's own profit and interest.

(Callicles, from Plato, *Gorgias*, 482–484) [49]

The dialogue *Gorgias* falls into three divisions to which the three characters of Gorgias, Polus, and Callicles respectively correspond. In the first division the question is asked—what is rhetoric? In the second division, Gorgias, bettered by the arguments of Socrates, transfers his arguments to Polus. Callicles, in whose house they are assembled, is the third sophist to appear on the scene.

CALLICLES: O Socrates, you are a regular declaimer, and seem to be running riot in the argument. And now you are declaiming in this way because Polus has fallen into the same error himself of which he accused Gorgias:—for he said that when Gorgias was asked by you, whether, if some one came to him who wanted to learn rhetoric, and did not know justice, he would teach him justice, Gorgias in his modesty replied that he would, because he thought that mankind in general would be displeased if he answered 'No'; and then in consequence of this admission, Gorgias was compelled to contradict himself, that being just the sort of thing in which you delight. Whereupon Polus laughed at you deservedly, as I think; but now he has himself fallen into the same trap. I cannot say very much for his wit when he conceded to you that to do is more dishonourable than to suffer injustice, for this was the admission which led to his being entangled by you; and because he was too modest to say what he thought, he had his mouth stopped. For the truth is, Socrates, that you, who pretend to be engaged in the pursuit of truth, are appealing now to the popular and vulgar notions of right, which are not natural but only conventional. Convention and nature are generally at variance with one another: and hence, if a person is too modest to say what he thinks, he is compelled to contradict himself; and you, in your ingenuity perceiving the advantage to be thereby gained, slyly ask of him who is arguing conventionally a question which is to be determined by the rule of nature; and if he is talking of the rule of nature, you slip away to custom: as, for instance, you did in this very discussion about doing and suffering injustice. When Polus was speaking of the conventionally dishonourable, you assailed him from the point of view of nature; for by the rule of nature to suffer injustice is the greater disgrace because the greater evil; but conventionally, to do evil is the more disgraceful. For the suffering of injustice is not the part of a man, but of a slave, who indeed had better die than live; since when he is wronged and trampled upon, he is unable to help himself, or any other about whom he cares. The reason, as I conceive, is that the makers of laws are the majority, who are weak; and they make laws and distribute praises and censures with a view to themselves and to their own interest; and they terrify the stronger sort of men, and those who are able to get the better of them, in order that they may not get the better of them; and they say, that dishonesty is shameful and unjust; meaning by the word injustice, the desire of a man to have more than his neighbours; for knowing their own inferiority, I suspect that they are too glad of equality. And therefore the endeavour to have more than the many, is conventionally said to be shameful and unjust, and is called injustice, whereas nature herself intimates that it is just for the better to have more than the worse, the more powerful than the weaker; and in many ways she shows, among men as well as among animals, and indeed among whole cities and races, that justice consists in the superior ruling over and having more than the inferior. For on what principle of justice did Xerxes invade Hellas, or his father the Scythians? (not to speak of numberless other examples). Nay, but these are the men who act according to nature; yes, by Heaven, and according to the law of nature: not, perhaps, according to that artificial law, which we invent and impose upon our fellows, of whom we take the best and strongest from their youth upwards, and tame them like young lions,—charming them with the sound of the voice, and saying to them, that with equality they must be content, and that the equal is the honourable and the just.  But if there were a man who had sufficient force, he would shake off and break through, and escape from all this; he would trample under foot all our formulas and spells and charms, and all our laws which are against nature: the slave would rise in rebellion and be lord over us, and the light of natural justice would shine forth.  And this I take to be the sentiment of Pindar, when he says in his poem, that

'Law is the king of all, of mortals as well as of immortals;' this, as he says,

'Makes might to be right, doing violence with highest hand; as I infer from the deeds of Heracles, for without buying them—'

—I do not remember the exact words, but the meaning is, that without buying them, and without their being given to him, he carried off the oxen of Geryon, according to the law of natural right, and that the oxen and other possessions of the weaker and inferior properly belong to the stronger and superior.

(Isocrates, *Panegyricus*, 75–78)

In the excerpt below, Isocrates points out the high qualities of the former citizens of Greece and indicates that they were responsible for the later achievements of the citizens of Hellas.

Now the men who are responsible for our greatest blessings and deserve our highest praise are, I conceive, those who risked their bodies in defence of Hellas; and yet we cannot in justice fail to recall also those who lived before this war and were the ruling power in each of the two states; for they it was who, in good time, trained the coming generation and turned the masses of the people toward virtue, and made of them stern foemen of the barbarians.  For they did not slight the commonwealth, nor seek to profit by it as their own possession, nor yet neglect it as the concern of others; but were as careful of the public revenues as of their private property, yet abstained from them as men ought from that to which they have no right.  Nor did they estimate well-being by the standard of money, but in their regard that man seemed to have laid up the securest fortune and the noblest who so ordered his life that he should win the highest repute for himself and leave to his children the greatest name; neither did they vie with one another in temerity, nor did they cultivate recklessness in themselves, but thought it a more dreadful thing to be charged with dishonour by their countrymen than to die honourably for their country; and they blushed more for the sins of the commonwealth than men do nowadays for their own.

(Isocrates, *Panegyricus*, 78–79)

The reason for this was that they gave heed to the laws to see that they should be exact and good—not so much the laws about private contracts as those which have to do with men's daily habits of life; for they understood that for good and true men there would be no need of many written laws, but that if they started with a few principles of agreement they would readily be of one mind as to both private and public affairs.

(Demosthenes, *On the Embassy*, 296–297)

In the following passage Demosthenes attacks Eubulus for defending Aeschines. He expresses his belief in what justice in a democratic state should be.

I would have no man acquitted or doomed, to please any individual. Only let us be sure that the man whose actions acquit or condemn him will receive from you the verdict he deserves. That is the true democratic principle.

(Demosthenes, *On The Crown*, 123–124)

Demosthenes criticizes Aeschines' method of attacking him and suggests the proper method of bringing a culprit to justice.

The difference between abuse and accusation is, I imagine, that an accusation is founded upon crimes, for which the penalties are assigned by law; abuse, upon such slanders as their own character leads enemies to utter about one another.

And I conceive that our forefathers built these courts of law, not that we might assemble you here and revile one another with improper expressions suggested by our adversary's private life, but that we might convict any one who happens to have committed some crime against the State.

## 11. COMPARATIVE GOVERNMENT

### (Aeschylus, *Prometheus Bound*, l. 225–229)

In this passage, Prometheus reveals his story to the chorus. He tells of the service he was to Zeus and how ill Zeus repaid him for his service.

PROMETHEUS: Such profit did the tyrant of Heaven have of me and with such foul return as this did he make requital; for it is a disease that somehow inheres in tyranny to have no faith in friends.

### (Euripides, *The Suppliants*, l. 399–456)

A messenger arrives from Creon warning Theseus not to make war on Thebes. The ensuing discussion between the messenger, who lauds dictatorship, and Theseus, who upholds democracy, is similar to modern discussions on the subject.

HERALD:  Your despot, who?—to whom must I proclaim
The words of Creon, lord of Cadmus' land
Since Etcocles by the hand was slain
Of Polyneices by the sevenfold gates?
THESEUS:  First, stranger, with false note thy speech began,
Seeking a despot here.  Our state is ruled
Not of one only man: Athens is free.
Her people in the order of their course
Rule year by year, bestowing on the rich
Advantage none; the poor hath equal right.
HERALD:  One advantage hast thou given me, as to one
That playeth draughts:—the city whence I come
By one man, not by any mob, is swayed.
There is none there who, slavering them with talk,

This way and that way twists them for his gain,
Is popular now, and humours all their bent;
Now, laying on others blame for mischief done,
He cloaks his faults, and slips through justice' net.

How should the mob which reason all awry
Have power to pilot straight a nation's course?
For time bestoweth better lessoning
Than haste.  But yon poor delver of the ground,
How shrewd soe'er, by reason of his toil
Can nowise oversee the general weal.
Realm-ruining in the wise man's sight is this,
When the vile tonguester getteth himself a name
By wooing mobs, who heretofore was naught.
    THESEUS:  An eloquent herald this, a speech-crammed bab-
        bler!
But, since thou hast plunged into this strife, hear me:—
'Twas thou flung'st down this challenge unto parley:—
No worse foe than the despot hath a state,
Under whom, first, can be no common laws,
But one rules, keeping in his private hands
The law: so is equality no more.
But when the laws are written, then the weak
And wealthy have alike but equal right.
Yea, even the weaker may fling back the scoff
Against the prosperous, if he be reviled;
And, armed with right, the less o'ercomes the great.
Thus Freedom speaks:—"What man desires to bring
Good counsel for his country to the people?"
Who chooseth this is famous: who will not,
Keeps silence.  Can equality further go?
More—when the people piloteth the land,
She joyeth in young champions native-born:
But in a king's eyes this is hatefullest:
Yea, the land's best whose wisdom he discerns,
He slayeth, fearing lest they shake his throne.

How can a state be stablished then in strength,
When, even as sweeps the scythe o'er springtide mead,
One lops the brave young hearts like flower-blooms?
What boots it to win wealth and store for sons,
When all one's toil but swells a despot's hoard?
Or to rear maiden daughters virtuously
To be a king's sweet morsels at his will,
And tears to them that dressed this dish for him?
May I die ere I see my daughters ravished!
Such answering shaft to thine do I hurl back.

(Herodotus, *History*, Book III, 80–81)

The following excerpt consists of a comparison of oligarchic, monarchical, and democratic forms of government. Otanes, a Persian, is
speaking, but there can be no doubt that the ideas belonged to Herodotus.

When the tumult had subsided and more than five days
had elapsed, those who had risen against the Magians began
to take counsel about the general state, and there were spoken
speeches which some of the Hellenes do not believe were really
uttered, but spoken they were nevertheless.  On the one hand
Otanes urged that they should resign the government into the
hands of the whole body of the Persians, and his words were
as follows: "To me it seems best that no single one of us should
henceforth be ruler for that is neither pleasant nor profitable.
Ye saw the insolent temper of Cambyses, to what lengths it
went, and ye have had experience also of the insolence of the
Magian: and how should the rule of one alone be a well-ordered
thing, seeing that the monarch may do what he desires without
rendering any account of his acts?   Even the best of all men,
if he were placed in this position, would be caused by it to
change from his wonted disposition; for insolence is engendered
in him by the good things which he possesses, and envy is
implanted in man from the beginning; and having these two
things, he has all vice; for he does many deeds of reckless
wrong, partly moved by insolence proceeding from satiety, and
partly by envy.  And yet a despot at least ought to have been

free from envy, seeing that he has all manner of good things.
He is however naturally in just the opposite temper towards his
subjects; for he grudges to the nobles that they should survive
and live, but delights in the basest of the citizens, and he is
more ready than any other man to receive calumnies. Then of
all things he is the most inconsistent; for if you express admira-
tion of him moderately, he is offended that no very great court
is paid to him, whereas if you pay court to him extravagantly,
he is offended with you for being a flatterer. And the most important matter of all is that which I am about to say,—he
disturbs the customs handed down from our fathers, he is a
ravisher of women, and he puts men to death without trial. On
the other hand the rule of many has first a name attaching to it
which is the fairest of all names, that is to say 'Equality'; next,
the multitude does none of those things which the monarch
does: offices of state are exercised by lot, and the magistrates
are compelled to render account of their action; and finally all
matters of deliberation are referred to the public assembly. I
therefore give as my opinion that we let monarchy go and increase the power of the multitude; for in the many is contained
everything."

This was the opinion expressed by Otanes; but Megabyzos
urged that they should entrust matters to the rule of a few, saying these words: "That which Otanes said in opposition to a
tyranny, let it be counted as said for me also, but in that which
he said urging that we should make over the power to the multitude, he has missed the best counsel; for nothing is more sense-
less or insolent than a worthless crowd; and for men flying from
the insolence of a despot to fall into that of unrestrained popular power, is by no means to be endured; for he, if he does anything, does it knowing what he does, but the people cannot
even know; for how can that know which has neither been
taught anything noble by others nor perceived anything of itself, but pushes on matters with violent impulse and without
understanding, like a torrent stream? Rule of the people then
let them adopt who are foes to the Persians; but let us choose

a company of the best men, and to them attach the chief power; for in the number of these we shall ourselves also be, and it is likely that the resolutions taken by the best men will be the best."

(Herodotus, *History*, Book V, Section 97)

Herodotus illustrates a shortcoming in democracy—that is, that the multitude is more easily deceived than a monarch or tyrant.

Aristagoras the Milesian, ordered away from Sparta by Cleomenes the Lacedaemonian, arrived at Athens; for this was the city which had most power of all the rest besides Sparta. And Aristagoras came forward before the assembly of the people and said the same things as he had said at Sparta about the wealth which there was in Asia, and about the Persian manner of making war, how they used neither shield nor spear and were easy to overcome. Thus I say he said, and also he added this, namely that the Milesians were colonists from the Athenians, and that it was reasonable that the Athenians should rescue them, since they had such great power; and there was nothing which he did not promise, being very urgent in his request, until at last he persuaded them: for it would seem that it is easier to deceive many than one, seeing that though he did not prove able to deceive Cleomenes the Lacedaemonian by himself, yet he did this to thirty thousand Athenians.

(Pericles, from Thucydides, II, 60) [50]

The Athenians, upset by their losses in the Peloponnesian War, turn on their leader, Pericles. He answers them in the following manner, reprimanding them for their lack of foresight.

'I was expecting this outburst of indignation; the causes of it are not unknown to me. And I have summoned an assembly that I may remind you of your resolutions and reprove you for your inconsiderate anger against me, and want of fortitude in misfortune. In my judgment it would be better for individuals themselves that the citizens should suffer and the state flourish than that the citizens should flourish and the state suffer. A private man, however successful in his own dealings, if his country perish is involved in her destruction; but if he be an unprosperous citizen of a prosperous city he is more likely to recover. Seeing then that the states can bear the misfortunes of individuals, but individuals cannot bear the misfortunes of the state, let us all stand by our country and not do what you are doing now, who because you are stunned by your private calamities are letting go the common hope of safety, and condemning not only me who advised, but yourselves who consented to, the war.

(Thucydides, *History*, Book II, 65)

Thucydides is referring to Pericles in the excerpt given below.

The reason of the difference was that he, deriving authority from his capacity and acknowledged worth, being also a man of transparent integrity, was able to control the multitude in a free spirit; he led them rather than was led by them; for, not seeking power by dishonest arts, he had no need to say pleasant things, but, on the strength of his own high character, could venture to oppose and even to anger them. When he saw them unseasonably elated and arrogant, his words humbled and awed them; and, when they were depressed by groundless fears, he sought to reanimate their confidence. Thus Athens, though still in name a democracy, was in fact ruled by her greatest citizen. But, his successors were more on an equality with one another, and, each one struggling to be first himself, they were ready to sacrifice the whole conduct of affairs to the whims of the people. Such weakness in a great and imperial city led to many errors, of which the greatest was the Sicilian expedition; not that the Athenians miscalculated their enemy's power, but they themselves, instead of consulting for the interests of the expedition which they had sent out, were occupied in intriguing against one another for the leadership of the democracy, and not only grew remiss in the management of the army, but became embroiled, for the first time, in civil strife.

216 SOCIAL THOUGHT AMONG THE EARLY GREEKS

(Thucydides, Book VIII, 97)

In the following extract, Thucydides is of the opinion that the Politeia which was established in Athens after the fall of the Four Hundred was not merely superior to democracy, but was the only good constitution that Athens had enjoyed in its lifetime.

When the news came the Athenians in their extremity still contrived to man twenty ships, and immediately summoned an assembly (the first of many) in the place called the Pnyx, where they had always been in the habit of meeting; at which assembly they deposed the Four Hundred, and voted that the government should be in the hands of the Five Thousand; this number was to include all who could furnish themselves with arms. No one was to receive pay for holding any office, on pain of falling under a curse. In the numerous other assemblies which were afterwards held they re-appointed Nomothetae, and by a series of decrees established a constitution. This government during its early days was the best which the Athenians ever enjoyed within my memory. Oligarchy and Democracy were duly attempered. And thus after the miserable state into which she had fallen, the city was again able to raise her head. The people also passed a vote recalling Alcibiades and others from exile, and sending to him and to the army in Samos exhorted them to act vigorously.

(Cleon, from Thucydides, III, 37) [51]

Cleon believes that a democracy cannot manage an empire well.

I have remarked again and again that a democracy cannot manage an empire, but never more than now, when I see you regretting your condemnation of the Mitylenaeans. Having no fear or suspicion of one another in daily life, you deal with your allies upon the same principle, and you do not consider that whenever you yield to them out of pity or are misled by their specious tales, you are guilty of a weakness dangerous to yourselves, and receive no thanks from them. You should remember that your empire is a despotism exercised over unwilling subjects, who are always conspiring against you; they do not obey in return for any kindness which you do them to your injury, but in so far as you are their masters; they have no love of you, but are held down by force. Besides, what can be more detestable than to be perpetually changing our minds? We forget that a state in which the laws, though imperfect, are unalterable, is better off than one in which the laws are good but powerless. Dullness and modesty are a more useful combination than cleverness and licence; and the more simple sort generally make better citizens than the more astute. For the latter desire to be thought wiser than the laws; they want to be always taking a lead in the discussions of the assembly; they think that they can nowhere have a finer opportunity of speaking their mind, and their folly generally ends in the ruin of their country; whereas the others, mistrusting their own capacity, admit that the laws are wiser than themselves: they do not pretend to criticise the arguments of a great speaker; and being impartial judges, not ambitious rivals, they are generally in the right. That is the spirit in which we should act; not suffering ourselves to be so excited by our own cleverness in a war of wits as to advise the Athenian people contrary to our own better judgment.

(Athenagoras of Syracuse, from Thucydides, Book VI, 39) [52]

I shall be told that democracy is neither a wise nor just thing, and that those who have the money are most likely to govern well. To which I answer, first of all, that the people is the name of the whole, the oligarchy of a part; secondly, that the rich are the best guardians of the public purse, the wise the best counsellors, and the many, when they have heard a matter discussed, the best judges; and that each and all of these classes have in a democracy equal privileges. Whereas an oligarchy, while giving the people the full share of danger, not merely takes too much of the good things but absolutely monopolises them.  And this is what the powerful among you and the young would like to have, and what in a great city they will never obtain.

(Lysias, *Defence Against A Charge of Subverting The Democracy*, XXV, l. 25–35)

Throughout his life, Lysias showed himself to be a true lover of democracy.  In the following speech, however, he comments on the weaknesses and dangers of a democratic form of government.

You know that Epigenes, Demophanes and Cleisthenes, while reaping their personal gains from the city's misfortunes, have inflicted the heaviest losses on the public weal.  For they prevailed on you to condemn several men to death without trial, to confiscate unjustly the property of many more, and to banish and disfranchise other citizens; since they were capable of taking money for the release of offenders, and of appearing before you to effect the ruin of the innocent.  They did not stop until they had involved the city in seditions and the gravest disasters, while raising themselves from poverty to wealth.  But your temper moved you to welcome back the exiles, to reinstate the disfranchised in their rights, and to bind yourselves by oaths to concord with the rest.  At the end of it all, you would have been more pleased to punish those who traded in slander under the democracy than those who held office under the oligarchy.  And with good reason, gentlemen: for it is manifest now to all that the unjust acts of rulers in an oligarchy produce democracy, whereas the trade of slanderers in the democracy has twice led to the establishment of oligarchy.  It is not right, therefore, to hearken many times to the counsels of men whose advice has not even once resulted in your profit.

And you should consider that, in the Piraeus party, those who are in highest repute, who have run the greatest risk, and who have rendered you the most services, had often before exhorted your people to abide by their oaths and covenants, since they held this to be the bulwark of democracy: for they felt that it would give the party of the town immunity from the consequences of the past, and the party of the Piraeus an assurance of the most lasting permanence of the constitution. For these are the men whom you would be far more justified in trusting than those who, as exiles, owed their deliverance to others and, now that they have returned, are taking up the slanderer's trade. In my opinion, gentlemen of the jury, those among our people remaining in the city who shared my views have clearly proved, both under oligarchy and under democracy, what manner of citizens they are. But the men who give us good cause to wonder what they would have done if they had been allowed to join the Thirty are the men who now, in a democracy, imitate those rulers; who have made a rapid advance from poverty to wealth, and who hold a number of offices without rendering an account of any; who instead of concord have created mutual suspicion, and who have declared war instead of peace; and who have caused us to be distrusted by the Greeks. Authors of all these troubles and of many more besides, and differing no whit from the Thirty,—save that the latter pursued the same ends as theirs during an oligarchy, while these men follow their example in a democracy—they make it their business to maltreat in this light fashion any person they may wish, as though everyone else were guilty, and they had proved themselves men of the highest virtue. (Nay, it is not so much they who give cause for wonder as you, who suppose that there is a democracy, whereas things are done just as they please, and punishment falls, not on those who have injured your people, but on those who refuse to yield their own possessions.) And they would sooner have the city diminished than raised to greatness and freedom by others: they consider that their perils in the Piraeus give them licence now to do just as they please, while, if later on you obtain deliverance through others, they themselves will be swept away, and those others will be advanced in power. So they combine to obstruct any efforts that others may make for your benefit. But their purpose is readily detected by any observer: for they are not anxious to hide themselves, but are rather ashamed not to be reputed villains; while you partly see the mischief for yourselves, and partly hear it from many other persons. As for us, gentlemen, we consider that you are bound by your duty towards all the citizens to abide by your own covenants and your oaths: nevertheless, when we see justice done upon the authors of your troubles, we remember your former experiences, and condone you; but when you show yourselves openly chastising the innocent along with the guilty, by the same vote you will be involving us all in suspicion. . . .

(Isocrates, To Nicocles, 14–17)

Speaking, then, of forms of government (for this was the subject I set out to lay before you), I imagine that we all believe that it is altogether monstrous that the good and the bad should be thought worthy of the same privileges, and that it is of the very essence of justice that distinctions should be made between them, and that those who are unlike should not be treated alike but should fare and be rewarded in each case according to their deserts. Now oligarchies and democracies seek equality for those who share in the administration of them; and the doctrine is in high favour in those governments that one man should not have the power to get more than another—a principle which works in the interests of the worthless! Monarchies, on the other hand, make the highest award to the best man, the next highest to the next best, and in the same proportion to the third and the fourth and so on. Even if this practice does not obtain everywhere, such at least is the intention of the polity. And, mark you, monarchies more than other governments keep an appraising eye upon the characters and actions of men, as everyone will admit. Who, then, that is of sound mind would not prefer to share in a form of government under which his own worth shall not pass unnoticed, rather than be lost in the hurly-burly of the mob and not be recognized for what he is? Furthermore, we should be right in pronouncing monarchy also a milder government, in proportion as it is easier

to give heed to the will of a single person than to please many
and manifold minds.

(Isocrates, *On The Peace*, 112–113)

Is it not true that when men obtain unlimited power they
find themselves at once in the coils of so many troubles that
they are compelled to make war upon all their citizens, to hate
those from whom they have suffered no wrong whatsoever, to
suspect their own friends and daily companions, to entrust the
safety of their persons to hirelings whom they have never even
seen, to fear no less those who guard their lives than those who
plot against them, and to be so suspicious towards all men as
not to feel secure even in the company of their nearest
kin? . . .

And when men who are of the foremost rank and of the
greatest reputation are enamoured of so many evils, is it any
wonder that the rest of the world covets other evils of the same
kind?

(Aeschines, *Timarchus*, 4–6) [58]

Aeschines gives a brief description of the three forms of government in
the following lines.

It is acknowledged, namely, that there are in the world
three forms of government, autocracy, oligarchy, and democracy: autocracies and oligarchies are administered according to
the tempers of their lords, but democratic states according to
established laws. And be assured, fellow citizens, that in a
democracy it is the laws that guard the person of the citizen and
the constitution of the state, whereas the despot and the oli-
garch find their protection in suspicion and in armed guards.
Men, therefore, who administer an oligarchy, or any government based upon inequality, must be on their guard against
those who attempt revolution by the law of force; but you, who
have a government based upon equality and law, must guard
against those whose words violate the laws or whose lives have

defied them; for then only will you be strong, when you cherish the laws, and when the revolutionary attempts of lawless men shall have ceased. . . .

(Demosthenes, *For The Liberty of the Rhodians*, 17–21) [54]

In this speech, Demosthenes supported the claim of the Rhodians against the oppression of Artemisia, widow of Mausolus of Caria. He failed in his attempt because there was much prejudice against Rhodes.

You may also observe, Athenians, that you have been engaged in many wars both with democracies and with oligarchies. You do not need to be told that; but perhaps none of you considers what are your motives for war with either. What, then, are those motives? With democracies, either private quarrels, when they could not be adjusted by the State, or a question of territory or boundaries, or else rivalry or the claim to leadership; with oligarchies you fight for none of these things, but for your constitution and your liberty. Therefore I should not hesitate to say that I think it a greater advantage that all the Greeks should be your enemies under democracy than your friends under oligarchy. For with free men I do not think that you would have any difficulty in making peace whenever you wished, but with an oligarchical state I do not believe that even friendly relations could be permanent, for the few can never be well disposed to the many, nor those who covet power to those who have chosen a life of equal privileges.

Seeing that Chios and Mytilene are ruled by oligarchs, and that Rhodes and, I might almost say, all the world are now being seduced into this form of slavery, I am surprised that none of you conceives that our constitution too is in danger, nor draws the conclusion that if all other states are organized on oligarchical principles, it is impossible that they should leave your democracy alone. For they know that none but you will bring freedom back again, and of course they want to destroy the source from which they are expecting ruin to themselves. Now, all other wrongdoers must be considered the enemies of those only whom they have wronged, but when men overthrow

free constitutions and change them to oligarchies, I urge you to
regard them as the common enemies of all who love freedom.
Then again, Athenians, it is right that you, living under a
democracy, should show the same sympathy for democracies in
distress as you would expect others to show for you, if ever—
which God forbid!—you were in the same plight.  Even if
anyone is prepared to say that the Rhodians are served right,
this is not the time to exult over them, for prosperous communities ought always to show themselves ready to consult the
best interests of the unfortunate, remembering that the future
is hidden from all men's eyes.

## 12. THE NATURE OF THE STATE

(Euripides, *Hecuba*, l. 629–657)

The chorus speaks these lines after Hecuba bemoans her fate and the
fate of her family and country.  Hecuba accuses Paris of bringing disaster
to Troy.  Thus the State's welfare is shown to be dependent upon the
individual's action.

CHORUS:  My doom of disaster was written,
The doom of mine anguish was sealed,
When of Paris the pine-shafts were smitten
Upon Ida, that earthward they reeled,
To ride over ridges surf-whitened,
Till the bride-bed of Helen was won,
Woman fairest of all that be lightened
By the gold of the sun.

For battle-toils, yea, desolations
Yet sorer around us close;
And the folly of one is the nation's
Destruction; of alien foes
Cometh ruin by Simöis waters.
So judged in the judgement given
When on Ida the strife of the Daughters
Of the Blessed was striven;

For battle, for murder, for ruin
Of mine halls:—by Eurotas is moan,
Where with tears for their homes undoing
The maidens Laconian groan,
Where rendeth her tresses hoary
The mother for sons that are dead,
And her cheeks with woe-furrows are gory,
And her fingers are red.

(Pericles, *Funeral Speech After The Corinthian War*,
from Thucydides, Book II, 35–43)

Pericles, who embodied all the lofty principles of Athenian democracy, sets out to describe the ideals and character of his people. This funeral oration was delivered over the men who had died in the first year of the war with Peloponnesus, 431 B.C. It is very likely that Thucydides colored this oration with his own thoughts; be that as it may, the work stands out as a remarkable treatise on the nature of life in Athens.

'Most of those who have spoken here before me have commended the lawgiver who added this oration to our other funeral customs; it seemed to them a worthy thing that such an honour should be given at their burial to the dead who have fallen on the field of battle. But I should have preferred that when men's deeds have been brave, they should be honoured in deed only, and with such an honour as this public funeral, which you are now witnessing. Then the reputation of many would not have been imperilled by the eloquence or want of eloquence of one, and their virtues believed or not as he spoke well or ill. For it is difficult to say neither too little nor too much, and even moderation is apt not to give the impression of truthfulness. The friend of the dead who knows the facts is likely to think that the words of the speaker fall short of his knowledge and of his wishes; another who is not so well informed, when he hears of anything which surpasses his own powers will be envious and will suspect exaggeration. Mankind are tolerant of the praises of others so long as each hearer thinks that he can do as well or nearly as well himself, but, when the speaker rises above him, jealousy is aroused and he begins to be incredulous. However, since our ancestors have set the seal of their approval upon the practice, I must obey, and to the utmost of my power shall endeavour to satisfy the wishes and beliefs of all who hear me.

I shall speak first of our ancestors, for it is right and becoming that now, when we are lamenting the dead, a tribute should be paid to their memory. There has never been a time when they did not inhabit this land, which by their valour they have handed down from generation to generation, and we have received from them a free state. But if they were worthy of praise, still more were our fathers, who added to their inheritance, and after many a struggle transmitted to us, their sons, this great empire. And we ourselves assembled here today, who are still most of us in the vigour of life, have chiefly done the work of improvement, and have richly endowed our city with all things, so that she is sufficient for herself both in peace and war. Of the military exploits by which our various possessions were acquired, or of the energy with which we or our fathers drove back the tide of war, Hellenic or Barbarian, I will not speak; for the tale would be long and is familiar to you. But before I praise the dead, I should like to point out by what principles of action we rose to power, and under what institutions and through what manner of life our empire became great. For I conceive that such thoughts are not unsuited to the occasion, and that this numerous assembly of citizens and strangers may profitably listen to them.

Our form of government does not enter into rivalry with the institutions of others. We do not copy our neighbours, but are an example to them. It is true that we are called a democracy, for the administration is in the hands of the many and not of the few. But while the law secures equal justice to all alike in their private disputes, the claim of excellence is also recognised; and when a citizen is in any way distinguished, he is preferred to the public service, not as a matter of privilege, but as the reward of merit. Neither is poverty a bar, but a man may benefit his country whatever be the obscurity of his condition. There is no exclusiveness in our public life, and in our private intercourse we are not suspicious of one another, nor angry with our neighbour if he does what he likes; we do not put on sour looks at him which though harmless, are not pleasant. While we are thus unconstrained in our private intercourse, a spirit of reverence pervades our public acts; we are prevented from doing wrong by respect for authority and for the laws, having an especial regard to those which are ordained for the protection of the injured as well as to those unwritten laws which bring upon the transgressor of them the reprobation of the general sentiment.

And we have not forgotten to provide for our weary spirits many relaxations from toil; we have regular games and sacrifices throughout the year; at home the style of our life is refined; and the delight which we daily feel in all these things helps to banish melancholy. Because of the greatness of our city the fruits of the whole earth flow in upon us; so that we enjoy the goods of other countries as freely as of our own.

Then, again, our military training is in many respects superior to that of our adversaries. Our city is thrown open to the world, and we never expel a foreigner, or prevent him from seeing or learning anything of which the secret, if revealed to an enemy, might profit him. We rely not upon management or trickery, but upon our own hearts and hands. And in the matter of education, whereas they from early youth are always undergoing laborious exercises which are to make them brave, we live at ease, and yet are equally ready to face the perils which they face. And here is the proof. The Lacedaemonians come into Attica not by themselves, but with their whole confederacy following; we go alone into a neighbour's country; and although our opponents are fighting for their homes and we on a foreign soil, we have seldom any difficulty in overcoming them. Our enemies have never yet felt our united strength; the care of a navy divides our attention, and on land we are obliged to send our own citizens everywhere. But they, if they meet and defeat a part of our army, are as proud as if they had routed us all, and when defeated they pretend to have been vanquished by us all.

If, then, we prefer to meet danger with a light heart but without laborious training, and with a courage which is gained by habit and not enforced by law, are we not greatly the gainers? Since we do not anticipate the pain, although, when the hour comes, we can be as brave as those who never allow themselves to rest; and thus too our city is equally admirable in peace and in war. For we are lovers of the beautiful, yet simple in our tastes, and we cultivate the mind without loss of manliness. Wealth we employ, not for talk or ostentation, but when there is a real use for it. To avow poverty with us is no disgrace; the true disgrace is in doing nothing to avoid it. An Athenian citizen does not neglect the state because he takes care of his own household; and even those of us who are engaged in business have a very fair idea of politics. We alone regard a man who takes no interest in public affairs, not as a harmless, but as a useless character; and if few of us are originators, we are all sound judges of a policy. The great impediment to action is, in our opinion, not discussion, but the want of that knowledge which is gained by discussion preparatory to action. For we have a peculiar power of thinking before we act and of acting too, whereas other men are courageous from ignorance but hesitate upon reflection. And they are surely to be esteemed the bravest spirits who, having the clearest sense both of the pains and pleasures of life, do not on that account shrink from danger. In doing good, again, we are unlike others; we make our friends by conferring, not by receiving favours. Now he who confers a favour is the firmer friend, because he would fain by kindness keep alive the memory of an obligation; but the recipient is colder in his feelings because he knows that in requiting another's generosity he will not be winning gratitude but only paying a debt. We alone do good to our neighbours not upon a calcula-tion of interest, but in the confidence of freedom and in a frank and fearless spirit. To sum up; I say that Athens is the school of Hellas, and that the individual Athenian in his own person seems to have the power of adapting himself to the most varied forms of action with the utmost versatility and grace.  This is no passing and idle word, but truth and fact; and the assertion is verified by the position to which these qualities have raised the state.  For in the hour of trial Athens alone among her contemporaries is superior to the report of her.  No enemy who comes against her is indignant at the reverses which he sustains at the hands of such a city; no subject complains that his masters are unworthy of him.  And we shall assuredly not be without witnesses; there are mighty monuments of our power which will make us the wonder of this and of succeeding ages; we shall not need the praises of Homer or of any other panegyrist whose poetry may please for the moment, although his representation of the facts will not bear the light of day.  For we have compelled every land and every sea to open a path for our valour, and have every-where planted eternal memorials of our friendship and of our enmity.  Such is the city for whose sake these men nobly fought and died; they could not bear the thought that she might be taken from them; and every one of us who survive should gladly toil on her behalf.

I have dwelt upon the greatness of Athens because I want to show you that we are contending for a higher prize than those who enjoy none of these privileges, and to establish by manifest proof the merit of these men whom I am now com-memorating.  Their loftiest praise has been already spoken.  For in magnifying the city I have magnified them, and men like them whose virtues made her glorious.  And of how few Hel-lenes can it be said as of them, that their deeds when weighed in the balance have been found equal to their fame!  Methinks that a death such as theirs has been gives the true measure of a man's worth; it may be the first revelation of his virtues, but is at any rate their final seal.  For even those who come short in other ways may justly plead the valour with which they have fought for their country; they have blotted out the evil

with the good, and have benefited the state more by their
public services than they have injured her by their private
actions.   None of these men were enervated by wealth or
hesitated to resign the pleasures of life; none of them put off
the evil day in the hope, natural to poverty, that a man, though
poor, may one day become rich.   But, deeming that the punishment of their enemies was sweeter than any of these things and
that they could fall in no nobler cause, they determined at the
hazard of their lives to be honourably avenged, and to leave
the rest.   They resigned to hope their unknown chance of
happiness; but in the face of death they resolved to rely upon
themselves alone.   And when the moment came they were
minded to resist and suffer, rather than to fly and save their
lives; they ran away from the work of dishonor, but on the
battle-field their feet stood fast and in an instant at the height
of their fortune, they passed away from the scene, not of their
fear, but of their glory.

(Isocrates, Areopagiticus, 26–28)

Isocrates, comparing the government of the founders of Athens with
the government as it existed in his day, finds the former far superior.

In a word, our forefathers had resolved that the people, as
the supreme master of the state, should appoint the magistrates, call to account those who failed in their duty, and judge
in cases of dispute; while those citizens who could afford the
time and possessed sufficient means should devote themselves
to the care of the commonwealth, as servants of the people,
entitled to receive commendation if they proved faithful to
their trust, and contenting themselves with this honour, but
condemned on the other hand, if they governed badly, to meet
with no mercy, but to suffer the severest punishment.   And
how, pray, could one find a democracy more stable or more
just than this, which appointed the most capable men to have
charge of its affairs but gave to the people authority over their
rulers.

(Xenophon, *Oeconomicus*, Chap. IV, 3-13)

This is a conversation between Socrates and Critobulus. The author (Xenophon) does not scruple to use Socrates as a mere mouthpiece to convey to the reader some of his own favorite ideas. "Which are the arts you would counsel us to engage in?" Critobulus asks. Socrates replies that they must not be ashamed to imitate the Persian king, who is said to set the highest value on the arts of war and agriculture. An account follows of the Persian system, in which militarism and the cultivation of the soil are helpmates of one another.

CRITOBULUS: Then which are the arts you counsel us to engage in?

SOCRATES: Well, we shall not be ashamed, I hope, to imitate the king of Persia? That monarch, it is said, regards amongst the noblest and most necessary pursuits two in particular, which are the arts of husbandry and war, and in these two he takes the strongest interest.

What! (Critobulus exclaimed); do you, Socrates, really believe that the king of Persia pays a personal regard to husbandry, along with all his other cares?

SOCRATES: We have only to investigate the matter, Critobulus, and I dare say we shall discover whether that is so or not. We are agreed that he takes interest in military matters; since, however numerous the tributary nations, there is a governor to each, and every governor has orders from the king what number of cavalry, archers, slingers, and targeteers it is his business to support, as adequate to control the subject population, or in case of hostile attack to defend the country. Apart from these the king keeps garrisons in all the citadels. The actual support of these devolves upon the governor, to whom the duty is assigned. The king himself meanwhile conducts the annual inspection and review of troops, both mercenary and other, that have orders to be under arms. These all are simultaneously assembled (with the exception of the garrisons of citadels) at the mustering ground, so named. That portion of the army within access of the royal residence the king reviews in person; the remainder, living in remoter districts of the empire, he inspects by proxy, sending certain trusty representatives. Wherever the commandants of garrisons, the captains of thousands, and the satraps are seen to have their appointed numbers complete, and at the same time shall present their troops equipped with horse and arms in thorough efficiency, these officers the king delights to honor, and showers gifts upon them largely. But as to those officers whom he finds either to have neglected their garrisons, or to have made private gain of their position, these he heavily chastises, deposing them from office, and appointing other superintendents in their stead. Such conduct, I think we may say, indisputably proves the interest which he takes in matters military.

Further than this, by means of a royal progress through the country, he has an opportunity of inspecting personally some portion of his territory, and again of visiting the remainder in proxy as above by trusty representatives; and wheresoever he perceives that any of his governors can present to him a district thickly populated, and the soil in a state of active cultivation, full of trees and fruits, its natural products, to such officers he adds other territory, adorning them with gifts and distinguishing them by seats of honor. But those officers whose land he sees lying idle and with but few inhabitants, owing either to the harshness of their government, their insolence, or their neglect, he punishes, and making them to cease from their office he appoints other rulers in their place. . . . Does not this conduct indicate at least as great an anxiety to promote the active cultivation of the land by its inhabitants as to provide for its defense by military occupation?

Moreover, the governors appointed to preside over these two departments of state are not one and the same. But one class governs the inhabitants proper, including the workers of the soil, and collects the tribute from them, another is in command of the armed garrisons. If the commandant protects the country insufficiently, the civil governor of the population who is in charge also of the productive works, lodges accusation against the commandant to the effect that the inhabitants are prevented from working through deficiency of protection. Or if again, in spite of peace being secured to the works of the land by the military governor, the civil authority still presents a territory sparse in population and untilled, it is the commandant's turn to accuse the civil ruler. For you may take it as a rule, a population tilling their territory badly will fail to support their garrisons and be quite unequal to paying their tribute. Where a satrap is appointed he has charge of both departments

Whereupon Critobulus: Well, Socrates (said he), if such is his conduct, I admit that the great king does pay attention to agriculture no less than to military affairs.

And besides all this (proceeded Socrates), nowhere among the various countries which he inhabits or visits does he fail to make it his first care that there shall be orchards and gardens, parks and "paradises," as they are called, full of all fair and noble products which the earth brings forth; and within these chiefly he spends his days, when the season of the year permits.

### 13. IDEAS ON WAR AND PEACE

#### (Pindar, *Fragment* 78) [10]

Harken! O War-shout, daughter of War! prelude of spears! to whom soldiers are sacrificed for their city's sake in the holy sacrifice of death.

#### (Pindar, *Fragment* 109)

Let him that giveth tranquillity to the community of citizens, look for the bright light of manly Peace, when from out his heart he hath plucked hateful faction, faction that bringeth poverty, and is an ill nurse of youth.

#### (Pindar, *Fragment* 110)

To the inexperienced war is pleasant, but he that hath had experience of it, in his heart sorely feareth its approach.

(Aeschylus, *The Persians*, l. 852–855)

After the spirit of Darius disappears, Atossa bewails the misfortunes that have come upon the state through her own son Xerxes. The chorus then makes the following remarks.

CHORUS: Ah me, in sooth it was a glorious and goodly life under civil government that we enjoyed so long as our aged and all-powerful King, who worked no ill and who loved not war, god-like Darius, ruled the realm.

(Aeschylus, *Agamemnon*, l. 434–456)

The chorus recite these lines when they learn that Troy has been conquered and the warriors are returning home. Aeschylus discusses the grim nature of war and its attendant hardships.

CHORUS: For Ares bartereth the bodies of men for gold; he holdeth his balance in the contest of the spear; and back from Ilium to their loved ones he sendeth a heavy dust passed through his burning, a dust bewept with plenteous tears, in place of men freighting urns well bestowed with ashes. So they make lament, lauding now this one: "How skilled in battle!" now that one: "Fallen nobly in the carnage,"—"*for another's wife*," men mutter in secret, and grief charged with resentment spreads stealthily against the sons of Atreus, champions in the strife. But there far from home, around the city's walls, those in their beauty's bloom are entombed in Ilian land—the foeman's soil hath covered its conquerors.

(Aeschylus, *Agamemnon*, l. 859–866)

Clytaemnestra replies thus to Agamemnon as he returns home to her after participating in the War of Troy for a number of years. Aeschylus depicts the sufferings of the women, who, although non-combatants, bear the brunt of war's unpleasantness.

CLYTAEMNESTRA: Untaught by others, I can tell of my own weary life all the long while this my lord lay beneath Ilium's walls. First and foremost, an evil full of terror is it for a wife to sit forlorn at home, severed from her husband, forever hearing malignant rumours manifold, and for one messenger after another to come bearing tidings of disaster, each worse than the last, and cry them to the household.

(Bacchylides, *Paeans*, 7) [11]

Moreover great Peace bringeth forth for men wealth and the flowers of honey-tongued songs, and for Gods the yellow flame of the burning of the thighs of oxen and fleecy sheep upon fine-wrought altars, and for the young a desire for disport of body and for flute and festal dance.

(Sophocles, *Aias*, l. 1185–1210)

The chorus of warriors recites the following lines just before Aias' burial. It is a lament on the horrors of war. The man who first taught men to do battle is cursed, and a real repugnance for war is indicated.

CHORUS: When shall the final count be told,
The endless coil be all unrolled
Of these long homeless-wandering years
Which bring the curse, the ceaseless strain
Of travail of the charging spears
Wide-swaying over Troyland's plain
For Hellas' sons' reproach and pain?

Oh had he vanished from men's sight,
Drowned in the heaven's abysmal height.
Or to all-havening Hades thrust,
Who first taught Greeks the leagued array
Of arms abhorred!—O battle-lust
Begetting battle-lust for aye!—
He ruined nations in a day.

No joy of garlands to enwreathe me,
    Nor wine-draughts deep,
Did that man's felon lore bequeath me,
No, nor sweet notes of flutes outpealing,
Nor any solace travail-healing
    Of nightly sleep.

'Tis long since dream of love beguiled me,
From love so wholly he exiled me.
Uncared for thus, thus utter-weary
I lie, while aye with dews thick-falling
My dank hair drips—all things recalling
One nightmare thought. 'By Troy the dreary
My watch I keep!'

(Sophocles, *Philoctetes*, l. 436–438) [55]

Neoptolemus tells Philoctetes of the death of a number of his friends. It is pointed out that the war affects the state adversely, since it takes the best of the young men and leaves the weaklings.

NEOPTOLEMUS: He too was dead. Lo, I will tell thee all
In one brief word:—war cuts off willingly
No villain, but the noblest evermore.

(Euripides, *Suppliants*, l. 476–495)

Creon's messenger tells Theseus and his people to beware of the war they are about to begin. He gives a graphic description of the evils of war.

HERALD: Look to it, nor, being chafed at these my
      words,—
Because forsooth a city free thou hast,—
Make arrogant answer from a weaker cause.
Hope is delusive; many a state hath this
Embroiled, by kindling it to mad emprise.
For, when for war a nation casteth votes,
Then of his own death no man taketh count,
But passeth on to his neighbour this mischance.
But, were death full in view when votes were cast,
Never war-frenzied Greece would rush on ruin,
Yet, of elections twain, we know—all know—
Whether is best, the blessing or the curse,
And how much better is peace for men than war;
Peace, she which is the Muses' chiefest friend,
But Retribution's foe, joys in fair children,
In wealth delights. Fools let these blessings slip,

And rush on war: man bringeth weaker man
To bondage; city is made city's thrall.
Thou helpest men our foes, and dead men they,
Wouldst win for graves them whom their insolence slew!

(Euripides, *Suppliants*, l. 745–749)

Adrastus speaks these lines when he hears that Theseus has been victorious in the battle with the Theban hosts.  This is almost a modern condemnation of war, with an appreciation of arbitration as a method of
settling quarrels between nations.

ADRASTUS:   Who strain the bow beyond the mark, and
     suffer
Much harm at justice' hand, and yield at last
Not to friends' mediation, but stern facts!—
O foolish states, which might by parley end
Feuds, yet decide them in the field of blood!

(Thucydides, *History*, I, 79)

When the Lacedaemonians had heard the charges brought
by the allies against the Athenians, and their rejoinder, they
ordered everybody but themselves to withdraw, and deliber-
ated alone.  The majority were agreed that there was now a
clear case against the Athenians, and that they must fight at
once.  But Archidamus, their king, who was held to be both
an able and prudent man, came forward and spoke as follows:—

'At my age, Lacedaemonians, I have had experience of
many wars, and I see several of you who are as old as I am,
and who will not, as men too often do, desire war because they
have never known it, or in the belief that it is either a good or
safe thing.

(Aristophanes, *The Acharnians*, l. 496–556)

Dicaeopolus, here dressed in beggar's garments, tells the chorus the
causes of the Peloponnesian War, pointing out that the people of Athens
have made war for frivolous reasons.

DICAEOPOLIS: Bear me no grudge, spectators, if, a beggar,
I dare to speak before the Athenian people
About the city in a comic play.
For what is true even comedy can tell.
And I shall utter startling things but true.
Nor now can Cleon slander me because,
With strangers present, I defame the State.
'Tis the Lenaea, and were all alone;
No strangers yet have come; nor from the states
Have yet arrived the tribute and allies.
We're quite alone clean winnowed; for I count
Our alien residents the civic bran.
The Lacedaemonians I detest entirely;
And may Poseidon, Lord of Taenarum,
Shake all their houses down about their ears;
For I, like you, have had my vines cut down.
But after all—for none but friends are here—
Why the Laconians do we blame for this?
For men of ours, I do not say the State,
Remember this, I do not say the State,
But worthless fellows of a worthless stamp,
Ill-coined, ill-minted, spurious little chaps,
Kept on denouncing Megara's little coats.
And if a cucumber or hare they saw,
Or sucking-pig, or garlic, or lump-salt,
All were Megarian, and were sold off-hand.
Still these were trifles, and our country's way.
But some young tipsy cottabus-players went
And stole from Megara-town the fair Simaetha.
Then the Megarians, garlicked with the smart,
Stole, in return, two of Aspasia's hussies.
From these three Wantons o'er the Hellenic race
Burst forth the first beginnings of the War.
For then, in wrath, the Olympian Pericles
Thundered and lightened, and confounded Hellas,
Enacting laws which ran like drinking-songs,

*That the Megarians presently depart*
*From earth and sea, the mainland, and the mart.*
Then the Megarians, slowly famishing,
Brought their Spartan friends to get the Law
Of the three Wantons cancelled and withdrawn.
And oft they asked us, but we yielded not.
Then followed instantly the clash of shields.
Ye'll say *They should not;* but what should they, then?
Come now, had some Laconian, sailing out,
Denounced and sold a small Seriphian dog,
Would you have sat unmoved?  Far, far from that!
Ye would have launched three hundred ships of war,
And all the City had at once been full
Of shouting troops, of fuss with trierarchs,
Of paying wages, gilding Pallases,
Of rations measured, roaring colonnades,
Of wineskins, oarloops, bargaining for casks,
Of nets of onions, olives, garlic-heads,
Of chaplets, pilchards, flute-girls, and black eyes.
And all the arsenal had rung with noise
Of oar-spars planed, pegs hammered, oar-loops fitted,
Of boatswains' calls, and flutes, and trills, and whistles.
This had ye done; and shall not Telephus,
Think we, do this?   We've got no brains at all.

(Aristophanes, *The Peace*, l. 335–360) [56]

The prospect of peace is delightful to the chorus.  They chant the woes of the long war and speak of the blessings of peace.

CHORUS:   I'm so happy, glad, delighted, getting rid of arms at last,
More than if, my youth renewing, I the slough of Age had cast.
TRYGAEUS:   Well, but don't exult at present, for we're all uncertain still,
But, when once we come to hold her, then be merry if you will;
Then will the time for laughing,

Shouting out in jovial glee,
Sailing, sleeping, feasting, quaffing,
All the public sights to see.
Then the Cottabus be playing,
Then the hip-hip-hip-hurrahing,
Pass the day and pass the night
Like a regular Sybarite.
    CHORUS:  Oh that it were my fortune those delightful
        days to see!
Woes enough I've had to bear,
Sorry pallets, trouble, care,
Such as fell to Phormio's share,
I would never more thereafter so morose and bitter be,
Nor a judge so stubborn-hearted, unrelenting, and severe;
You shall find me yielding then,
Quite a tender youth again,
When these weary times depart.
Long enough we've undergone
Toils and sorrows many a one,
Worn and spent and sick at heart,
From Lyceum, to Lyceus, trudging on with shield and spear.
Now then tell us what you would
Have us do, and we'll obey,
Since by fortune fair and good
You're our sovereign Lord today.

(Aristophanes, The Peace, l. 435–453)

    TRYGAEUS:  And as we pour we'll pray.  O happy morn,
Be thou the source of every joy to Hellas!
And O may he who labours well today
Be never forced to bear a shield again!
    CHORUS:  No; may he spend his happy days in peace,
Stirring the fire; his mistress at his side.
    TRYGAEUS:  If there be any that delights in war,
King Dionysus, may he never cease
Picking out spearheads from his funny bones.

CHORUS:   If any, seeking to make a Captain,
Hates to see Peace return, O may he ever
Fare in his battle like Cleonymus.

TRYGAEUS:   If any merchant, selling spears or shields,
Would fain have battles, to improve his trade,
May he be seized by thieves and eat raw barley.

CHORUS:   If any would-be General won't assist us,
Or any slave preparing to desert,
May he be flogged, and broken on the wheel.
But on ourselves all joy: hip, hip, hurrah!

(Aristophanes, *The Peace*, l. 551–581)

In this excerpt we find Trygaeus discoursing on the joys of peace.

TRYGAEUS:   O yes! O yes! the farmers all may go
Back to their homes, farm-implements and all.
You can leave your darts behind you: yea, for sword and spear
      shall cease,
All things all around are teeming with the mellow gifts of
      Peace;
Shout your Paeans, march away to labour in your fields today.

CHORUS:   Day most welcome to the farmers and to all
      the just and true,
Now I see you I am eager once again my vines to view,
And the fig-trees which I planted in my boyhood's early
      prime,
I would fain salute and visit after such a weary time.

TRYGAEUS:   First, then, comrades, to the Goddess be our
      faithful prayers addressed,
Who has freed us from the Gorgons and the fear-inspiring
      crest.
Next a little salt provision fit for country uses buy,
Then with merry expedition homeward to the fields we'll hie.

HERMES:   O Poseidon! fair their order, sweet their serried
      ranks to see:
Right and tight, like rounded biscuits, or a thronged festivity.

TRYGAEUS:   Yes, by Zeus! the well-armed mattock seems
         to sparkle as we gaze,
And the burnished pitchforks glitter in the sun's delighted rays.
Very famously with those will they clear the vineyard rows.
So that I myself am eager homeward to my farm to go,
Breaking up the little furrows (long-neglected) with the hoe.
Think of all the thousand pleasures,
Comrades, which to Peace we owe,
All the life of ease and comfort
Which she gave us long ago:
Figs and olives, wine and myrtles,
Luscious fruits preserved and dried,
Banks of fragrant violets, blowing
By the crystal fountain's side;
Scenes for which our hearts are yearning,
Joys that we have missed so long,—
—Comrades, here in Peace returning,
Greet her back with dance and song!

(Aristophanes, *The Lysistrata*, l. 586–596) [57]

This is the argument that Lysistrata has with the Magistrate when he
protests against the strike of the women. She points out that war inflicts
the greatest hardships on the women who stay at home.

MAGISTRATE:   Heard any ever the like of their impudence,
         these who have nothing to do with the war,
Preaching of bobbins, and beatings, and washing-tubs?
LYSISTRATA:   Nothing to do with it, wretch that you are!
We are the people who feel it the keenliest, doubly on us the
         affliction is cast,
Where are the sons that we sent to your battle-fields?
MAGISTRATE:   Silence! a truce to the ills that are past.
LYSISTRATA:   Then in the glory and grace of our woman-
         hood, all in the May and the morning of life,
Lo, we are sitting forlorn and disconsolate, what has a soldier
         to do with a wife?

*We* might endure it, but ah! for the younger ones still in their
  maiden apartments they stay,
Waiting the husband that never approaches them, watching
  the years that are gliding away.
MAGISTRATE:   Men, I suppose have their youth everlasting.
LYSISTRATA:   Nay, but it isn't the same with a man:
Grey though he be when he comes from the battlefield, still if
  he wishes to marry he can.
Brief is the spring and the flower of our womanhood, once let
  it slip and it comes not again;
Sit as we may with our spells and our auguries, never a husband
  will marry us then.

(Isocrates, Archidamus, 49–50)

Isocrates explains that peace is the best state of affairs for those who
wish to preserve the status quo.  Those whose position is unfortunate have
a great deal to gain from war.

There are those who condemn war and dwell on its pre-
cariousness, employing many other proofs, but particularly
our own experiences, and express surprise that men should see
fit to rely on an expedient so difficult and hazardous.

But I know of many who through war have acquired great
prosperity, and many who have been robbed of all they possessed through keeping the peace; for nothing of this kind is
in itself absolutely either good or bad, but rather it is the use
we make of circumstances and opportunities which in either
case must determine the result.  Those who are prosperous
should set their hearts on peace, for in a state of peace they
can preserve their present condition for the greatest length of
time; those, however, who are unforunate should give their
minds to war, for out of the confusion and innovation resulting
from it they can more quickly secure a change in their fortunes.

# APPENDICES

Since this book deals with the social thought of the early Greeks, it was thought advisable to include in separate appendices lists of the sources of the social thought of Plato, of Aristotle, and of the Hellenistic Age, so as to make available for those who might be interested a complete picture of Greek social thought. The source materials are classified in accordance with selected categories of social thought.

## APPENDIX I. *THE ATTIC AGE: PLATO* (427–347 B.C.)

1. Origin of Society and State
   *Republic*, II, 369
   *Republic*, IV, 433
2. The Social Mind
   *Republic*, V, 462
3. Origin of Classes in Society
   *Republic*, III, 415
4. On The Nature of Rulers in the State
   *Republic*, III, 412
   *Republic*, III, 414
   *Republic*, V, 473
   *Statesman*, 303
5. The Place of Eugenics in Plato's Ideal Society
   *Republic*, V, 458–462
6. On Poverty and Wealth
   *Republic*, IV, 421
   *Laws*, V, 742–744
7. On Community of Property
   *Republic*, III, 417
8. On Law
   *Statesman*, 294
9. Penology and Criminology
   *Laws*, IX, 862
   *Laws*, XI, 934
10. On the Position of Women
    *Republic*, V, 455–457

11. On Education
    *Laws*, VII, 796
    *Republic*, III, 410–411
    *Republic*, VII, 537
    *Republic*, VII, 540
12. Social Evolution
    *Laws*, III, 676–684

## APPENDIX II.  *ATTIC AGE:  ARISTOTLE*

1. Origin and Nature of Society and State
    *Politics*, I, 1–2
    *Politics*, II, 5–9
    *Politics*, III, 6
    *Nich. Ethics*, VIII, 12
2. Friendship
    *Nich. Ethics*, VIII, 1
    *Nich. Ethics*, VIII, 9
    *Nich. Ethics*, IX, 10
3. Origin of Government
    *Politics*, I, 2: 6–16
4. Comparative Government
    *Politics*, III, 1
5. On Private Property:  Aristotle's Criticism of Plato's Communism
    *Politics*, II, 2–7
6. Revolution and Its Causes
    *Politics*, V, 2
7. A Picture of the Ideal State
    *Politics*, VII, 4
    *Politics*, VII, 8–12
8. The Social Mean
    *Politics*, IV, 11
9. Influence of Physical Environment on Society
    *Politics*, VII, 7
10. On Education
    *Politics*, VIII, 1–3

## APPENDIX III.  *HELLENISTIC AGE*

1. Society as a Rational Process
    Zeus, from Diogenes Laertius, *Lives of Eminent Philosophers*, VII, 85 ff.
    Cicero, *The Tusculan Disputations*, IV, 23, 51
    Marcus Aurelius Antonius, *To Himself*, III, 4

*Ibid.*, VI, 14, 23
*Ibid.*, X, 2
Cicero, *De Officiis*, I, vii, 22
2. Stoic Conception of a World Society
    Seneca, *Ad Lucilium Epistulae Morales*, XCV, 51
    Cicero, *De Finibus*, Book III, xx, 67
    *Ibid.*, xix, 62
    Marcus Aurelius Antonius, *To Himself*, Book II, 16, 11
    *Ibid.*, Book IV, 4
3. The Individualism of Epicurus
    Diogenes Laertius, *Epicurus*, X, 140–141
    *Ibid.*, X, 148, 150–154
4. Friendship
    Cicero, *De Finibus*, Book I, XX, 66
    *Ibid.*, Book II, xxvi, 82
5. Social Evolution
    Polybius, *The Histories*, VI, 5–6
6. Checks and Balances in Government
    Polybius, *The Histories*, VI, 11–15
7. On the Nature of History: How It Should Be Written
    Polybius, V, 31–33
    *Ibid.*, VIII, 2
    *Ibid.*, XI, 19
8. The Influence of Geography in History
    Polybius, III, 57–59

# NOTES FOR CHAPTER I

[1] *Social Life in Greece from Homer to Menander* (London: The Macmillan Co., 1898), p. 1.

[2] "Sociology and the Epic," *American Journal of Sociology*, Vol. 6, p. 267.

[3] "All Peoples of whom we have records have had some thought about institutions, customs and human relations." (Charles A. Ellwood, *A History of Social Philosophy*, (New York: Prentice-Hall, Inc., 1938, p. 3).

Although Bogardus considers Comte the first to approach the study of society scientifically, he devotes a great deal of space to the Pre-Comtean period. He states that the Chinese "have furnished the most elaborate degree of social thought." (E. S. Bogardus, *A History of Social Thought*, U. of California, 1929, p. 44). Of Herodotus he states that he was "the first descriptive sociologist." (*Ibid.*, p. 72).

Frank Hamilton Hankins holds, too, to the view that sociology had its origins with the beginning of man as a thinking being. Although he considers Plato's *Republic* and Aristotle's *Politics* as the "two works that represent the highest achievements of the human mind in its efforts to answer the primary questions which have given rise to sociological inquiry," he accepts the social thinking of pre-Greek times as sociological in nature. This is clearly seen when he says: "Sociology is at once the oldest and the youngest of the social sciences. There probably was never a time during the past hundred thousand years when some men somewhere were not speculating on the origin of man and the meaning of human destiny. . . ." From this broad point of view it may be said that sociology began when philosophy and religion began, that is, with the origin of man himself." (Chapter VI, "Sociology," in Harry Elmer Barnes, *History and Prospects of the Social Sciences,* New York: Alfred A. Knopf, 1925, p. 255).

Othmar Spann would also trace sociology, not only to the Greeks, but back to man's conscious reflective thinking to include the Zend-Avesta of Zoroaster, Buddhism, and Pythagoras. (Hans Proesler, *Die Anfänge der Gesellschaftslehre,* verlag von Palm & Enke in Erlangen, 1935, p. 12).

"The beginnings of a scientific observation and classification of social facts, and of true generalizations from them, are preserved for us in the "Republic" and "Laws" of Plato, and in the "Politics" of Aristotle. . . ." (F. Giddings, *Principles of Sociology*, 1896, p. 5).

[4] Adolf Menzel, *Griechische Soziologie* (Vienna, Akademie der Wissenschaften, Sitzungsberichte, 216. Band, I., 1936).

[5] *Ibid.*, pp. 3–10, 10–13, 85–86.

[6] *Ibid.*, p. 14.

[7] See chapter II, section 7; chapter III, sections 1, 5; chapter IV, sections 2, 3, 4, 5, 6, 7, 8, 9, 11, 12.

[8] See Chapter IV.

[9] See Harry Elmer Barnes and Howard Becker, *Social Thought From Lore To Science* (New York: D. C. Heath & Co., 1938), Vol. I, pp. 5–10.

[10] Henry Osborn Taylor, *Ancient Ideals* (New York: The Macmillan Co., 1913) Vol. I, p. 151. Pericles' funeral speech, *Thucydides,* ii, 40, Jowett's translation.

[11] H. E. Barnes and H. Becker, *op. cit.*, p. 10.

[12] *Ibid.*, p. 146.

[13] See chapter IV, section 11.

[14] See p. 80.

[15] See p. 127.

[16] Joyce O. Hertzler, *The Social Thought of Ancient Civilizations* (New York: McGraw Hill Co., 1936), p. 337.

[17] See p. 128.

[18] See p. 131.

[19] See pp. 40–41.

[20] See p. 81.

[21] See p. 193.

[22] See p. 121.

[23] Karl Mannheim, *Ideology and Utopia,* (New York: Harcourt, Brace Co., 1936), p. 2. Translated by L. Wirth and E. Shils.

[24] J. B. Gittler, "Possibilities of a Sociology of Science," *Social Forces*, Vol. 18, No. 3, p. 350.

# NOTES FOR CHAPTER II

[1] *The Odyssey*, XI, 488ff., trans. by S. H. Butcher and A. Lang (New York: The Macmillan Co., 1930).

[2] John A. Scott, *Homer And His Influence* (Boston: Marshall Jones Company, 1925), p. 93.

[3] See Homeric *Hymn to the Delian Apollo*.

[4] C. M. Bowra, *Ancient Greek Literature*. (London: Thornton Butterworth, Ltd., 1933) p. 39.

[5] C. M. Bowra, "Sociological Remarks on Greek Poetry," *Zeitschrift fur Sozialforschung*, Jahrgang VI, Heft 2 (1937), p. 387.

[6] See p. 33, (*Odyssey*, I, 46–62).
See pp. 35–36, (*Odyssey*, XVIII, 130–142).

[7] See p. 34, (*Odyssey*, I, 230–244).
See pp. 34–35, (*Iliad*, XXIII, 862–871).
See pp. 36–37, (*Iliad*, IX, 533–534).

[8] See p. 35, (*Odyssey*, XIV, 83–84).
See p. 35, (*Odyssey*, XVIII, 130–142).
See p. 36, (*Iliad*, II, 591–600).

[9] See pp. 38–40.

[10] See pp. 47–48.

[11] See pp. 40–41.

[12] See pp. 5off.

[13] See pp. 54ff.

[14] See chapter II, section 6.

[15] See chapter II, section 7.

[16] All excerpts from *The Odyssey* are taken from the translation of S. H. Butcher and A. Lang, 1930. By permission of the Macmillan Company, New York.

[17] All excerpts from the *Iliad* are taken from the translation by Andrew Lang, Walter Leaf, Ernest Myers, 1927. By permission of the Macmillan Company, New York.

[18] *Hesiod, The Homeric Hymns, and Homerica*, translated by Hugh G. Evelyn-White, 1914. Loeb Classical Library. All the excerpts from Hesiod are taken from this translation.

[19] That is, in the poor man's fare as "bread and cheese."

[20] W. C. Lawton, *Successors of Homer* (London: Innes, 1898), p. 16.

[21] Early in May.

[22] In November.

# NOTES FOR CHAPTER III

[1] Howard P. Becker, *Ionia and Athens: Studies in Secularization* (Ph.D. thesis, University of Chicago, 1930).

[2] *Alcman* (c. 650 B.C.) was a Lydian of Sardis who came to Sparta as a slave. There he was liberated and given the rights of a citizen. He has been considered the inventor of love-songs, although he composed many hymns, paeans, processionals, and maiden-songs as well. Fragments of his verse are very scanty, most of it having been destroyed.

[3] *Lyra Graeca*, Vol. 1, edited and translated by J. M. Edmonds (The Loeb Classical Library, 1922). All the fragments in this chapter are numbered in accordance with this translation unless otherwise noted. Notation as to place of origin of the excerpt can be obtained by reference to the works themselves. It should be understood that all the excerpts from the same writer come from the same translations unless otherwise stated.

[4] *Elegy and Iambus*, Vol. 2, edited and translated by J. M. Edmonds (Loeb Classical Library, 1931).

*Semonides of Samos* (c. middle of the 7th century) was a native of Samos and founded a colony in the neighboring island of Amorgos. The longest fragment of his verse that has been preserved is the one quoted in the text comparing women to various animals. (Section 6.)

[5] *Lyra Graeca, op. cit.*, vol. 1.

Alcaeus (c. 600 B.C.) was a member of one of the noble families of Mitylene. He was a contemporary of Sappho and ranks high among the poets of this period. He took part in the war against the Athenians (606 B.C.) and was forced into exile by political enemies. Many of his poems are directed against the tyrants whom he hated, and against all his political enemies. At the close of his life he was pardoned by Pittacus.

[6] *Elegy and Iambus*, vol. 1, edited and translated by J. M. Edmonds (Loeb Classical Library, 1931).

[7] *Solon* (c. 638 B.C.) was one of the greatest of Athenian statesmen. As a young man he became widely known for his love of poetry, and later, for his fiery political poetry. Throughout his life Solon was extremely active in affairs of state and was famous for his economic and constitutional reforms in Athens. After his reforms were instituted, he was faced by much opposition, and to escape from it, he left Athens for approximately ten years. During this period he traveled a great deal, visiting Cyprus, Egypt, and Lydia. When he returned

to Athens there was much civil strife and his friend Peisistratus became tyrant. Solon is said to have died about 558 B.C.

[8] *Anaximander* (c. 611–547 B.C.) was a citizen of Miletus and was reputed to be a pupil of Thales. He was a member of the group of physical philosophers who flourished during this period. Little is known of his life. His reputation rests on the work he did on *Nature*.

[9] All excerpts from Anaximander are taken from the translations by John Burnet, *Early Greek Philosophy* (London: A. & C. Black, Ltd.).

[10] *Xenophanes* (c. 3rd or 4th decade of the 6th century B.C.) was born in Colophon, was exiled from his home, and lived both in Sicily and Catana until he settled in southern Italy in a colony called Elea. He was the founder of the Eleatic school of philosophy. He expressed many of his ideas, with much vigor, in long poems. He lived to a considerable age and had many disciples.

[11] *Elegy and Iambus, op. cit.,* Vol. 1.

[12] *Elegy and Iambus, op. cit.,* Vol. 1.

*Theognis* (c. 545 B.C.) was a native of Megara. He lived during the democratic revolution in the sixth century, and this fact is probably responsible for the attitudes expressed in his poetry. His reputation as a moralist was upheld for many years after his death. His poetry is well-balanced and filled with sound common-sense.

[13] *Simonides of Ceos* (c. 556–469 B.C.) was born at Iulis on the island of Ceos. He taught music and poetry on the island until he was invited to Athens by Hipparchus, patron of literature and art. Upon the death of Hipparchus, he went to live in Thessaly, where he received the patronage of two Thessalian families. After the battle of Marathon, Simonides returned to Athens for a short time. Hieron of Sicily extended an invitation to him, and Simonides spent the remaining portion of his life at the court of Hieron. Simonides was widely known and was held in great esteem by the most powerful and prominent men of his day. His poetry commanded great prices and was very much sought after.

[14] *Lyra Graeca,* Vol. 2, edited and translated by J. M. Edmonds (The Loeb Classical Library, 1924).

[15] Arthur Fairbanks, *First Philosophers of Greece* (London: K. Paul, Trench, Trübner & Co., 1898).

*Heracleitus* (c. 540–475 B.C.) was born at Ephesus into a noble family. The facts of his life are not available. He was considered one of the foremost of Greek philosophers and has been called the founder of metaphysics. His philosophy was based, in part, on the theories of the Ionian school.

[16] C. M. Bakewell, *Source Book in Ancient Philosophy* (New York: Charles Scribner's Sons, 1907).

[17] *Elegy and Iambus, op. cit.,* Vol. 2.

[18] *Mimnermus* (c. 630–600 B.C.) was born in Colophon. Nothing is known about his life. Most of his poetry (which he set to music) was on the theme of love.

[19] *Elegy and Iambus, op. cit.,* Vol. 2.

*Anacreon* (c. 560 B.C.) was born in Teos, a city on the coast of Asia Minor. It is probable that he went into exile with a large number of his townsmen when Cyrus the Great was conducting a war on the Greek cities of Asia (545 B.C.). This group founded a colony in Thrace. Anacreon acted as a tutor to Polycrates of Samos, upon whose death Hipparchus, who was then ruler in Athens, sent for Anacreon. At the Athenian court Anacreon made the acquaintance of Simonides. He fitted well into this court atmosphere and was highly popular for his gay wit and clever verse. When Hipparchus was assassinated, Anacreon returned to Teos, where he died a few years later. His poems are characteristically light court poetry with the emphasis upon love and drinking.

[20] *Elegy and Iambus, op. cit.,* Vol. 1.

*Phocylides* (c. 560 B.C.) was born in Miletus and was a contemporary of Theognis. Details of his life are not available. Very little of his poetry has been preserved.

[21] *Lyra Graeca,* Vol. 3, edited and translated by J. M. Edmonds (The Loeb Classical Library, 1927).

[22] *Elegy and Iambus, op. cit.,* Vol. 2.

*Archilochus* (c. 650 B.C.) was born at Paros. His father, a nobleman, founded a colony at Thasos to which Archilochus removed when he was hard-pressed for funds. Thasos was in frequent wars, in one of which Archilochus fought. Soon after this battle Archilochus travelled to Sparta, where he was banished because of his cowardice and the tone of his verse. From there he proceeded to Italy, and finally returned home, where he was slain in battle. The invention of Iambic poetry is attributed to him as well as its use in satiric poetry.

[23] *Lyra Graeca, op. cit.,* Vol. 2.

*Stesichorus* (c. 640–555 B.C.) was a native of Himera in Sicily. There are no available details of his life. He has been referred to as the poet "most like Homer" because of his epic verse.

[24] *Lyra Graeca, op. cit.,* Vol. 2.

*Ibycus* (c. 540 B.C.) was born in Rhegium, in Italy. He was a contemporary of Anacreon and spent some time at the court of Polycrates, ruler of Samos. Most of his life was spent in wandering from place to place. His lyric verse was mainly erotic in character.

[25] *Elegy and Iambus, op. cit.,* Vol. 1.

*Tyrtaeus* (c. 680 B.C.) lived in Sparta, but there is some question as to his place of birth. The second Messenian war was raging during his lifetime, and it is said that he took part in it. In his verse he tried to settle the internal disputes in Sparta and was highly interested in political affairs. Only twelve fragments of his poetry have come down to us.

[26] *Elegy and Iambus, op. cit.,* Vol. 1.

*Callinus* (c. 650 B.C.) of Ephesus is known as the creator of the political and warlike elegy. His countrymen were engaged in a protracted war with the Magnesians during his lifetime, and this fact is probably responsible for the character of his poetry, which sought to arouse patriotism among the Ionians. With the exception of a few fragments, his poetry has been lost.

[27] *Lyra Graeca, op. cit.*, Vol. I.

*Sappho* (c. 600 B.C.) was a native of Lesbos and was of aristocratic lineage. She has been called the greatest Greek poetess. Many tales have grown up about Sappho's life, but none of them are verifiable. Her poems, written to her pupils and friends, are in the nature of love lyrics reflecting the aristocratic way of life.

# NOTES FOR CHAPTER IV

[1] All the excerpts from the plays by Aeschylus are taken from the translations by Herbert Weir Smyth (Loeb Classical Library, 2 Vols., 1927). Volume I contains the following plays: *The Suppliant Maidens, The Persians, Prometheus Bound, The Seven Against Thebes.* Volume II contains *Agamemnon, The Libation Bearers, Eumenides, Fragments.*

Aeschylus (525–456 B.C.) was born at Eleusis into a family distinguished for its bravery in battle. Aeschylus himself fought at Marathon, and this fact is said to have influenced his life and his work greatly. He was a member of the old aristocratic party in Athens which was opposed to the democratic party. Twice he retired to Sicily because of a disagreement with political factions in the state. It is known that he was tried for impiety in his plays, but nothing remains of that trial. Aeschylus ranks as one of three greatest Greek tragedians.

[2] *Synopsis of 'The Persians' by Aeschylus.* Xerxes, the young king of Persia, goes forth to war with Greece and is prompted to do this in order to avenge his father Darius' cruel defeat at Marathon. The court hears no news of him for a long while. Then Atossa, the Queen Mother, comes to the Elders and asks them to interpret her dream, which predicted disaster for her son Xerxes. A courier arrives at the scene and tells of the annihilation of the Persian fleet at Salamis. Atossa performs sacrifices at her husband's tomb, and the chorus awakens Darius' spirit, which says that there shall be no further invasion of Greece, that the Persians will be hopelessly defeated at Plataea, and that all this is due to the foolish pride of Xerxes. Xerxes appears at the end of the play utterly downcast.

[3] *Synopsis of 'Agamemnon' by Aeschylus.* When Helen had fled to Troy with Paris, her husband Menelaus and his brother Agamemnon vowed to avenge this insult to Zeus, the guardian of the rights of hospitality. And so they called to arms countless numbers of men and made ready to set sail in their ships. But the goddess Artemis was angry with the kings, and caused the ill winds to blow and they were unable to sail. Therefore, in order to pacify Artemis, Agamemnon was required to sacrifice his young daughter Iphigenia. The Trojan war dragged for ten years. In the meantime Clytaemnestra, Agamemnon's queen, because she was lonely and embittered against Agamemnon for the slaying of their daughter Iphigenia, took as a lover Aegisthus, an old enemy of Agamemnon. As the play opens these two plotted Agamemnon's death, and after he returns victorious from the Trojan war, Clytaemnestra murders him and his captive, Cassandra, who had warned the Elders that disaster would befall their king.

⁴ All the excerpts from Sophocles are taken from the translations by Arthur S. Way (London: Macmillan & Co., Ltd.), in 2 parts; Part I, 1926; Part II, 1914. Part I contains translations of the following plays: *Oedipus The King, Oedipus at Kolonus, Antigone*. Part II contains *Aias, Electra, Trachinian Maidens, Philocteles*.

*Sophocles* (495–405 B.C.) was born at Colonus, a town about one mile from Athens, and he lived in Athens all his life with the exception of the time spent in military service. Sophocles received the broad education of Athenian youth and his accomplishments in music and gymnastics made his name famous even as a youth. In 468 B.C. Sophocles presented his first play in Athens, and between that date and his death he wrote one hundred and thirteen plays. Sophocles has been described as a man typical of the high ideals of the Periclean age of Athens. A much loved and widely known figure, he was highly prominent in the affairs of Athens.

⁵ *Synopsis of 'Aias' by Sophocles*. After Achilles was slain in the last year of the Trojan War, it was proclaimed that his armour would be given as a prize to the greatest of Greek heroes. Both Aias and Odysseus sought the prize. Odysseus was awarded the prize because his warcraft had done the greatest damage to the enemy, although Aias was considered the mightiest warrior among the Greeks. Aias was enraged by loss of the prize and he determined to kill Odysseus. Then the goddess Athena drove him to madness in order to protect Odysseus, and so Aias roamed the fields, killing cattle and sheep. When he was restored to his senses, he was horrified and killed himself. Menelaus, seeking to punish him, refused to allow him a burial. Odysseus, however, showing his nobleness, insisted that Aias, his enemy, be buried with all the honor due him.

⁶ *Synopsis of 'Oedipus The King' by Sophocles*. Laius, king of Thebes, sent to the oracle of Delphi to discover whether he would have a child. The oracle spoke and said that Laius was to have a son who would murder his father. Therefore, when a son was born to him, he pinned the child's feet together with a spike and ordered him to be put on Mount Kithairon to die. In a strange way, the child was saved and adopted by the king of Corinth, who called him Oedipus, which means "swollen-footed." When Oedipus grew up he consulted the oracle of Delphi in regard to his parentage and was told that he was destined to kill his father and marry his mother. Fearing this, he fled to Thebes. On the way he slew an old man and his servants. He delivered Thebes from the Sphinx, and so the people made him king, since Laius had never returned from a pilgrimage to Delphi. He then married Iokasta. Some time after this a pestilence fell on Thebes, and this brought to light that Oedipus had slain Laius, his own father, and married Iokasta, his mother, and the gods were punishing Thebes for his sins. When Oedipus discovered what he had unwittingly done, he put out his eyes and bewailed his fate.

⁷ *Synopsis of 'Oedipus at Kolonus' by Sophocles*. This play is an extension of *Oedipus The King*. (See note 6.) In this play Oedipus, blind and miserable, remained in Thebes until his sons had grown up. Then they disputed each other's right to be king and the people thought that Oedipus was to blame and

he was therefore exiled and made to wander in his old age with only his daughter Antigone to take care of him. When Oedipus and Antigone reached Kolonus, they settled there, Theseus promising Oedipus that he might be buried in that land.

[8] *Synopsis of 'Antigone' by Sophocles.* When Oedipus died, Polyneikes, his son, led the host of Argives against Thebes. His brother, Eteokles, the king, decided to fight against the invader. In the course of the battle the two brothers killed each other. Thus Kreon, their uncle, was left sole ruler of Thebes. The following day Kreon commanded, on pain of death, that no one bury Polyneikes because he had been a traitor. His sister, Antigone, not heeding Kreon's cruel declaration, attempted to bury Polyneikes. She was apprehended and sentenced to die. Her betrothed, Haimon, son of Kreon, in anger at the King's sentencing his beloved to death, committed suicide.

[9] *Pindar* (c. 522 B.C.) was a native of Thebes and a member of one of the most illustrious of Theban families. Although he was born in the Lyric Age, most of his contributions were made during the Attic Age. The great Persian War, in which Greece was victorious, coincided with the time of Pindar's life. As a young man, he went to Athens to study poetry. Upon his return to Thebes he became a professional poet, writing hymns of praise to various Theban heroes. One period of his life was spent in visiting his various patrons at Syracuse, Agrigentum, and Aegina. His poetry reflects the religious and mystical beliefs of his day and is highly moralistic in character.

[10] *The Odes of Pindar,* translated by Sir John Sandys (Loeb Classical Library, 1930). All excerpts from Pindar are taken from this translation.

[11] *Lyra Graeca,* Vol. 3, edited and translated by J. M. Edmonds (The Loeb Classical Library, 1927).

Bacchylides (c. 470 B.C.) was born at Iules, in the island of Ceos. Bacchylides lived at the court of Hieron of Syracuse, as did Simonides and Pindar, and is said to have been extremely popular within court circles. Practically no details of his life are known other than these few facts.

[12] *Synopsis of 'Trachinian Maidens' by Sophocles.* Deianeira was married to Herakles after he had conquered the River Achelous. As they were crossing the ford of the Evenus, the Centaur Nessus seized Deianeira, and so Herakles shot him with a poisoned arrow. Nessus told Deianeira to take his blood as a love charm and use it to win back her husband's love if she should ever lose it. Some time later Herakles fell in love with Iole. When the news of this came to Deianeira, she took out her love potion, smeared Herakles' garments with it, and sent them to him by way of a messenger. When Herakles put the garments on, he became poisoned and was near death. Deianeira, realizing that the love potion was really poison, killed herself. Then Herakles commanded his son Hyllus to place him on the funeral pyre and burn him, and to take Iole as a wife. This Hyllus did.

[13] All excerpts from Euripides' plays are taken from the translation by Arthur S. Way, in 4 volumes (Loeb Classical Library). Volume I (1925) contains: *Iphigenia at Aulis, Rhesus, Hecuba, The Daughters of Troy, Helen.* Volume II (1924) contains: *Electra, Orestes, Iphigenia in Taurica, Andromache,*

*Cyclops.* Volume III (1925) contains: *Bacchanals, Madness of Hercules, Children of Hercules, Phoenician Maidens, The Suppliants.* Volume IV (1928 contains: *Ion, Hippolytus, Medea, Alcestis.*

Euripides (485–406 B.C.) was born on the island of Salamis. He is said to have received an excellent liberal education under some of the best teachers of his day. His married life is said to have been exceedingly unhappy and this fact supposedly led him to make many bitter attacks on women in his plays. His first play was presented in 455 B.C., and the total number of plays he wrote was ninety. Of these only eighteen have survived. Euripides spent the last portion of his life at the court of King Archelaus at Macedon. Of the three great tragedians of Athens, Euripides is known as the greatest realist and the least didactic. His plays were widely popular during his lifetime and long after his death.

[14] *Synopsis of 'Medea' by Euripides.* Medea, after helping Jason to win the Golden Fleece, leaves her home to go with Jason to Greece. They reside in Corinth, and Medea bears Jason children. After ten years Jason is betrothed to the daughter of the king of Corinth, and Medea is banished from the land. Medea, angered over Jason's faithlessness, upbraids him and plots revenge. She sends her children with a gift to the bride, but as soon as the bride dons the apparel Medea has sent, she dies; for the garments have been poisoned. Her father, in attempting to save her, dies too. Medea then murders her own children, knowing well, that they would be slain in any case. When Jason hears that his children are dead, he is filled with anguish. Medea flees to her refuge in Athens, predicting her husband's death.

[15] *Synopsis of 'Hecuba' by Euripides.* Hecuba, the wife of Priam, and her daughters Cassandra and Polyxena, along with the other women of Troy, are enslaved by the Greeks after the capture of Troy. Polyxena is carried away to die as a sacrifice on the tomb of Achilles. Polydorus, Hecuba's son, had fled to his father's friend, Polymester, king of Thrace, with a great treasure. Polymester, desiring Polydorus' treasure, murders him and throws his body into the sea. His body is washed up to the shore of the Greek camp, where Hecuba lives. She vows vengeance upon Polymester. When Polymester comes to the camp, she entices him into her tent and there murders his children and puts out his eyes. He, in turn, predicts her death, the death of her daughter Cassandra, and the death of Agamemnon.

[16] All excerpts from Aristophanes' plays are taken from the translation by B. B. Rogers (Loeb Classical Library), in three volumes. Volume I (1927) contains the following plays: *The Acharnians, The Clouds, The Knights, The Wasps.* Volume II contains: *The Peace, The Birds, The Frogs.* Volume III (1924) contains: *Lysistrata, Thesmophoriazusae, Ecclesiazusae, The Plutus.*

Aristophanes' (448–388 B.C.) works remain the only source from which the facts of his life can be gathered. It is known that he wrote fifty-four plays, eleven of which have survived. It has been conceded by all critics of Greek literature that Aristophanes raised Greek comedy to its highest level. Aristophanes' habit was to select a burning question of the day and satirize mercilessly. Many of Aristophanes' plays are still being produced. His comedies were highly popular in his day, the audience relishing the clever mockery of all important Athenians.

[17] *Synopsis of 'The Birds' by Aristophanes.* In *The Birds*, two elderly citizens of Athens, dissatisfied with the atmosphere in their own city, set out to find a completely satisfactory city. In the course of their search they visit the Hoopoe, a bird who once was a man. The two Athenians, Pisthetaerus and Euelpides, suggest to the Hoopoe that the birds build a city in the air and become masters of the universe. The birds take up this proposal with great enthusiasm. Pisthetaerus and Euelpides each assume a task in building the new city, which is called Nephelococcygia ("cloudcuckootown"). When the city is finished, a messenger arrives from Zeus, who protests the lack of sacrifices being made. Meanwhile a bird brings the news that mankind is highly in favor of the new bird-city, and many are applying for feathers. Prometheus arrives and relates that the gods are starving. He tells Pisthetaerus that he must demand Zeus' sceptre and Basileia for a wife. Paseidon and Hercules, as envoys of Zeus, come in and finally accede to Pisthetaerus' demands. The play ends with the marriage of Pisthetaerus and Basileia amid much rejoicing.

[18] All excerpts from the speeches of Isocrates are taken from George Norlin's translations (Loeb Classical Library, 1928–29, 2 Vols.)

*Isocrates* (436 B.C.–339 B.C.) was born in Athens and his childhood was spent amid the devastation of the Peloponnesian War. During his long lifetime he saw Athens weak and besieged time after time. Isocrates lost his inheritance during the Peloponnesian War and was forced to seek a profession. In 392 B.C. he opened a school in Athens and had many distinguished pupils. Isocrates himself was a poor orator and many of his speeches were written for publication or for other men to deliver.

[19] *Synopsis of 'Archidamus' by Isocrates.* After the disastrous battle of Leuctra in 371 B.C., which was followed by three Theban invasions, the Spartans became exceedingly frightened. Epaminondas had entered Sparta and had established the city of Messene with fugitive helots and Messenians. Sparta's allies became anxious and sued Thebes for peace. A condition which Thebes insisted upon was that the city of Messene be recognized as independent. When the allies met to consider this, Archidamus III, son of king Agesilaus, arose and delivered this speech, declaring that Sparta ought to die rather than give up Messene, its rightful possession. The speech was written for him by Isocrates, and is a masterpiece of eloquence. It was written when Isocrates was ninety years of age.

[20] *Synopsis of 'On The Peace' (355 B.C.) by Isocrates.* In this speech Isocrates voices his idea of what might be a lasting peace for Athens. He urges that she give up the idea of empire and again be a leader of the Hellenic states, protecting each Hellenic state's freedom and independence from outside aggression. It is much the same idea as he expressed in the *Panegyricus;* he proposes a voluntary union of free states with a chosen leader.

[21] *Synopsis of 'Areopagiticus' (355 B.C.) by Isocrates.* Isocrates here makes a comparison of Athens in former days and Athens as it existed in his own. In the fourth century the citizens of Athens were taking much less part in actively

governing themselves. Isocrates points out the manner in which their fore-fathers had guided the state. He feels that there is an over-abundance of "freedom." He does not believe in pure democracy, but rather in a limited democracy of the Solonic type—a leadership by the best citizens for the benefit of all the citizenry. It is an eloquent speech and one which was received with much enthusiasm among certain groups.

<sup>22</sup> *Synopsis of 'Antidosis' by Isocrates.* It was customary for the wealthy citizens of Athens to bear the expense of public services. A trierarchy (fitting out a ship for war) was often the duty to be performed. Anyone who had to perform such a service could challenge another citizen to take over this service or to exchange property with him. The challenge was called "antidosis." Apparently, Isocrates went through such a trial and had to undertake a trierarchy. After the trial, Isocrates felt he had been misunderstood and consequently wrote this speech in defence of "his thought and whole life." This is essentially what the speech deals with, and is largely a defence of himself as a teacher.

<sup>23</sup> Arthur W. Pickard, *The Public Orations of Demosthenes*, Vol. I (Oxford: The Clarendon Press, 1912). Excerpts from *On The Embassy* are taken from this volume.

*Synopsis of 'On The Embassy' by Demosthenes.* In 346 B.C., when the Second Embassy, of which Aeschines was a member, gave their report to the Board of Auditors, Timarchus and Demosthenes announced that they would take proceedings against Aeschines for alleged misconduct of the Second Embassy, whereupon Aeschines attacked Timarchus for immoralities which he had practised in his youth and therefore had him disqualified as a prosecutor. Later (343), however, Demosthenes brought the charge of corruption as an ambassador against Aeschines. The trial was presided over by the Board of Auditors and held before a large jury. Aeschines was acquitted by thirty votes. The trial dealt essentially with Aeschines' policies and it is difficult to know whether he was guilty of disloyalty to the state. His views and methods differed from Demosthenes', but his sincerity is not to be greatly doubted. There is no doubt that Demosthenes believed that Aeschines had been bribed.

<sup>24</sup> *Demosthenes* (384–322 B.C.) was born in Athens. His father, a rich sword-maker, died when Demosthenes was seven years of age, leaving the boy to be brought up by his mother and his guardians. At the age of eighteen he claimed his father's estate, but his guardians refused to give it to him. This led to a long court trial in which Demosthenes pleaded his own case with much success. During this period he studied with Isaeus and learned a great deal about judicial procedure and rhetoric. Since his guardians had dissipated his estate, he was forced to support himself by writing speeches. As his fame grew he became more and more active in the affairs of Athens, and he has been called by many one of Athens' great statesmen. His most important speeches were on public matters.

<sup>25</sup> All excerpts from the speeches of Aeschines are taken from the translations by Charles D. Adams, *The Speeches of Aeschines* (Loeb Classical Library, 1919).

*Aeschines* (390–314 B.C.) was an Athenian by birth. There is some evidence to show that his parents were humble people, a fact which made it necessary for Aeschines to work during his childhood. His education seems to have been neglected. As a young man, he was first an actor and then a clerk; finally he emerged into political life. Aeschines carried on a lifetime feud with Demosthenes, and two of his most famous speeches were attacks on the life and work of Demosthenes. After losing a case in 330 B.C., he retired to Rhodes, but there is no record concerning his life there, or the year of his death.

[26] *Synopsis of 'On The Embassy' by Aeschines.* The occasion of this speech was the trial of Aeschines for treason on the second embassy. Aeschines had delayed this trial by bringing Timarchus, a friend of Demosthenes', to trial. The trial took place in the summer of 343 B.C., three years after the event. By this time popular sentiment had turned against Aeschines because of the disastrous results of the peace treaty of Philocrates. Demosthenes claimed that Aeschines had been bribed by Philip and had furthered Philip's plans. Aeschines gives the defense of his actions in this speech. He was acquitted by the court, but failed to right himself in public opinion.

[27] J. M. Edmonds, *Lyra Graeca*, Vol. 3 (Loeb Classical Library, 1927).

[28] *Works of Xenophon.* Translated by H. G. Dakyns (New York: Macmillan Co., 1897), Vol. 3. All excerpts from *Hiero* and *Oeconomicus* are taken from this volume.

*Xenophon* (431–357 B.C.) was an Athenian by birth. He was influenced greatly by Socrates in his youth. After the fall of Athens he was invited by Cyrus, a Persian Prince, to help him in wresting the throne from his brother Artaxerxes. He joined this expedition, writing an account of his adventures in the *Anabasis*. On his return, he served under the Spartan king Agesilaus at the Battle of Coronea in 394 B.C. against his own countrymen. Xenophon was much more sympathetic with the Spartan way of life than with the Athenian democracy. The Spartans awarded him an estate near Olympia, where he occupied himself with literary work.

[29] *Synopsis of 'Prometheus Bound' by Aeschylus.* Cronus was king in heaven until the gods revolted against his rule. The Olympians wanted to crown Zeus, his son, as king, but the Titans fought against Zeus and his friends. Prometheus, who was a Titan, warned by his mother Earth that only by craft would the battle be won, and knowing that the Titans relied solely on their own strength, rallied to Zeus' cause. When Zeus had triumphed, he assigned to each of the gods a function, and decided to destroy man and create a better race. Prometheus upset this plan because he was moved by pity for man's plight. He taught man the use of fire and also the arts and crafts. Zeus decided to punish him for this disobedience, and decreed that Prometheus be bound to a rock on the brink of the ocean for an untold length of time. Although Prometheus knows that he must suffer this punishment, he is helped by his knowledge that he has been treated unfairly, and also is possessed of a secret in regard to Zeus that will ultimately free him from his torture.

[30] All excerpts from Herodotus are taken from *The History of Herodotus*, translated by G. C. Macaulay (New York: Macmillan Co., 1914), 2 volumes.

*Herodotus* (490–428 B.C.) was born at Halicarnassus, in Caria. His family was a highly cultured one with a deep interest in antiquity. When thirty years of age, Herodotus was forced to leave home because of political quarrels. There followed a ten year period of extensive travelling for him, and he finally settled at Thurii, an Athenian colony in southern Italy. His great work is *The History*, which gives an account of the conflict between the Greeks and the 'Barbarians' which ended in the Persian wars. Although many portions of the book are highly unreliable, it is a remarkable work. Herodotus has been called the "father of history."

[31] All excerpts from Thucydides are from B. Jowett's translation (Oxford: Clarendon Press, 1881).

*Thucydides* (470–398 B.C.) was born in Athens, and had reached maturity at the outbreak of the Peloponnesian War. His family was wealthy and distinguished, and he apparently received all the advantages of a well-born Athenian youth. He was a general in command of an Athenian fleet during the war, but was relieved of his command because of his failure successfully to defend an Athenian possession in northern Greece. This led to his exile for twenty years, an extremely fortunate occurrence for him because it enabled him to follow the war very closely on both sides. This interest led to the publication of his great work *History of the Peloponnesian War*. Further facts about Thucydides' life are unknown.

[32] From *Greek Historical Thought* by Arnold J. Toynbee (New York: E. P. Dutton & Co., 1924). All Hippocrates' writings are taken from this translation.

*Hippocrates* (c. 460 B.C.) was born on the island of Cos, off the coast of Asia Minor. He is often referred to as the "Father of Medicine," and is said to have belonged to a famous family of physicians. Much legend has grown up around the life and character of Hippocrates, but the tales have not been substantiated. It is known that Hippocrates travelled extensively, having taught at Thrace, Thessaly, Delos, and Athens. Tribute has been paid to him for his wide knowledge of medicine and his conception of the role of a physician.

[33] *Lyra Graeca*, Vol. 2, edited and translated by J. M. Edmonds (Loeb Classical Library, 1924).

*Timocreon* (c. 520 B.C.) was known to have been a Rhodesian. Legend has it that he sold himself to the Persians when they occupied Rhodes. He has been described as a buffoon in classical literature, but little is known about his life.

[34] *Synopsis of 'The Plutus' by Aristophanes*. The plot of this play turns about the question of why the wicked are always prosperous, while the good are always poor. In the play the answer is suggested. Wealth must be blind. And so Aristophanes contrives to give Wealth back his sight, and in consequence the good are allowed to prosper.

[35] *Synopsis of 'Ecclesiazusae' by Aristophanes*. The title of this play gives some indication as to its character. It may be translated as "Women attending the Athenian legislative assembly." The play, in brief, has Praxagora and a group of women, disguised in their husbands' clothes, plotting to take over the government. They go to the assembly thus disguised and succeed in pushing through a proposal which gives the state over to the women. Praxagora has been elected to carry out this policy. She tells of the new methods and ideas

they are about to put into effect: everything is going to be held in common—all wealth, meals, and sexual relations. The rest of the play deals with these reforms, out of which many ludicrous situations arise. We see, in this play, Aristophanes' opinion of communism.

[36] All excerpts from the speeches of Lysias are taken from the translations by W. R. M. Lamb (Loeb Classical Library, 1930).

*Lysias* (459–380 B.C.) was not a native of Athens, but lived there for a number of years. His family was wealthy and widely known in Athens. Lysias studied rhetoric under Tisias at the colony of Thurii. When the thirty tyrants attacked the resident aliens in Athens, Lysias barely escaped imprisonment and fled to Megara. After the restoration he returned to Athens, but found his fortune gone. He took up the profession of speech writing for others, and his genius lay in being able to write speeches in character for the Pleaders.

[37] M. L. W. Laistner, *Greek Economics* (London: J. M. Dent & Sons, Ltd., 1925), pp. 52–62.

[38] Excerpts from "On The Crown" are taken from Arthur W. Pickard, *The Public Orations of Demosthenes* (Oxford: Clarendon Press, 1912), Vol. II.

*Synopsis of 'On The Crown' by Demosthenes.* Demosthenes was an important public figure of his time. He concerned himself primarily with the foreign policy of Athens, although he did make several speeches against men who proposed illegal legislation. At various periods of difficult diplomatic upheaval, Demosthenes was sent as his country's ambassador. He had a record for unusual success in these diplomatic feats. In the speech "On The Crown" he defends himself against the charges of Aeschines (long his enemy) that it was illegal to propose to crown any man until the Board of Auditors had examined him, and Demosthenes had not so been examined; that a grant of a crown could not be proclaimed at the Dionysia unless it was made by a foreign state; and lastly, that the description of Demosthenes' career which entitled him to the crown was based on falsehoods. A golden crown was often voted by the Athenians to outstanding citizens at the Dionysia. In reality, this speech was a defense of Demosthenes' entire career as well as of his ideas.

[39] *Synopsis of the speech 'Panegyricus' by Isocrates.* This discourse was published when Athens found itself in a miserable state. Her leadership in Greece had been broken by the Peloponnesian War. Sparta was continually making war on the Greek city-states, and factionalism was rife in Greece. Circumstances had grown intolerable, and it was at this time that Isocrates wrote this speech. Its theme, in essence, was that there must be concord among the Greeks and together they must conquer the "Barbarians"—that is, the Persians. The question of leadership arises, and Isocrates feels that Athens has unquestioned right to the leadership of the Greeks. He points out that Athens has always suffered for the sake of freedom for all the Hellenes. There is little question in Isocrates' mind that his plan is entirely practicable, and he outlines it very eloquently in this discourse.

[40] *Synopsis of the play 'Hippolytus' by Euripides.* Hippolytus, the son of Theseus (king of Athens) and Hippolyta (Queen of the Amazons), reveres Artemis, Goddess of the Chase, and is scornful of Aphrodite, Queen of Love.

This angers Aphrodite greatly, and she contrives to have Phaedra (his father's young wife) fall violently in love with Hippolytus. Phaedra's love is revealed to him and he is horrified. Phaedra, overcome by her love, dies. Theseus then blames his son for her death. He instantly wishes for Hippolytus' death, and, because of a previous promise by Poseidon, his wish is fulfilled. Later, Theseus learns that he has been mistaken, but it is too late to save Hippolytus, for he must now die. His father and the chorus are reconciled to his death because they realize that these events have been caused by the divine will.

[41] *Synopsis of the play 'Orestes' by Euripides.* After murdering his mother (Clytaemnestra) and her lover (Aegisthus), to avenge his father's death, Orestes is beset by madness as punishment for matricide. Electra, his sister, nurses him, and after a time his fury subsides. The citizens of Argos refuse to let Orestes rule, and are ready to stone him to death. The council meets and decides that Orestes must slay his sister and then kill himself. Menelaus, his kinsman, does nothing to help save Orestes and Electra. Orestes, wishing to avenge himself on Menelaus, kills Helen, Menelaus' wife. Suddenly Apollo appears and tells Orestes that he is to live in the Parrhasian land for a year, and then, cleansed in Athens from the stain of his mother's blood, he will marry Hermione, Helen's daughter. Electra will marry Pylades, and Orestes will rule at Argos so long as Menelaus rules at Sparta.

[42] *Synopsis of 'The Knights' by Aristophanes.* The play opens with two slaves discussing their stupid master Demus (the Athenian people). Demus has bought a Paphlagonian slave whom he adores, and he mistreats all others. As the play proceeds, it becomes clear that the Paphlagonian slave is Cleon. A struggle then ensues between Cleon and a sausage-maker for the leadership of Greece. After much violent abuse, the sausage-maker becomes ruler and rejuvenates Demus. The play is a direct attack on Cleon.

[43] *Synopsis of 'The Acharnians' by Aristophanes.* Dicaeopolis, a citizen of Athens, is anxious to make peace, and since the Assembly will not make peace with Sparta, he sends a messenger to make a private peace for him. The Acharnians, the war party in Athens, hear about this and attempt to stone Dicaeopolis to death. However, after argument to and fro, all opposition to Dicaeopolis disappears. The rest of the play shows the great blessings which Dicaeopolis has gained.

[44] *Synopsis of the speech 'Against Ctesiphon' by Aeschines.* Ctesiphon, a friend of Demosthenes, carried a motion in the senate that Demosthenes be awarded a golden crown at the Dionysia with a proclamation of Demosthenes' devotion to the state. In the Assembly, Aeschines claimed that the motion was illegal. The trial did not take place until six years had passed. Aeschines had the law on his side in claiming that Ctesiphon had made the motion illegally. However, the trial, in actuality, was a political contest between Aeschines and Demosthenes. In it, one of the two men had to lose his public position of prominence. Aeschines underestimated Demosthenes' popularity, and thus Demosthenes received a clear acquittal.

[45] *Synopsis of 'Electra' by Sophocles.* When Agamemnon returned home from the Trojan War, his wife, Clytaemnestra, with the help of her lover,

Aegisthus, murdered him. They also attempted to kill her young son, Orestes, so that no one would avenge Agamemnon's murder. Electra, his sister, sent him away to Phocis with a faithful old servant. Aegisthus and Clytaemnestra lived together and ruled Argos. Electra and her sister Chrysothemis lived in the palace with their father's murderers and hated them, waiting only for the day when Orestes would avenge their father's death. Orestes devised a plan whereby a messenger was sent to Clytaemnestra to say that Orestes was dead. Both Clytaemnestra and Aegisthus were taken off their guard by this news. Electra was broken-hearted. Soon Orestes arrived, and told her of his plot to kill his mother and her lover, and thus avenge his father's death. His plans were successful and he killed first Clytaemnestra and then Aegisthus.

[46] *Synopsis of 'The Suppliants'* by Euripides. When Theseus, a good king, ruled Athens, war broke out between Argos and Thebes. In the course of the war, many were slain. It was a customary practice to allow the enemy to carry away their dead and bury them. Now, when the Argives, who had been defeated, requested the bodies of the slain men of Thebes, Creon refused to give them up. Since lack of burial was the worst thing that could befall a man in Greece, the mothers of these men pleaded with Theseus to intercede in their behalf. Theseus was reluctant to do so at first, but later he led a battle against Thebes, was successful, and so brought back the bodies to their relatives. These were then given a rightful burial.

[47] *Works of Xenophon,* translated by H. G. Dakyns (New York: Macmillan & Co., 1897), Vol. 3.

Hippias (c. middle of fifth century) was a sophist, a contemporary of Socrates, and, like him, a teacher. His aim in teaching was to give his pupils weapons for winning arguments rather than to impart knowledge. Socrates attacked his methods again and again.

[48] Translated by B. Jowett (Oxford University Press, 3rd edition). All excerpts from Plato's *Republic* are taken from this edition. Material on the life of Thrasymachus is very meager. He was one of the later sophists.

[49] Translated by B. Jowett (Oxford University Press, 3rd edition). All excerpts from *Gorgias* are taken from this edition. Callicles was one of the later sophists.

[50] Pericles (c. 490–429 B.C.) was born in Athens into a distinguished family. His father was a commander of the Greek fleet and his mother was connected with the former tyrants of Sicyon. Pericles was taught by Damon in music, by Zeno in the powers of dialectic, and by Anaxagoras in philosophy. These men exerted a great deal of influence on his life and work. In 436 B.C., he helped to prosecute Cenion on charges of bribery, and from that period until his death he played an active part in Athenian politics. During his lifetime Athens reached its highest peak of prosperity and security. Democracy made great strides during this period because of the numerous reforms instituted by Pericles. Pericles has been called the greatest of Greek statesmen.

[51] *Cleon* (d. 422 B.C.) was an Athenian politician during the Peloponnesian War. He was the first prominent politician springing from the commercial classes in Athens. During Pericles' lifetime Cleon opposed him strongly, but

when Pericles died and Cleon became the head of the government, he too fought for democratic reforms. Cleon's rule was strongly criticized in both Aristophanes' and Thucydides' writings.

[52] *Athenagoras* (c. 415 B.C.) was a popular leader in Athens. Details of his life are not available.

[53] *Synopsis of the speech 'Timarchus' by Aeschines.* In this speech, Aeschines brings action against Timarchus for breaking the law. The specific charges are immorality and corruptness in public life.

[54] J. H. Vince, *Demosthenes*, (Loeb Classical Library, 1930).

[55] *Synopsis of 'Philoctetes.'* An oracle revealed that Troy would not be captured save by the son of Achilles, with the arrow of Heracles in the hands of Philoctetes, in the tenth year of the Trojan War. Consequently, Odysseus was delegated to bring Philoctetes back from the island of Lemnos, where the Greeks had put him because he had a wound from a snake-bite which was so unpleasant that the Greeks could not bear the smell of him. For nine years Philoctetes had remained on the island, nursing a hatred of the Greeks for having treated him in such a foul manner. The play is an account of how Odysseus and Neoptolemus succeeded in bringing him back.

[56] *Synopsis of 'The Peace' by Aristophanes.* Trygaeus, an Athenian citizen, mounts a giant beetle and flies aloft to Heaven, intending to ask Zeus why he has allowed the Peloponnesian War to continue. When he arrives in Heaven, however, he finds only Hermes. The rest of the gods, disgusted by the Greeks, have gone to live on a remote summit, leaving Polemus (War) to do whatever he wishes. The Peace-goddess has been buried in a cave. Polemus leaves for a short while and Trygaeus seizes this opportunity to summon those who are friends of Peace to rescue her. They are about to begin to save her when Hermes returns and threatens to reveal their plans to Zeus. They bribe him with gifts and set to work. After a short delay, they set Peace and her handmaids free. Great rejoicing follows and the play ends with much gaiety.

[57] *Synopsis of 'The Lysistrata' by Aristophanes.* Lysistrata summons the Greek women to combine and stop the Peloponnesian War. Her plan is to refuse all the men of the Greek states sexual intercourse until they cease fighting. The women, after much discussion, agree. The Athenian women barricade themselves in the Acropolis. One of the men, Cinesias, who is longing for his wife, Myrrhine, comes to take her away. She promises to go home with him, and at the last moment changes her mind. Finally, after much altercation, the two semi-choruses consisting of a men's chorus and a women's chorus, become reconciled and form one chorus. Lysistrata makes friends with the Spartan and Athenian envoys and they proceed to a banquet to make merry.

# INDEX

Achaeans, 20.

*Acharnians, The,* 189–90, 237–38; synopsis of, 264.

Aeschines, 117, 130, 192, 221–22; biographical sketch of, 260–61.

Aeschylus, 115, 118, 119, 120, 122, 132, 185, 210, 233; biographical sketch of, 255.

*Against The Corn Dealers,* 157–62.

*Agamemnon,* 119, 120, 122, 185, 233; synopsis of, 255.

*Aias,* 120, 121, 195, 234–35; synopsis of, 256.

Alcaeus, 76, 84, 93, 104–5, 106; biographical sketch of, 251.

Alcibiades, 113.

Alcman, 11, 75, 76, 89; biographical sketch of, 251.

Aliens, position of: in Attic Age, 114.

Anacreon, 85, 86, 87, 105, 107–8; biographical sketch of, 253.

Anaxagoras, 115.

Anaximander, 78; biographical sketch of, 252.

Anthropological thought: in the Attic Age, 118, 132 ff.

*Antidosis,* 128, 191–92; synopsis of, 260.

*Antigone,* 122, 123, 124, 195, 196; synopsis of, 257.

*Archidamus,* 127, 242; synopsis of, 259.

Archilochus, 89, 103–4, 109; biographical sketch of, 253.

Architecture: in Lyric Age, 73.

*Areopagiticus,* 128, 229; synopsis of, 259.

Aristocracy: during the Homeric Age, 20.

Aristophanes, 9, 10, 11, 125, 145–50, 150–57, 181–83, 187, 188, 189, 190, 237, 238, 239, 240, 241, 242; biographical sketch of, 258.

Aristotle, 8, 117, 247; sources of social thought in the writings of, 244 ff.

Athenagoras of Syracuse, 217–18, 266.

Attic Age: ideas on propaganda in, 118, 185 ff.

Attic Age: ideas on public opinion in, 118, 185 ff.

Attic Age, 7, 8, 10, 11, 12, Chapter IV; anthropological thought in the, 118, 132 ff; citizens in the, 114; comparative government in the, 118, 210 ff; conception of social competition in the, 118, 193 ff; conceptions of social control in the, 118, 181 ff; economic factor in society, 118, 144 ff; economic thought and theory in the, 118, 150 ff; gods and their relation to man, 118 ff; historical background of the, 110 ff; ideas on justice in the, 118, 195 ff; ideas on law in the, 118, 195 ff; ideas on leadership in the, 118, 185 ff; literature in the, 115–16; ideas on the nature of the state, 118, 223 ff; ideas on peace in the, 118, 232 ff; ideas on propaganda in the, 118, 185 ff; ideas on public opinion in the, 118, 185 ff; ideas on tradition in the, 118, 181 ff; ideas on war in the, 118, 232 ff; position of aliens in the, 114; position of women in the, 114; relation of physical environment to human life, 118, 141 ff; religions in the, 115; slaves in the, 114; social classes in the,